Our Journey

Women

Lessons we learned along the way!

Visionary & Publisher Dr. LaQuita Parks and 20+ Extraordinary Co-Authors

Dr. LaQuita Parks
Tracey Adams ~ Mary Beal ~ Jacinda Beason
Diontrise Blake ~ Masiya Bomoni ~ Gwendolyn Bradley
Carolyn Coleman ~ Jacquiline Cox
Shanita Dawson-Ugwuoke ~ LaMonique Fairbanks
Shelia Hardison ~ Jewel L. Howard
Mz. Inez ~ Jacqueline L. Jackson Homer
Dr. Monica Y. Jackson ~ Renea Jones-Hudson
Dr. Patricia O. Lawton ~ Cecelia Myers
Ninotchka Phillips ~ Leticia Reeves
Denice Richardson ~ Chyanne Thomas~
Desiree Williams ~Vaneeka Robinson

Foreword by Melissa Summers

Our Journey From Girls To Women

The body of work titled Our Journey From Girls To Women Lessons we learned along the way.

Copyright © 2024 by Pa-Pro-Vi Publishing

Cover Design by Pa-Pro-Vi Publishing

No part of this publication may be reproduced, stored in a retrieval system, or transmitted in any form or by any means, electronic, mechanical, photocopying, recording, or otherwise, without the written permission of the publisher. the only exception is brief quotations in printed reviews.

For information regarding permission, contact Pa-Pro-Vi Publishing @ www.paprovipublishing.com.

ISBN 978-1-959667-57-5

To Jenny Owens, I thank GOD every day for allowing our paths to cross. Keep doing what you are doing, you are a true blessings to me and my daughter.

Love,
Shanita Dawson-Ugwuoke

WARNING
SOME OF THE STORIES IN THIS ANTHOLOGY MAY BE TRIGGERING TO SOME READERS.

TRAUMA TRIED TO KILL ME!

Excerpt

During this time, my sister called me while I was out and said my mom told her to tell me I could not come back home. I called the guy and asked him if I could live with him, and he said yes. Now remind you, he had no idea I was a teenager because I had a child and a job when we met. After a couple of weeks, I took him to meet my maternal grandmother and she immediately said, "Shanita he is a devil you need to go back home to your mother!" Needless to say, I did not listen! I continued with him because at the time, he seemed like an angel sent from heaven.

Shanita Dawson-Ugwuoke

Our Journey From Girls to Women

Table of Contents

Dedication 6

Foreword by Melissa Summers 7

The Ride of a Lifetime by LaQuita Parks- Publisher 12

I'm Not Like Them by Tracey Adams 21

Middle Child, Middle Girl by Mary Beal 37

Unsolicited Advice by Jacinda Beason 55

Finding My Delight by Diontrise Blake 71

From Pieces To Peace by Masiya Bomoni 89

The Impact Of Prayer On My Life by Gwendolyn Bradley 112

Guess What, I Grew Up by Carolyn Coleman 125

The Me You See by Jacquiline Cox 135

Trauma Tried To Kill Me by Shanita Dawson-Ugwuoke 146

Surviving Her Cancer by LaMonique Fairbanks 162

The Beauty God Made Me In by Sheila Hardiman 174

Young Girls by Jewel L. Howard 181

From Scaredy Cat to All That by Mz. Inez 199

Silence Kills Speaking Heals by Dr. Monica Y. Jackson 222

Hello Food by Jacqueline L. Jackson Homer 231

Rising From Trauma by Renea Jones-Hudson 244

Walking On The Edge Of Purpose by Dr. Patricia Lawton 260

Throughout My Journey God Was There by Cecelia Myers 274

Life Was Good by Ninotchka Phillips 288

Grace Through The Storm by Leticia Reeves 295

Born Fabulous by Denice Richardson 303

The Darkest Gray by Vaneeka Robinson 313
I Carried Her With Me by Chyanne Thomas 336
When You Ask The Lord Why by Desiree Williams 363
Afterwords 387

Dedication

To the women who have paved the way with their strength, courage and unyielding faith.

To the women who walk beside us, facing life's challenges with grace, resilience, and unwavering determination.

And to the women who will come after us, may these stories inspire you to embrace your power, honor your truth, and continue the legacy of pain, progress, and victory.

This book is for every woman who dares to rise, to heal, to overcome, and to thrive.

Foreword

Melissa Summers- **Beauperthuy**

From the moment I became acquainted with Dr. LaQuita Parks, her zeal for life, her tenacity to achieve, and her genuine love for people moved me to want the world to know just who she is. Most have no idea of the literal 'pain' she fights through on a daily basis. Yet, not only does she persevere but she finds the time and strength to uplift and encourage others.

This book, *Our Journey from Girls to Women*, is a must read. Through this anthology of many women sharing their "Journey's", you will more than likely find some of your own heart-stories through their stories. Each journey is a testament to resilience, hope, and transformation.

As I write this foreword, I feel deeply connected to the stories within these pages. My own journey is beautifully intertwined with those of the sisters featured in this book. Dr. Parks has a remarkable ability to resonate personally and directly with each story, including mine, and I am confident that you, too, will discover your story through theirs.

This is more than a book—it's an experience of shared triumphs and the collective power of our voices.

About Melissa

The Melissa Summers-Beauperthuy

BACKGROUND

Melissa Summers' career spans close to 25 years in radio and television, beginning while in the United States Army. She has hosted many features for various TV and Radio network affiliates throughout the country. Her voice and image has been both seen and heard around the world from appearances on "The Dating Game" and "Lifetime Television for Women", to co-hosting an internationally syndicated radio show Lost in the 80's, a program that aired in the United States, Bosnia, and in the U.S. Virgin Islands and she has broadcast live across the country including her most recent stint in Atlanta.

In the Atlanta market, Summers was known as "Atlanta's Girlfriend" and was the noted midday personality for V-103, and was former host for Atlanta's adult station, KISS 104.1 where she also served as Assistant Program Director. It was this juncture in her career that she was impressed to leave the secular realm of music for religious reasons, thus Summers segued into the gospel arena and joined gospel radio as morning show host of "The Inspiration Morning Show" on Praise 97.5FM, as the morning drive host and was one of the only women hosting a Morning Show solo anywhere in major market radio in the country and in less than one year garnered third place ratings for her show. From here God guided her steps to the state of Illinois to work for one of the largest Christian Television Networks in the world, "Three Angels Broadcasting Network" (3ABN), where she hosted an internationally viewed TV program called "Issues and Answers" and served as a program coordinator for the network.

Melissa pressed even further to become Director of Programming for a Worldwide Television Satellite Network called Global Family Network (GFN). Summers was responsible for providing programming for a Global viewing audience.

Currently she is Executive Director/Producer of a video production company, DVI Global Productions, Inc. and Co-Director of "M&M Powerhouse Health" along with her husband, Mario Beauperthuy. They now travel worldwide, together, speaking and teaching how to restore optimum health through God's natural methods.

COMMUNITY SERVICE
A firm believer in church and community involvement, Summers participates in many professional and charitable organizations including serving as Communications Director for her church, Decatur Seventh-day Adventist Church, where she is a member, she serves on the Georgia Avon Breast Cancer Survivors Mass Choir Committee, the Board of Directors for the Atlanta Day Shelter for Women & Children, the Advisory Board of Directors for the American Red Cross's campaign "The Power Is In You", the President's Advisory Board for the Metropolitan Atlanta Coalition of 100 Black Women, the Health Disparities Committee for Emory Healthcare. She is a board member of Good Choices, Inc., Life Member of NAACP, Life Member of the National Council for Negro Women, and the Atlanta Business League. Summers has also contributed to the works of The American Cancer Association, Big Brothers /Big Sisters, The American Business Women's Association, and the Sickle Cell Foundation among many others. In 1999, Summers created "In the Name of Love," a charity drive benefiting battered women, sickle cell victims and education programs both locally and nationally.

GREAT ACCOMPLISHMENTS

One of Summers' greatest accomplishments is earning the trust of her listeners. She specifically recalls the relief and joy of convincing a listener not to commit suicide. Summers was able to reach out to the listener through love, understanding and humor to convince her that she was not alone and that "life is truly worth living." She thanks God that the listener is now doing very well. "Knowing that my audience views me as their "girlfriend who's always there for them means more to me than any award I could ever receive," Melissa says.

HONORS & AWARDS

Summers' trailblazing achievements in radio and the community have earned her many notable honors and awards, including the distinct honor of being one of only eleven Georgians invited by President Bush's top Republican Party Leaders to represent Georgia on his Republican Presidential Roundtable. Summers graciously and boldly declined stating "It is an incredible honor to receive such a prestigious invitation. However, I will not accept because I am not a Republican and wish not to misrepresent my ethics."

She's listed in the New Millennium Edition of Who's Who in Black Atlanta. She also received the "Pronet Sojourner Truth Pioneer Award," the "Women's Shining Star Award" by the National Organization of Elected Legislative Women, Black Radio Exclusive Magazine's Shannon Dell "Breaking the Glass Ceiling Award." Summers was inducted into the Metropolitan Atlanta Coalition of 100 Black Women and assigned to the President's Advisory Board. She is recognized by the Atlanta Business League as one of "Atlanta's Top 100 Women of Influence." She was nominated as "Best Radio Personality" by the NAACP Phoenix Awards and "Urban AC Personality of the Year" by Radio & Records Industry

Achievement Awards for four consecutive years. Summers was also named "Broadcaster of the Week" by Billboard Magazine as well as numerous nominations by Billboard for Personality of the year, named "Best On Air Girlfriend" by Atlanta Magazine, and noted as "the Oprah of the Airwaves" by Heart and Soul magazine just to name a few.

The Ride of a Lifetime

Visionary & Publisher
Dr. LaQuita Parks

I have had several memorable, life defining experiences on my journey from a girl to a woman.

The fun times...

As a child I had a curiosity for things most children already have the opportunity to explore. I rarely knew what it was like to run and play outside. Due to a serious leg injury at the age of four, I didn't get the chance to play in the snow or splash puddles in the rain. While everyone else was outside playing, I was usually watching from the window. I watched the sunshine and the flowers bloom just like I watched the kids riding bikes and jumping rope. I would get lost in my thoughts and wonder what life for me would be like if I had "good" legs like everyone else. Even as a child, I reclined to think that I was only going to be able to do just so much.

One day I was given the opportunity to participate in a program that would allow me to travel and have experiences that I never dreamed I could have. My travels would take me on a scenic route from Georgia to Birmingham, Alabama; Little Rock, Arkansas; Oklahoma City, Oklahoma; Amarillo, Texas; Albuquerque, New Mexico and Flagstaff, Arizona.

When I boarded the luxury bus headed to the West Coast, I was not prepared for the scenery that would be embedded in my memory forever. Although I was excited to be taking this adventure, I didn't want to spend hours on a bus. I figured being on a bus for days on end would be horrible. I had no idea that I was about to embark on the bus ride of a lifetime. What I didn't know then was that I was about to experience a rebirth.

It was a pleasant July morning when the trip began. The itinerary that I had been given said we were departing Atlanta, Georgia and our destination was going to be Los Angeles, California with quick tours in the states we would be driving through. I was young and still had a touch of the "are we there yet" syndrome. A part of me was wondering how I was going to survive a three-thousand-mile bus trip.

First stop was Alabama to the city of Birmingham where we toured the downtown site of some of the most tragic and historical events of the Civil Rights movement of the 1950's and 60's. As I stood in downtown Birmingham, I imagined what it must have been like to live during the time when black people and white people couldn't even dine in the same restaurants or drink from the same water fountains. After getting a brief city history, we were off to our next destination.

Little Rock, Arkansas was our next stop. We headed to North Little Rock near the Arkansas River and went to Old Mill Park. This park was actually an old mill that operated in the 1800's and became famous because it was the background for the opening of "Gone with the Wind." It was interesting to see that the water wheel was still turning. The flowers were in total bloom and it was quite pretty.

Our next stop was the State of Oklahoma. I found out a lot of African American history in Oklahoma City when we took a tour of what is called the Bricktown Canal. To see an entire town built with red brick was fascinating too me. Not only did Henry Ford open an assembly plant in 1915 but Bricktown was also the home of the first black newspaper that was founded by Roscoe Dunjee. Bricktown right in the heart of Oklahoma City was known as the birthplace for social diversity.

I can honestly say that I had an opportunity to "get my kicks on Route 66." Amarillo, Texas was our next tour site. Since we were taking the scenic route to California and had just left Oklahoma, it seemed only sensible that we would take an easy journey down Route 66. I had a chance to stop and view some of the Texas landscape. It was fun acting like I was in an old western movie. As we were driving down Route 66 the most memorable part of the trip for me was watching the sunset because you could see the curves of the earth for miles and miles.

We continued on Route 66 to Albuquerque, New Mexico where we took in the quiet scenes at Roosevelt Park. I learned that the park is named after President Franklin Roosevelt and was built during the Great Depression. We didn't spend much time in the park but I remember looking at the tall trees in amazement thinking I had never seen trees that tall before, not to mention the number of gorgeous hills that covered the park. This adventure was turning out to be much more than I had ever anticipated.

So far I had been to places that I had never even consider visiting before. We had walked through cities made of brick and driven down Route 66 where the song named for the highway was now embedded in my head plus we relaxed in a park named after a famous president. None of that prepared me for the sight I was about to behold. The place we went to next would forever be etched in my memory and be credited with my rebirth. Next stop was Flagstaff, Arizona.

The Grand Canyon took my breath away. It took us about three hours to drive up the canyon from Flagstaff. All you could see was what looked like molded rock after molded rock with water in between. As we started up the canyon, the weather was cloudy and you could tell that rain was near. Even though it was hot and muggy outside, no one seemed to care because we were all so intrigued. I wasn't sure which I was the most excited or scared. All I knew was that this was the first time in my life that I had been on an adventure of this sort. The higher we got the more nervous I became. As we got closer to the top of the canyon, the rain began to fall. I kept thinking, how much longer. It started to really pour and I wasn't sure if we would be able to get off the bus.

When we finally reached the top of the canyon, the rain stopped. Curiosity outweighed my fear because the sight from the top of the Grand Canyon was the most astonishing thing I had ever laid eyes on. The rain had been replaced by sunshine and you could actually see the steam coming from the rocks within the canyon. I was totally mesmerized by the view. The clouds appeared to be riding on top of the mountains and I thought the rocks were gleaming with magnificent color.

It was many years ago when I boarded that bus headed to the west coast. I had no way of knowing the impact it would have on my life. The exceptional beauty of the Grand Canyon with its mountain of rocks and waterfalls will remain in my memory forever because it was the day of my rebirth, a semblance of stability!

The "Not So Fun" times...

As a child, born to a teenage mother, the only time I can remember having a stable home was the five years we lived with my grandmother from the age of nine until I was fourteen. Prior to that, we were evicted from every place we ever lived. As hard as my mom tried, she struggled financially and having three children, plus a child that required special attention and frequent trips to the doctor and one therapist or another wasn't easy. I recall clearly (on more than one occasion) walking up the street or getting off the bus and seeing our stuff on the street. These memories have lived in my mind since I was a child. After going through a horrible divorce, my goal was to make sure that my children had a stable environment. I never wanted them to feel the pain of eviction and homelessness. No matter what, no matter how I felt, no matter the level of pain, I made sure that my children had consistency and stability.

As I take a trip back down memory lane, I remember the tears and the look of desperation and despair on my mother's face. She was tired and she was broken but she didn't quit. I didn't know it at the time but I was learning from my environment. I was learning what not to do.

My mother was what I call "straight, no chaser!" She had no problem telling you exactly what was on her mind. If your feelings got hurt, it wasn't personal; it was just Sheila Gail or "Sister Sledge," as my uncle affectionately called her. My mother liked to drink from as far back as I can remember. My mother was an alcoholic. There would always be some Budweiser, Schiltz Malt Liquor Bull, Henessy, or Canadian Mist in our house at any time. When her friends visited, they would often come with a package or two in hand.

I will never forget an incident that happened one Sunday evening while we were still living at my grandmother's house. My grandmother had a small three-bedroom house, and I was the "lucky one" who had to share a bedroom with my mother. There were very few times I can recall my mom not having a beer. This day was no different. It was almost bedtime, and as I ran into the room and felt the cool liquid hit my foot, I knew immediately that I was in trouble. I had accidentally knocked over my mother's beer, her last one at that. I started crying as I nervously grabbed a towel to clean up the spill. She angrily asked me what I was crying for. Through my sobbing, I said, "I was crying because I was scared I was going to get a whopping!" The next thing I knew, my mother had grabbed the belt and started hitting me with it. After all was said and done, she claimed that she whopped me because I was crying (according to her, she was giving me something to cry about). In my heart, I believe she whipped me because I knocked over her last can of beer. This is one of the things I learned not to do. The one thing I learned was how to be strong, and that's what I taught my children.

I taught my children that no one was going to give them anything, they had to be strong and work hard to get what they wanted in this life. My childhood caused me to teach my children that "only the strong survive!"

Ensuring my children were raised with the stability I didn't have was no easy task but I made a promise to myself that I would not allow my children to be products of my environment. I didn't know what it felt like to be whole but I was committed to figuring out how I was going to give it to them. I can readily admit that something was missing and I didn't know what until I was invited to a bible study. I was asked to forget everything I thought I knew about the bible and be willing to learn the Word by the Word. After studying and obeying the gospel, I realized what was missing. I was trying to make our lives whole without building a relationship with God. Although stability is important, trying to have it without Christ was an effort in futility.

Today my children are adults living in their perspective homes with their perspective careers. They have never known the pain of eviction.

In 2009, my mother passed away and it broke my heart. In missing her, I learned to appreciate everything she tried to do for me. Life wasn't easy for her. I didn't understand that then but I do now. With God's grace and mercy, and the lessons I learned (good and bad) I was able to provide a life of stability for my children and me. Although life wasn't easy, it was stable and has been quite the ride!

About Dr. LaQuita

Dr. LaQuita Parks (Hon), is the Founder and CEO of Pa-Pro-Vi Publishing and A Failure 2 Communicate LLC as well as a 6x International Best-Selling Author, Relationship Communication Coach, Writing Coach, Motivational Speaker and Mentor with a passion for people and their well-being.

LaQuita received her Doctor of Humane Letters (Honoris Causa) and the Credential of Global Fellowship in Leadership Principles from Mainseed Christian University. She is also the recipient of the 2024 Presidential Lifetime Achievement Award. LaQuita is a 2024 It's In A Book Award recipient, was the 2022 Making Headline News Woman of the Year Award Recipient as well as the 2022 recipient of Trivia's Inspirational Radio Community Excellence Award. She is also the host of her own podcast show, "My Heart on Pages" and "So, What's Your Story. LaQuita has been a contributing writer and sponsor for I Am International Magazine since January 2021 and is also a contributing writer for the award-winning magazine, Listen Linda.

LaQuita created the Pa-Pro-Vi Publishing platform to help people start the healing process because she believes there is power in YOUR story and that writing and sharing your story can be therapeutic.

Walking Limitations is LaQuita's first published book and the true story of how she went into the hospital to have a simple procedure and it left her crippled for life at the hands of a nurse. This created a medical tsunami that has affected her life for the last fifty years. Writing her story started the healing process for her and she helps others do the same with their story.

Since starting Pa-Pro-Vi Publishing in 2020, LaQuita has been coaching people through the process of writing their stories. LaQuita has been able to help hundreds of people around the world take their stories from a "thought to a realization." LaQuita has written and published numerous books of her own including two co-authored children's books.

LaQuita is a faithful Christian and the mother of three adult children, Shante', Curtis and Alexis and the Nanna to 5 precious heartbeats, Carter, Amir, Christian, Gabriella and Arya. LaQuita has a Business Degree from Shorter University.

Connect with Dr. LaQuita at www.paprovipublishing.com

Email: laquita@afailure2communicate.com

Linked In: https://www.linkedin.com/in/dr-laquita-parks-honoris-causa-a03647a/

I'm Not Like Them

TRACEY ADAMS

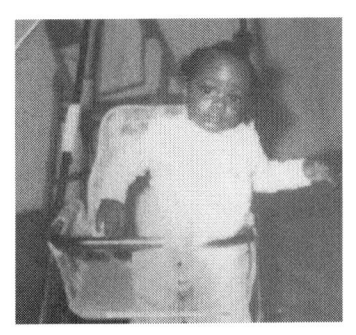

Growing up in Kansas City, Missouri, I imagine it was like growing up in any city across the country. My childhood had some emotional ups and downs. Some of those emotional downs I still carry with me even today. Growing up when I did and how I did, shaped and molded me into the adult that I am today. I am the youngest of seven children and there are huge age gaps between me and my brothers and sisters. Even at a very young age, I knew that I was not like them. I had three sisters, and they were teenagers when I was born. My oldest sister is seventeen years older than me. The next sister is fifteen years younger than me and then my next older sister is thirteen years older than me. The oldest sibling is our brother Richard. He is twenty years older than me. And my brother Price is seven years older than me.

Growing up, I saw all three of my sisters involved in not so healthy relationships. Relationships that involved emotional and physical abuse. Seeing this as a little girl, a teenager, and even as an adult had an effect on me and how I approach being in relationships. I was determined not to allow any man to put his hands on me. I am not like them. However, I learned from them how to verbally communicate with the opposite sex. I saw a lot of verbal abuse between my sisters and their partners.

I didn't realize until years later that I learned how to communicate by watching how they communicated with their partners. I saw how they communicated with other people including each other and the rest of the family. They didn't listen and if they did, they only listened to respond and not to understand. I carried this trait into my relationships as I became an adult. And that includes relationships with men, girlfriends, and more importantly, my family. Whenever there was a problem, instead of going to the person and discussing it, I shut down and stopped talking. Very unhealthy. When I graduated high school and moved from Denver, my oldest sister and I were not on the best of terms. When I left, I left with a lot of unresolved issues.

My sisters made their fair share of mistakes that even I had to learn from. From what I was told, my sister Linda dropped out of school and ran away from home at the age of 16. She was in the streets for as long as I can remember. She used drugs and was in several abusive relationships. She used to steal to get her fix. She even stole from us, her family. My mother was so disappointed. She prayed for her constantly, but my sister could not leave the drugs alone.

Linda and I got into a physical fight because I was tired of her stealing my clothes and taking my money. Once, I confronted her about taking my leather jacket that my aunt bought me for school, and she cursed me out. I ran up to her and tried to snatch my jacket off of her and the fight was on. My other sister had to break us up. It didn't stop there. The stealing continued for years. My sister's life of drug addiction went on for years. She was in and out of jail and prison. Her relationships landed her in the hospital beaten and bruised. We lost her 3 years ago. She was chased down and shot down by some guy she got into an argument with. My mother was devastated. WE were devastated. Our mother had to bury another child due to gun violence. I love my sister dearly however I am not like her.

My three sisters were gangsters. Always ready to pop off and fight anybody that was disrespectful. My three sisters treated me like their baby. They had to look after me while mommy worked. They did my hair and took me places with them. They protected me from the kids at school who would bully me. I was not like them. I was quiet and shy. I hated getting into fights. Lord, the bullies growing up! I was teased and bullied incessantly because of my dark skin and because my hair was not long and wavy. Even my brother Price and his friends constantly dogged me out. Calling me *black* and saying my hair is *so* nappy.

It really hurt my feelings being made fun of for something that I could not help. I was born with a mole on my nose and that made the teasing even worse. The kids at school would sometimes talk about me from the time I got on the school bus in the morning until the time I got off the bus in the afternoon. I came home crying many times because of it. My mother told me that the kids were jealous because I was born with something different from them and because I was smarter than them. I was a smart little girl. I talked a lot in class but that didn't take anything away from me learning. I received several academic awards in elementary school and some of the kids had ugly things to say about that too. I couldn't win. I was not like them.

In middle school, I became very quiet and reserved. I figured the less I said the less the kids would bother me. My grades were not the best but for the most part I maintained a B average. I remembered being nervous going to middle school because I was afraid that I was going to be bullied. It wasn't as bad as in elementary school. I had an occasional verbal confrontation with a few of the girls but once they figured out that I wasn't afraid to speak up for myself, they pretty much left me alone. Most of them were bossy, wore makeup, and was boy crazy. I was not like them.

I avoided confrontations from childhood into adulthood. Even now it takes me a long time to say how I really feel about people and situations. Our oldest brother is laid back and doesn't bother anybody unless they bother him first. My brother Price is the same way. Richard moved out of the house when he was 17 years old and has lived on his own ever since. He stayed away for a long time. I was an adult when I found out that my brother was gay. Through the family grapevine, I heard that the reason my brother moved away and stayed away for many years was because my dad had my cousins to beat him up because he was gay.

They thought that he would try to *"do something"* to our brother Price. Me and my older siblings have different fathers. Me and my brother Price have the same father, and our older siblings had different fathers. My father is no longer alive for me to ask him about what actually happened. Neither is my mother. So, we will never know the whole truth. It is no big deal! I love him just the same. I don't judge him or put him down. He is my big brother, and I am not like them.

I learned from my brothers as well. I learned from my oldest brother to stay in my own lane, drive my own speed limit and you won't get into any accidents. He is very private and tight-lipped about his relationships, and I understand. In fact, I had never seen my brother with anyone. He never brought anyone he was involved with around for us to meet. Now that I am a whole grown adult, I totally understand. Whatever goes on in your relationship between you and your partner, should stay between you and your partner. You don't need your family's 15 cents about what you should do within your relationship. Whatever decision you make should be strictly *your* decision and not based on the biases of family. This was very helpful to me when I was going through a divorce.

My brother Price on the other hand was very sloppy with his relationships. He displayed the typical behavior of men who have no self-control. He was playing between two women, his oldest daughter's mother and his youngest daughter's mother. They found out about each other, and it was a total mess. I was on the sidelines as a young 21-year-old woman watching this chaos. All I knew was that whenever I decided to be involved with someone, I wanted be with someone who liked me as much as I liked them. Who liked me enough to at least respect me with loyalty and truth. And not put me in a situation where I have to fight somebody because of him.

I moved to Denver to live with my oldest sister and her three children at the age of fifteen. It was the summer of 1990, and my father had just died. My sister was moving away to get away from an abusive relationship and to make a better life for herself and her children. She dropped out of high school, but later went back and got her GED. She worked several jobs over the years to take care of her children. One of her children was totally disabled and I figured it would be good for me to move with her and help her with my nephew. Life was really difficult living in my mother's house.

At the time my sister Linda and my brother Price were dealing dope out of my mother's house. My father had just died, and my mother had just found out that she was a diabetic. Talk about life doing too much! Anyway, when my sister moved to Denver, I begged my mother to let me move with her. We went back and forth about it all summer until finally she caved and let me go. I was tired of being there knowing that at any time the police could kick in the house, or somebody would come and shoot up the house. My mother was enabling them by not calling the police and putting them out of the house. I felt like that was my chance to escape the madness that was going on at home.

My sister and her children moved to Denver earlier in the Spring of 1990. I finished my freshman year in high school in Kansas City and I was so ready to go later that summer. When my cousin drove to Kansas City from Denver that summer to visit her mother, I was in her van on my way to Denver when she drove back. I enrolled in high school as a sophomore and started what I *thought* at the time was a peaceful life. Boy oh boy! My sister, and her kids! We had fun times! My niece and nephews are around the same age, so we grew up as sisters and brothers.

School was great! I made the principal's honor roll my sophomore, junior, and senior year! I was nominated as Who's Who Among American High School my junior and senior year. I joined the pep club. We performed during our high school's homecoming with the cheerleaders. My high school counselors were very supportive and kept me on task with the credits that I needed to graduate. Life in Denver was going pretty good until my big sister became a big emotional and financial bully!

My dad was in the military, and he was a disabled veteran. When he died, his disability benefits were passed down to me. My mother received those benefits on my behalf while I lived under her roof, but once I moved with my sister, those benefits transferred to her and since I was a minor at the time, she had to sign off on the benefits as my guardian. Well, needless to say, she took advantage of that. Always needing money, wanting money, demanding money. I could not save a dime because she was always demanding money. I told my mother about it, and she chin checked my sister for it. She told her that since I was living under her roof, I could *pay* her $100 a month for living there! Who charges a 15-year-old kid rent for living under their roof? Not just any random 15-year-old but, your 15-year-old *baby* sister?! Who *does* that?!

Not only would I pay her the $100 a month but she would come back in the middle of the month begging for more! Not to mention, she wore my clothes every chance she got *AND* I was helping take care of her disabled son. I didn't mind taking care of my nephew because I loved him. However, several times she would fall asleep and leave him sitting in his wheelchair tired and sleepy. There were times when I would come upstairs exhausted after hours of studying and doing my homework to find my nephew rubbing eyes from exhaustion and sitting in a puddle of his urine in his wheelchair.

Everyone else had long gone to sleep. His brother, his sister, and his mother. I would run his bath water, lift his heavy body out of his wheelchair, and lay him in the tub so I could bathe him. After bathing him and dressing him, I would take his wheelchair apart, pour his urine in the toilet, and spray it down with cleaner so I could take it outside and spray it down with the hose. After drying it off, I'd put his wheelchair back together so it would be ready for him to go to school the next day.

As time went on, I became so frustrated with my sister. I called my mother and told her that I wanted to come home. She told me to come on! She would pay for my ticket. My mother of course called my sister and cursed her out! Telling her that taking care of her son was not my responsibility and that lifting him was too much for me to be doing by myself. She told my sister that I was coming home. Of course, my sister begged my mother to let me stay. Didn't want to let that money go. Mommy told her that it was my decision if I wanted to stay. I decided to stay because I was doing well in school, and I wanted to finish high school in Denver.

High school was much more comfortable for me. The bullying had subsided considerably. I think it was because the kids were more into being seen, playing sports, and being in relationships than they were in bullying somebody. I felt more relaxed in high school because I minded my own business and stayed out of the radar. I didn't have a boyfriend or go to the prom because well I didn't have the *look* that the boys in Denver looked for. The girls who were not all-black or not black at all were the ones who had dates for the prom. I was not like them, and I was not bothered in the least because my focus was on being on the principal's honor roll and going to college.

I did not have time or space to worry about who liked me or who didn't. I had one boyfriend in high school. He was nice and all, but I was so nervous and inexperienced that I broke up with him after a week. I quickly decided that being in a relationship was not for me, especially at the ripe age of 16. I had a friend who lived next door to us, and she was very active. She got pregnant at sixteen and had a baby girl. It was not more than a year later when she got pregnant again and had another baby. No judgment or shade. I just knew that that wasn't the life for me. I continued to be her friend, but we grew apart because she was busy being a teenage mother and I was busy being a teenager. I was not like her.

June 1, 1993. It was my graduation day! I was super excited! I was excited about graduating high school with honors. I was excited being accepted to three colleges. A college recruiter from the University of Colorado in Boulder contacted me about enrolling in their engineering program. At the time, I wanted to be an engineer. I wanted to attend a historically black college as well, so I researched the schools in the Atlanta University Center and decided to apply to Clark Atlanta University and Morris Brown College. I was accepted into both schools but decided to attend Morris Brown. I also received acceptance to the University of Colorado, but I declined the offer. I was Atlanta bound to Morris Brown College. Surprisingly, my whole family came to see me walk across the stage and receive my high school diploma. Including my brother Price.

After graduation, I decided not to go to Atlanta in the fall. I wanted to work and save some money before going to Atlanta. The whole time while I was in Kansas City I had to hear and see the negativity again. Only this time, it wasn't going on in my mother's house. The shenanigans had moved to another house. Across the street from my mother's house. Me and my mother worked through it the best way we could. We both worked two jobs. Mommy was determined to help me all she could to get me to and through college. In some way, I believe we both worked two jobs in order to escape the chaos that was going on.

The whole time I was home, I had to listen to my brother and sister go on and on about me leaving again to go to college. They did not support me moving. They always had some negative comments to make. Especially when me or my mother mentioned anything about me going away to college. Linda: "I am not impressed about you going to school in Atlanta. If you want to impress somebody then go to college overseas like to Paris or Italy somewhere!" I could not roll my eyes hard enough. I told her: "I am not trying to impress nobody and who are you that I need to try to impress?!" Me graduating from high school was impressive. Me getting accepted into college, impressive. I am not like her. My mother said something to me when I was a little girl that stayed with me, she said that my sisters saw something in me that they didn't see themselves. They saw determination. They saw a little girl who was determined to make something of herself. She said they felt bad because they wasted their life dropping out of school and running the streets when they were teenagers. Mommy said they had the same opportunities that I did but they decided to throw it away in the streets.

I could care less about what they said or thought. I was not like them, and I was determined not to be like them. The only one who did not give their 15 cents about me leaving for college, or their 15 cents about any of the decisions that I made in life, was my sister Marcie. She *never* told me what *SHE* thought I should do. Surprisingly, she is my coolest sister. She is nonjudgmental. She didn't judge me when I decided to leave home to go to college. She didn't judge me when I got married. She didn't judge me when I got divorced. She respected my decisions and supported me. Even To this day.

December 30, 1993, was moving day. It was time for me to head south to Atlanta. It took me weeks to find a van and someone to drive the van to Atlanta. My brother knew a lot of people and could have asked somebody to drive me, but he did not. Days before the trip, I finally found a van and reserved it immediately. Now, I only needed to find a driver and we would be on our way. Mommy was coming with me. My big god-brother found someone to drive us, and I never felt so relieved. My enrollment was complete, and I had received my official letter of acceptance. I had already paid for my dorm for the first two semesters. Student loans were approved, and the funds were ready to pay for my tuition. This was an adventure that I will never forget. This was the beginning of my life as a young adult.

When we arrived in Atlanta we stopped by my mother's first cousin's house in College Park. They spent hours catching up on family and talking about the good ole days. My cousin kept saying that her son and his wife were going to come over and take us around the city. More hours passed and me and my god-brother were bored out of our minds. We decided to take a walk. I needed some air after that long ride from Kansas City and from being couped up in the house. That walk led us to the nearest bus station. Once we were at the bus station we decided to get on and see where it took us. The bus took us to the College Park train station. Once we got to the train station we got on the train and ended in downtown Atlanta at Five Points. We walked and explored and shopped! We even had the nerve to get something to eat! When we got back to my cousin's house they were pissed! My mother went off! And her cousin didn't make matters better by telling us how dangerous Atlanta was. We tried to show them what we bought and tell them about all the sights we saw but they were not having it.

The next morning, they moved me into my dorm, and I could tell my mother was getting emotional. So was I but could not let her see that. I wanted to be in Atlanta, and I knew I was going to experience a lot of new things. I was excited and nervous at the same time. We said our goodbyes on the steps of the towers. My god-brother who is a photographer took a picture of us hugging each other. I still have that picture. I get teary-eyed every time I look at it.

I knew my mother was scared for me to be so far away from home with no family, but this was my life and my journey. In time, she came to accept me being away from her. I had every intention of making her proud of me.

Fast forward. I got married at the tender age of 23. I just wanted to be loved and to be wanted and so I married the first man that asked me. In my mind, I was not like my sisters or my friends because a man wanted to marry me and not just lay up with me. I didn't understand my worth and value or who I was as a woman. I didn't know what to expect from men and how I should have been treated. My father had been dead for a few years, and I didn't have that male role model to learn from. All I heard from my mother is that all men are doggish and that they cheat. I was not like her. I chose not to believe that. However, the men in my life showed me otherwise. My father and my brother cheated. I saw the guys in college juggle girls around like tennis balls. The men I was involved with after I got divorced had more than woman. Seeing these patterns in men should have made me believe what my mother said however, through it all, I chose not to believe that. As I entered into womanhood, I had to consider my behavior and decisions. I learned that you teach people how to treat you by having standards and setting boundaries.

I became a woman in my marriage. My marriage taught me that I needed to clearly communicate my feelings, set boundaries, and stand on them. Motherhood taught me how be patient and compassionate. The friendships I had in my life taught me how to listen and not pass judgment. I have learned in my current relationship to forgive quickly and move forward. I am still learning to not hold onto offenses. It's hard when people are deliberately disrespectful and egregiously offensive. It makes you question the love they claim to have for you. It makes you question yourself. Am I good enough? Did I nag too much? Am I too much? Did I ask for too much? And the answer is NO! I have concluded that I have been too much for the wrong people. And it is okay because I also know that I am just enough for the right people! I have learned in the last two years that I am a deeply empathetic person. When I love, I love with my whole heart and soul and that is the reason I hurt so badly when the people I love the most hurt me.

I would never, ever, *PURPOSELY* on purpose hurt the people that I love. I reminded myself that I am not like them. If I am not like them, then who am I?

**ated*I am Tracey.*
A natural chocolate beauty with smooth buttery skin.
I am not like them.

My hair is kinky, and my brows are not perfectly waxed.
I am not like them.

My body isn't snatched or flat. It hurts sometimes.
My nails are short, and not covered by acrylic.
I am not like them.

I love deeply with my whole heart and soul.
I am not like them.

I see things that others don't.
I am not like them.

Comfort and stability bring me peace and I work hard for it.
I am not like them.

The world and those in it don't owe me anything.

It is up to me to protect my peace and distance myself from negative energy.
I am not like them.

Show me one time that I am not your one and only and I am gone...forever.
I am not like them.

I forgive quickly and I try to forget,
But sometimes the hurt keeps rehearsing in my mind.
I am not like them.

Loyalty is my fault and trust is my weakness.
I am not like them.

Who am I?
I am Tracey.
Mother. Teacher. Writer and author.
A sister and an aunt.
A girlfriend, a best friend.
(His) Queen, love, and confidant.
Who am I?
I AM God's daughter.
Deeply loved by The Most High!
I am Tracey...

I am NOT like them!

About Tracey

Tracey Nicol Adams was born in Kansas City, MO and is the youngest of seven children. She moved to Atlanta, GA in 1994 to attend and eventually graduate from the prestigious Morris Brown College. She has been an elementary and special needs teacher for 24 years. Tracey began writing stories as a child and started keeping journals while in college. She has always wanted to be an author. She has read a plethora of books over the years from various authors and always thought to herself, "I can do this!"

Due to school, marriage, career, children, divorce, and just...life, Tracey put writing on the back burner for nearly 20 years. She began writing again in 2016 and decided that one day she was going to become a published author. She wrote her first book in March of 2016. It is called *Maya and the Ants* and it's a story about her oldest daughter and how she reacts to her baby sister inviting ants to live in their house. In late November 2016, after her college track coach passed away, Tracey started writing her second book, a realistic fiction novel called *While I Run This Race*.

Tracey's first book was published in 2022 and is currently live and available for purchase. It is entitled *How William Got His Wings.* she was initially going to collaborate with William and call it *William's Journey* but unfortunately

William gained his wings before starting the project. With permission from William's dad, Tracey wrote *How William Got His Wings* soon after William's passing in July 2022. A portion of the proceeds from the book goes to his family to honor his memory.

During the time that William was sick and later transitioned, Tracey's mother was also sick, and she passed away 2 weeks after William. While mourning William and her mother, the sequel, *How William Met Mommy*, was birthed.

Her current projects are *How William Met Mommy* and *Too Much of a Good Thing: A Runner's Journey*. They are currently in the illustration and editing process.

Tracey is extremely excited about this journey in her life and career. She is establishing her book distribution platform and business: TNA Literary Works Presents. Her goals are to share her stories while encouraging various audiences. Tracey wants to write screenplays and TV series based on her realistic fiction books.

For more information about Tracey's books and upcoming projects, visit her site at: **https://sites.google.com/view/tna-literary-works/home**

Middle Child – Middle Girl

MARY BEAL

Early Childhood

Join me in the first quarter of my life journey from childhood to adulthood. Over the years, I have heard many discussions about middle children. Wikipedia describes the middle child syndrome as the idea that the middle children of a family, those born in between siblings, are treated or seen differently by their parents from the rest of their siblings. Trust and believe there is more than an ounce of truth to this belief based on this middle-girl, middle child's experiences. The positive side of being a middle child is that I was born to experienced parents, had older siblings to learn from and explore with, and had younger siblings to experiment with. For example, I learned to braid hair, first by plaiting blades of grass and graduating to my siblings' hair.

I am the seventh child of ten children and the third daughter born to the same parents, James and Luella. My siblings included five brothers and four sisters. We were all born on a farm on the Old Leonard Estate in rural South Georgia, where my extended paternal family occupied with my grandfather as the patriarch. There were four separate households on the Old Leonard Estate. Uncle Pate and his family occupied the house about one mile west of our homestead. Aunt Leila (Doll) and her family lived with

Granddaddy and Grandma Magnolia (Mag) in what we called the Big House. My father's childless oldest sister, Aunt Eva, and her husband, Uncle Dan, moved into the smallest house, less than one-half mile from the Big House. Before Aunt Eva and Uncle Dan moved to the Old Leonard Estate, they resided on the Evans Estate in the Drayton community. The Drayton community is located west, about fifteen miles from the town of Americus and approximately the same distance from my mother's hometown of Montezuma to the north. My parents conducted most of their shopping in Cordele, located approximately ten miles southeast of the Old Leonard Estate.

Our house became a little crowded because after I was born, my mother gave birth to three more children, almost like clockwork, one every two years. My three oldest brothers were born in the first four years of my parents' marriage, and there was an eight-year gap before my oldest sister, Christine, was born. There are two siblings between Christine and me, Elijah (Buster) and Ruby. I refer to Ruby as my fifteen-month-old twin.

However, all ten children never lived together at the same time for several reasons. I experienced grief at age three and one-half years because my oldest brother, John Frank (JF), died in his sleep from an epileptic seizure. A few months later, my second oldest brother, James (Happy), left home to apprentice with a master brick mason in the adjacent county. He got married about three years later and started his own family. Less than two years later, my third oldest brother, Marion, enlisted in the U.S. Army and served during the Korean Conflict. My oldest brother, JF, died before my last two siblings were born. My youngest brother was born six months after my oldest brother JF died; I went to live with my childless Aunt Eva and Uncle Dan in the Drayton Community for less than two years. Around the same time frame, Elijah went to Brooklyn, New York, to live with my father's second oldest brother, Uncle Frank, and his wife, Aunt Novella, who were childless.

There always appeared to be some comings and goings in our household. When Christine was ten years old, she was accidentally hit on the head, and later, a brain tumor was diagnosed. This resulted in many days and nights away from home in a hospital in Augusta, Georgia. Once Christine was released from constant medical observation after brain surgery, her vision became impaired, therefore Mama enrolled her at the Blind Academy in Macon, Georgia. There, she stayed in the dormitory and only came home on holidays and special occasions. Christine was brave and intelligent, while I was a crybaby and afraid of my own shadow until I was eight. I missed her so much when she was away from the house because, as my big sister, I looked up to her for daily guidance.

There were external events in society that impacted some of the comings and goings in our household. For instance, when Emmet Till was killed in 1955, my father insisted that Buster return home to Georgia because he had become friendly with one of Uncle Frank's Italian neighbors. Daddy was an avid newspaper reader, and the newspapers' account of Emmet Till's brutal murder really upset him. This occurred shortly after the Brown vs. Board of Education in Topeka, Kansas. That legislative decision affected our household because it resulted in the subsequent closure of rural schools. We attended Piney Grove Church Country School, and because of its forecasted closure, Mama and Daddy allowed Ruby to live with a well-known local educator, Mrs. Clara Scott. Less than one year later, Piney Grove Church School closed, and our immediate family moved from the Old Leonard Estate to the City of Cordele.

At the age of ten, I moved with my family to the Newtown suburb of Cordele. Daddy moved to Broward County, Florida, to obtain work within two months of moving. Newtown was more populated than the Piney Grove community, and the entire family became familiar with our new neighborhood and made new friends. Many of my new friends were my classmates, so we walked to and from school together. Some became life-long friends.

The Drayton, Georgia, community is where our home church, Macedonia Missionary Baptist, is located, and some of my family members have continued to worship there. Also, the church cemetery, about twenty miles from Newtown community in Crisp County, is the final earthly resting place for many of my paternal ancestors.

I no longer hear the sound of the classroom loudspeaker announcing, "All Beal children report to the principal office immediately!" The time of day and the urgent tone were symbolic of chaos in the family. The principal informed us that we were being dismissed because our mother had summoned all of us to come home immediately. When we arrived home, we noticed a shotgun lying on the back porch. Mama informed us that Buster, age fourteen, had been accidentally killed with Granddaddy's shotgun. My Irish twin sister, Ruby and I infrequently discuss that incident. Unfortunately, this incident created another departure from the house, but this time it was permanent. I did not realize until forty-five years later that my grieving for Buster was an unresolved emotional issue in my life.

Buster would typically have been in school on the day and time of his death; however, he was on suspension for shooting a rubber band in the classroom. Mama was highly upset when she discovered that Buster had been suspended, and she had not been contacted about the infraction he had committed before his suspension. She could not get any satisfaction from the high school principal, so when it was time for my sister Ruby to enroll in high school, Mama enrolled her in the historic Holsey-Cobb Institute, a private Christian school operated by the Christian Methodist Episcopal (C.M.E.) Church. One year later, when I graduated from elementary school, I also began high school at Holsey-Cobb Institute. Holsey-Cobb was about one mile from our house, and we walked to school. Regrettably, Holsey-Cobb Institute closed one year before Ruby and two years before I graduated high school.

Teenage Years

The closing of the Holsey-Cobb Institute caused the family to face another financial challenge. We commuted daily to Holsey-Cobb Institute, where we paid a small tuition but did not have the expense of room and board. To complete our high school education in a Christian high school meant we would need to seek enrollment at Boggs' Academy in Keysville, Burke County, Georgia. Enrolling at Boggs' Academy was not a viable option for our family because, at the time of Holsey-Cobb's closing, there were three family members in high school. It was too cost-prohibitive to send three children away to boarding school. Also, the principal at the public high school at that time was our neighbor, Mr. George Tutt, and the Beal family had established strong relationships with our neighbors. Therefore, Mama felt confident that Mr. Tutt was honorable, and they developed a strong communication channel. They often sought each other for advice and guidance on behaviors, education, and career choices for me and my siblings.

When I and several of my classmates from Holsey-Cobb transferred to the public high school, A. S. Clark, in the Fall of 1962, we were high school juniors. A. S. Clark had three homerooms for each grade, comprising twenty-five to thirty-five students. I did make some new friends; however, those who transferred from Holsey-Cobb tended to stick together.

During my two years at A.S. Clark High School, I spent a lot of time assisting the clerical staff in the principal's office. Daddy purchased a blue typewriter for me when I was fifteen years old. By the time I left high school, I could type over seventy words per minute with over ninety percent accuracy. Hence, when Daddy died in June of 1963, I asked Mama if I could quit school and get a job to help earn money to support the family. This was one of those instances when Mama sought Mr. Tutt's advice. He told her that I could excel in college. He recommended that I not drop out or attend summer school to earn the three credits I needed to meet the State of Georgia graduation requirements.

Therefore, I stayed in school and graduated with my 1964 class. Because of family caregiving chores and my sister Christine's blindness, I did not have time for dating during high school. Dating was complicated because most of my contemporaries did not have access to a vehicle, and we lived on the outskirts of town; plus, Mama had some strict curfews.

College Years

During the Fall of 1964, I joined my sister, Ruby, and enrolled at Savannah State College as a Business Administration student. In my first year, I lived off campus on West 35 Street with Mr. Eugene Jackon and his wife, Mrs. Harriett Jackson. He was a member of the Savannah State College faculty, and I rode to campus with him in the morning and back home with him at the end of the day. I met Pamela Perry and Gwendolyn Cutter in the registration line during freshmen enrollment, and we became friends throughout my time at Savannah State College. They both lived off campus, Pamela owned a blue Ford Falcon, and we would ride with her to Victory Drive to purchase our lunch.

In my second year, I was required to live in the newly constructed Lockett Hall Dormitory and experienced sharing a room with someone other than a family member. I also became exposed to cafeteria food. Growing up on a farm and learning to cook at an early age, I was not impressed, nor did I like cafeteria-prepared food. Thank God for Mama; she had the foresight to send us to a college in a city where she had close family and friends. Mama had five first cousins and one aunt who lived in Savannah. Her Aunt Victoria Toomer lived with her daughter, Rosa Emerson, on the Savannah Transit Authority bus route. I got to eat many home-cooked meals on weekends.

During my junior year in College, I thought that I wanted to get married to a neighbor who had returned home from Vietnam. I got a ride with a minister who was the pastor of my grandfather's church in Dooly County and went to Cordele. My heart was not in it, so I did not see him, and I got a ride back to Savannah with the minister. Since I performed work study during my undergraduate career, I didn't have or make time for dating.

My third oldest brother, who was called Mama's Big Baby, Marion, drove from Broward County, Florida, to Cordele, picked up Mama, my youngest brother Jimmy, and drove to Savannah for my college graduation on a very hot, and humid day in August 1968. We took a few pictures, congratulated some fellow students, and departed immediately for August, Georgia, to visit my oldest sister, Christine, who had been in a coma since April of that same year.

I was not emotionally prepared for what I saw when I entered Christine's hospital room. She appeared to have tubes connected to every open pathway on her body and more. I had to remain strong and not break down because Marion had informed me earlier that I had to drive the family to Cordele because he was exhausted from the excessive driving he had performed without sufficient rest. I exited the hospital room and visited the ladies' restroom to pray and compose myself. Five years earlier, I entered my father's room and observed him dying. I saw the same thing with Christine except for the tubes. It troubled me that we were waiting for the medical staff to pronounce her dead when she was already dead and was being kept alive by machines and tubes.

Work Career

I returned home to Cordele with my B.S. Degree and resume and visited the unemployment office to look for a job. Based on my summer work experiences and work-study jobs during College, along with my degree, I was told, and I quote, "You are overqualified" for every job I applied for in Cordele. After about one and a half weeks, I became restless and traveled to Syracuse, New York, to visit two high school friends, Rosa Dunn and Gwendolyn Riley. I was reluctant to travel to Syracuse because I felt in my spirit that I could be summoned home any day because of Christine's condition. My spirit man was nudging me to stay active; therefore, with the encouragement of my classmate, Rosa, I departed Cordele.

When I arrived in Syracuse, I found the weather to be beautiful compared to the hot and humid conditions I had experienced all my life in Georgia during that time of year. Uneven terrain and hilly landscapes were appealing compared to the flat land in South Georgia. The houses were often multi-storied and contained radiator central heating. I shared a room with Rosa's sister, Betty. They resided on the second floor of a three-story house at the top of Madison Street hill across from the entrance to Thornton Park. Since Rosa and Gwen worked, Betty helped familiarize me with the neighborhood. She introduced me to many of their friends and acquaintances.

I started applying for jobs after being in Syracuse for a couple of days. Remember, this was 1968, and very few women were employed as auditors and accountants. I recall an incident with one company when I called to set up an appointment for an accounting position; the gentleman boldly asked, "Madame, are you calling for an interview for yourself?"

I responded, "Yes, Sir."

He boldly responded, "Forget it, we do not hire women," and hung up the phone!

The second place I applied hired me as a junior accountant and assigned me clerical duties. I had not worked for two weeks when I received a call informing me that Christine died on my twenty-second birthday. I returned home to Georgia for the funeral. After the funeral, I returned to Syracuse and worked for that company for about nine months.

I was introduced to many Syracuse University undergraduate and graduate students between September and December. I met students from various African countries, east, west, north, south, the Middle East, the Caribbean Islands, and throughout the United States. I developed close friendships with several students from South Africa, Southwest Africa, Ghana, Nigeria, Sierra Leone, Sudan, Liberia, Ivory Coast, Botswana, Malawi, Honduras, Kenya, Zimbabwe, Tanzania, Zambia, and multiple states in the U.S. I developed a long-time intimate relationship with an undergraduate student from South Africa.

During the very first snowfall in the winter of 1968, I fell and broke three bones in my face. Medical personnel at Upstate Medical Center were so busy the night I visited the hospital, and a nurse mistakenly sent me home. The streets were covered with snow and black ice, making it difficult to travel by auto or on foot because I lived at the top of Madison Street.

Several months after the surgery to repair broken facial bones, I began working for the nonprofit organization P.E.A.C.E., Inc. The acronym stands for People's Equal Action Community Empowerment, Inc., and was my second employer in Syracuse. P.E.A.C.E., Inc. provided me with the opportunity to learn and develop supervisory skills and simultaneously a chance to become familiar with community needs and community involvement. It enabled me to hone my interpersonal skills in training and supervising others and communicating with executive staff. This assignment also taught me a lot about collaboration, budget formulation, and overall personnel management. It provided an excellent opportunity to meet and interact with Syracusans.

Several of my colleagues at P.E.A.C.E., Inc. enjoyed playing the card game Bid Whist, and we would alternately host Bid Whist parties at one another's homes or apartments. On other occasions, we would attend parties hosted by various African students, usually in the University area. Sometimes, we traveled to Cornell in Ithaca, New York, where a well-known entertainer was scheduled to perform. I recall that I made a very costly mistake trying to attend a concert by the Edwin Hawkins singers. I was the driver with a carload of friends and should have been traveling to Oswego, New York, but I headed towards Otsego, New York, instead. Our friend

LeRoy Wright did not let me off the hook for several years. This incident occurred before the invention of the global positioning system (GPS) we constantly used road atlas to travel to other cities, towns, and states.

In addition to working, my cultural knowledge grew tremendously from my association with international students. I frequently received invitations to attend events, parties, and homes of international students and families. Attending many of these events made me familiar with cuisines, music, and dances from various countries. I also became familiar with different women's attire and hairstyles and even learned words and phrases in several African languages.

In the latter part of 1969, my sister, Beatrice, next to me in birth order, decided to move from Jersey City, New Jersey, to live in Syracuse. We shared an apartment while Beatrice attended Onondaga Community College to become a licensed practical nurse. Later, she got her apartment and shared it with a fellow nursing student. Two years later, I invited my second oldest sister, Ruby, to live with us in Syracuse because her teaching contract with the Macon County Georgia Board of Education was not renewed.

Graduate School

Several events changed my career trajectory between late 1970 and late 1972. I was offered a position as a cost analyst with General Electric (G.E.) Corporation in the Electronics Division located in Liverpool in Onondaga County. While working at G.E., I met a staff member who shared information about an M.B.A. program at Syracuse University. He encouraged me to apply for admission to the program. The program was funded by a government grant which included a monthly stipend for each student. I was selected into the graduate program and resigned from G.E.

because I could not align my course schedule with my work schedule. Therefore, I became a full-time student again.

While enrolling in the M.B.A. program, I met several students from the Newhouse School of Communication and the School of Engineering. After being in the M.B.A. program for about eight months, an acquaintance from Kenya informed me about an upcoming summer's East African Study Abroad Program. I applied, was accepted, and traveled to East Africa with approximately twenty-two other graduate students from the U.S. and Africa. This is an account of my first quarter-century journey of living an abundant life in the United States of America.

Except for a weekend trip to Toronto, Canada, I had not performed any international travel before departing for Nairobi, Kenya, in the summer of 1973. When I visited Canada, I was only required to show my driver's license as identification. This new adventure required me to have a passport and a visa for each foreign country I visited. Traveling to Africa required me to get certain immunization vaccinations. It appeared that everyone I encountered after receiving the vaccinations wanted to hug me and or touch the arm in which I had received the vaccinations. My arm was sore for several days. The blessed part of that was the vaccinations lasted for several years.

It took me several weeks and months to prepare for my trip to East Africa since I had predetermined that if I liked my initial visit, I would seek work and stay longer. Yahweh answered my prayer and provided a way to achieve my objectives. Through interpersonal relationships in Syracuse, NY, I found a letter at the Brunner Hotel, our first stop in Kenya. Little did I know that the letter paved the way for a successful African journey. The letter was from a former Syracuse University student, a native of Southwest Africa, and a member of the Southwest Africa People Organization (SWAPO). His letter introduced me to SWAPO's Chief of Staff in Dar es Salaam.

The SWAPO Chief of Staff was a humble gentleman of great integrity. He soon became my protector, advisor, chauffeur, shoulder to cry on, and older brother, all wrapped up in one person. I contacted him before visiting Tanzania because Dar es Salaam was scheduled towards the end of our East African Study Tour.

The East African Study Tour allowed participants to earn university credit hours. It required us to attend lectures at the University of Nairobi and the University of Dar es Salaam. We visited the archeological site, Olduvai Gorge, where the most continuously known record of human evolution was discovered. The Olduvai Gorge and the Serengeti Plains are part of the Ngorongoro Conservation Area in northern Tanzania. Ngorongoro Crater is the habitat of much of Tanzania's wildlife.

My adopted older big brother drove to Bahari Beach, where our group stayed during the Tanzania leg of our tour, to meet me. He instructed me to inform him upon my return to Dar es Salaam so that he could pick me up at the train station. After three days in Dar es Salaam, the study tour returned to Kenya. We participated in several more lectures at the University of Nairobi before the group departed home to the U. S., and I returned to Dar es Salaam, Tanzania.

A funny thing happened at the East African Train Station in Nairobi as I attempted to begin my overnight train ride to Dar es Salaam. It dawned on me that I had never traveled on an overnight commuter train, and I was at a loss on how to board and did not know anything about train compartments. Aha, I experienced one of my reversed cultural shocks. According to Mama, commuter trains stopped operating in my home area when I was a toddler. We traveled mostly by private auto, Greyhound, or Trailway Buses in Georgia. It was fascinating to watch wildlife from the train window as daylight appeared.

I started working for the Tanzania Ministry of Finance at the School of Accountancy in October 1973. About three weeks before beginning my work assignment, I met Andrea Metzger at a public function. I learned she was single and had applied for a teaching position at a girls' school. She rented a room from another African American living in Dar es Salaam for several years. We toured the city of Dar es Salaam together. We used the SWAPO office as our meeting place or to leave messages for one another when we had different schedules. On one particular occasion, we teamed up with some other young people we had become acquainted with and hitch-hiked to Bahari Beach. After we both became gainfully employed, our outings were conducted on weekends.

Little did we know that after one month of being assigned a house together, I was transferred to the Lake Victoria region. I became the senior instructor and assisted with opening a branch of the School of Accountancy at Mwanza. I stayed with Andrea Sania Metzger whenever I visited Dar es Salaam for work or pleasure. There is so much more to share about our fifty-one years of friendship, but I must capture those in my memoirs. We have both matured and experienced successful careers over the last half-century. I am honored to share Sania's own words:

The Kinetic Energy of Mary Beal

"True friendship, the late and honorable Percy Sutton of New York once said, "does not require daily attendance." True friendship is what I am honored to share with my amazing friend Mary Beal. Once Mary touches your life, her humanity and sincerity leave an indelible mark.

Mary first touched my life in 1973, 51 years ago this month. We met at the Y.M.C.A. in Dar-es-Salaam, Tanzania. Mary had traveled from her hometown in Cordele, Georgia, to Dar-es-Salaam to contribute to the educational goals of that then-recently decolonized, progressive nation.

We became fast friends drawn together by our mutual love of Africa, its promise, and its challenges in overcoming centuries of the trans-Atlantic slave trade and centuries of colonization. During her stay, Mary spent over three years teaching in Mwanza, Tanzania, and became fluent in Swahili.

Three words that come to mind when thinking about my dear friend Mary are intelligence, communication, and humanitarian. Mary is an avid reader and immerses herself in facts, data, and antidotes about national and world events that impact vulnerable individuals and communities around the globe.

Her educational background and passions allow her to analyze and explain complex economic, political, and spiritual concepts to the audience. Mary has a unique ability to use her intellect to inform and connect with audiences comprised of members of Generation Z as well as Baby Boomers. Because of Mary's insatiable thirst for knowledge in service of humanity, she maintains multitudes of friendships with people around the country and the world, from Syracuse, New York, to Johannesburg, South Africa, to Germany and the United Kingdom, to name only a few locations.

As a communicator, Mary has been gifted with the ability to express her ideas on health, politics, and religion through the written and spoken word. Mary is a published author. It is Mary's engagement with audiences that is uniquely impressive. Her thought-provoking presentations connect with all participants, as evidenced by the comments and questions that enrich the "conversations."

One might ask what motivates Mary to continue to lead such an active life when others have opted for the living room sofa and the T.V. remote. Mary is and has always been a humanitarian who cares profoundly about her family, neighbors, fellow Americans, and global brothers and sisters, especially those seeking a bare existence against socio-economic barriers and century-old prejudices. This passion to assist humanity has made Mary a citizen of the world.

I am so proud to call Mary Beal my lifelong friend. Mary is a true Renaissance woman. Her love for humanity is boundless. Mary is a ball of kinetic energy.

Sania Metzger deVeaux, Esq.

Bronx, New York

September 14, 2024

Message from the Author

My message to readers concerning my personal life journey is this- life is multi-faceted with many joys and sorrows. However, my life journey is a testament to Jeremiah 29:11-14 from God's Word Translation. "I know the plans that I have for you, declares the Lord. They are plans for peace and not disaster, plans to give you a future filled with hope. Then you will call to me. You will come and pray to me, and I will hear you. When you look for me, you will find me. When you wholeheartedly seek me, I will let you find me, declares the

Lord. I will bring you back from captivity. I will gather you from all the nations and places where I've scattered you, declares the Lord. I will bring you back from the place where you are being held captive."

God's plans for my life journey are still in effect, and I am unable to share much of the magnificent details of God's plans for my life that have already been manifested in this document. Please consider this contribution to 'Our Journey from Girls to Women' as an initial peep (first twenty-eight years of life) into my memoirs. Having played and was lettered in girls' basketball in high school, I view my life in quarterly segments. Unlike in basketball, I fouled out in a couple of games but thank God I am in the fourth quarter of my life's journey and still in the game at seventy-eight years old.

Stay tuned and follow me on social media for the rest of my life's story, told in quarterly segments!

You are loved and appreciated! The author, Mary L Beal

In remembrance of deceased family members and friends and in honor of those still alive!

End

Our Journey From Girls to Women

About Mary

Mary L Beal

Author, Family Historian, Consultant, Mentor, Speaker

About Mary

Mary is passionate about helping families reunite and restore family values. She has been featured in Southwest Georgia News, I Am Magazine, BizTalk with Zondra, on Our Global Family TV Show, WIMTV Broadcast and WSST TV. She has international travel and work experience on four continents, including the United States. She has developed a global family mindset. Mary is the author of six nonfiction books including three anthologies.

Speaking Topics
- Reuniting Families
- Restoring Family Values
- Live Your Legacy
- Why Do Families Separate
- Importance of Family History

Testimonials "

Mary Beal is dedicated to the family in its entirety. She carries a legacy that spans indefinitely. Mary's quest to empower families is intergenerational, global, and far reaching. Her tireless effort can transcend and transform generations.

Services Offered
- Workshops
  - Health & Wellness
  - Estate Planning
  - Family Unity
- Keynote Speaker
- Panel Discussion

Let's Work Together

mlbealconsultingllc@gmail.com

www.mlbealconsultingllc.com

https://www.facebook.com/LongtimeTraveler/

linkedin.com/in/mary-beal-beal-82a4a421/

https://www.instagram.com/marylbeal/

MLBeal Consulting, LLC, P. O. Box 1064, Cordele, Georgia, USA (229) 401-8308

Unsolicited Advice

Jacinda Beason
*A Message for My Sons
Relationships, Faith, & Family*

The way of a fool is right in his own eyes, but a wise man listens to advice. **Proverbs 12:15 ESV**

INTRODUCTION:

WHY I'M WRITING:

In 2020, my three sons were transitioning in their personal journeys as young adulthood, COVID-19 was declared a pandemic, and I was mourning the deaths of many friends and acquaintances. The possibility of death had me reflecting on the relationships in my life. I spent 15 years at home raising my sons, and now they are all out of the house. We call each other to catch up, reminisce, plan visits, and occasionally, they still ask for my opinion on their life challenges. It's moments when they ask for my advice that get me wondering if I have prepared them enough for life. When they were home, I could watch the situation unfold each day, pick up hints of their conflict, and observe their demeanor. It's not that I am concerned about the ethics of their decision-making. I know they carry the word of God in their heart and their Father's principles in their consciousness. I don't want to take for granted that I have time on this earth to share all my wisdom from my life experiences! LOL! There are stages in which you teach your children the soft skills of relationships and divulge life lessons wrapped in your experiences. We are shaped by our experiences as children. However, as time passes and you acquire knowledge, your perspective of that same memory may evolve. I want my sons to have these words of advice as encouragement and as my way of sharing with them and the generations to follow.

I do not have a favorite child. I love them all equally. The truth is that your children can frustrate you sometimes (dare I say get on your last nerve) but each of my sons have uniquely added a joy to my life that has allowed me the freedom to reveal different parts of me as a person. Thus, my relationship is different with each of them and my love is non-competing. I find myself reminding people that they are still learning about themselves, how to express their emotions, and how to communicate their likes and dislikes. It's not to say that they are not mature or have not been given the tools to make good choices. However, with time comes different experiences and hopefully, wisdom and understanding. So, where do we start?

IN THE BEGINNING: Ages 3-10:

MY DEMOGRAPHICS:

I was born in the early 1970s in Kankakee, Illinois, a small midwest city (yes, it's classified as a City!) an hour away from Chicago, IL. I am the youngest of my parents' two daughters. My father's people are from Mississippi. They owned a farm in Pembroke, IL, near Kankakee, where my father was raised. My mother's family originated from Alabama, and they moved to Pembroke, via Chicago, when my mother was a teenager. I spent my early years surrounded by my grandparents, aunts, uncles, cousins, and extended family. It was a big family. The majority of my parents' siblings lived in Kankakee. I remember we had lots of fun together; both families could come together like one. We traveled to Detroit, Cincinnati, and Indiana at least once a year to visit my grandmother's siblings, who also had big families. My parents' first cousins would also visit. I would hear stories of their experiences growing up and having fun as a family. Growing up in a small city with a large family was great. My parents would be considered "upper middle class' and were well known in the community.

My paternal grandparents were pioneers in Pembroke. As a child, I felt like I was part of royalty on both sides of my family. Everywhere I went, my family knew people, or people would identify me as an heir to the family name with high esteem and respect. I reaped the benefit of their work ethics, social engagement in society, and community activism. Unlike my classmates, I had hands-on experience of what entrepreneurs in a cooperative community looked like - starting with my paternal grandparents farm life, watching the behind the scene planning of the Pembroke Day parade and rodeo, walking through the forestry of the plains to check on neighbors, picking and planting fruits and vegetables, and the unfortunate knowledge that I was eating the farm animals I had befriended and named. In my mind, my environment was a microcosm of my two favorite shows - Sesame Street and Little House on the Prairie.

As a child, the core family consisted of the father, the primary provider; the mother, who provided direction and wisdom; and the children, who were always respectful, didn't ask questions that weren't their business, and did not tell the family's business. I also saw that although my maternal grandmother and paternal aunt were widows, they did not take advantage of the family or highlight their circumstances for attention. I did not notice any favoritism or competition for love and attention from either side of my family. I never felt a need to really make friends because all I needed was my family.

When I was around 3, we moved from Chestnut Street to a big house on Harrison. It didn't seem like a big deal, but everyone else understood the "come up." I didn't have a chance to get to know the neighborhood kids when we lived on Chestnut like my sister did. I only knew our next-door neighbors who also had two daughters; one a year older than my sister and the other a year younger than me. When we moved to the house in Harrison, we didn't have any neighbors! We were closer to downtown, and our property was half the block. I didn't know it then, but the house was a historical mini-mansion that needed a lot of work. We lived in the house while the work was being done. I enjoyed the mystic and adventure of sleeping on the floor, eating cereal (which was a treat) on crates, having a "secret" back stairway from the kitchen to our playroom, to the attic, an unfinished basement with rooms that had dirt floors, the huge unobstructed backyard with only two trees; a pear tree and the other would become our tree house. It was Utopia...until it wasn't.

MY FAITH:

When I think about the foundation of my life it has been rooted in faith, family, and community. My mother chose to live her life for Christ somewhere between my sister being a toddler and my conception. Through my mother, her siblings, brothers-in-law, and her mother also "got saved." My father did not attend church. Oddly, his father went to church every Sunday and served on the usher board. I grew up in the church and perceived it as family and community. I was baptized by my uncles at the age of seven. The church was the catalyst for my learning about God, faith, and the discernment of the holy spirit - what the world called instinct. My mother encouraged me to have a relationship with God and to know him for myself. Church in Kankakee and Bible Witness Camp in Pembroke was where I learned more about God's power, grace, and faithfulness through people's testimonies. I also got to be around kids my age who enjoyed praise and worship. We all could participate in fasting, speaking in tongues, and experiencing God's presence without age discrimination. My faith was strong, and God answered my most earnest prayer and the one I prayed often - that my parents would divorce.

LITTLE FOXES DESTROY THE VINE:

If someone asked me if I had a happy childhood, I would say yes. As the saying goes, "Two things can be true." Although my parents had an unhealthy marriage, many of my childhood memories are positive. I was a daddy's girl. My father taught me how to play chess, he did my hair and spent quality time with us. He is why breakfast is my favorite meal. He called me his champ, and he was my protector. I sometimes got up early on Saturday mornings with him to do chores, and then we watched Bruce Lee movies or Sugar Ray Leonard boxing. I was entertained by the sport of combat. It did not seem violent to me at the time, but soon I would have a different perspective. On occasion, I was a spectator to the combative incidents between my mother and father. I did not understand why the arguments would escalate to physical altercations. I had heard about my father getting into fights mainly to defend himself or a family member. It was traumatizing to see his blind anger unleashed on my mother. I don't know if he even knew I was present most of the time, but when he did notice, my sister and I were either put out of the house with my mother or kept from her for a few days as what felt like retaliation. What troubled me even more was why my mother stayed, but I thought if she could still love him and no one from the family seemed to say anything or treat him differently, it must be ok. When my mother took me with her to seek counsel from our pastor at the time regarding her marriage, I listened as she [the pastor] used the bible to convince my mother to stay with my father despite him breaking God's covenant of marriage. My mother's words rang very true at that moment, "You must know the Lord for yourself." I knew what I was hearing was not of God, even at that young age. I began to pray, and when we had a fast at the church, that was my focus.

When my parents divorced, I was ten years old. Suddenly, I felt ostracized from my father's family. I had a difficult time reconciling the contradiction of my feelings regarding some of my family members' love for me and mine for them. Still, it was equally my father's responsibility to ensure we were not casualties of his choices. Despite some devastating emotional traumas, I never lost my faith in God! Just as Moses reminded the people when God delivered them to the promised land, "And you shall tell your son on that day, saying, It is because of what the Lord did for me when I came out of Egypt." I know I am who I am because God has delivered me, and He will do the same for you.

THE ADVICE - *Relationships, Faith, & Family*

"Love the Lord your God with all your heart and with all your soul and with all your mind." Matthew 22:37 NIV

God has brought me through a lot, and my legacy will not be what I give you in this world but what I teach you spiritually. Just as my mother told me, you need to have your own personal relationship with God, continue to have your personal relationship with God, know Him for yourselves, and know the word for yourselves. This is the stage in your life where you will be challenged the most about who you are and your relationship with God, family, friends, and societal norms. We are inundated with temptations, false accusations, and subliminal messages used for manipulation that blind us from the basic truth of what is righteous. I pray for you all every day that you will have wisdom and discernment in everything you say and do in your life. Don't take prayer or those who pray for you for granted. The church is a community meant for worship, fellowship, and ministry with people. Pastors are teachers to help you better understand the word of God. If you study God's word, you won't be misled by people who misuse it and weaponize it to pass judgment on others. Let your life be a living testimony of what God has done for you and us. Colossians 3:17 (NIV) "Whatever you do, whether in word or deed, do it all in the name of the Lord Jesus, giving thanks to God the Father through him." Proverbs 3:6: "In everything you do, put God first, and He will direct you and crown your efforts with success." (TLB)

ADULTHOOD:

I learned that "doing the right thing," as you see it, does not mean it is right. As a child, you were taught to respect your elders by not disputing what they say, giving deference to their authority by addressing them as sir or ma'am, and to "stay in a child's place," which covers a plethora of scenarios. When you are transitioning into adulthood - graduating from high school, getting a job, going to college - people want your actions to be independent as an adult but not your mind. Don't be apprehensive about challenging the authority of someone who is abusing their authority. The 90s encompassed big milestones for me. I graduated from college, got married, and had my first child in that order. Unfortunately, my childhood frame of reference regarding adults and relationships impeded my ability to recognize my authority as an adult. I now understand the quandary my mother faced when married to my father. She was trying to do what was right for the love of her children, for the covenant of marriage, and to just keep peace in the family (hers and her in-laws). When your admirer (love interest, family/future in-laws, friend, boss, etc) becomes your antagonist, they undermine the sincerity of your effort to do what is right. Their exploitation of your geniality negates the value of the relationship. You have to teach people how to treat you, especially when that person has been unchallenged in their mistreatment of others. The dictionary defines a bully as someone who habitually seeks to harm or intimidate those they perceive as vulnerable. The Bible refers to this type of person as a fool, saying, "For the fool speaks folly, and his heart is busy with iniquity, to practice ungodliness, to utter error concerning the LORD, to leave the craving of the hungry unsatisfied, and to deprive the thirsty of drink." Isaiah 32:6 (ESV)

How do you know when you are being bullied or fooled? Bullies are skilled manipulators capable of subtly camouflaging their vain intentions. When their presence brings about stress, fear, or shame. When you feel you must explain or cover for their mean words or behavior to protect the one(s) you love. When those who have been there for you can no longer be around you or speak the truth to you because you are indoctrinated in oppressive treatment by a fool. The "right thing to do" is to seek out what God says about the situation and the person. The wrong motives can turn what seems like an act of kindness into a trap. Don't let your acts of kindness be rooted in guilt or withhold it because of hurt and anger. When you put on the full armor of God in preparation for the battle, let HIM go before you as your protector, and you can rest in peace. Just because you are in battle with someone does not make them your enemy, but it also does not mean you are allies. Reconciliation comes in God's time, so let Him choose who you need to stay connected to, whether it's a season or for life. Your Auntie

Jewel would say, "Care, but don't carry." I carried the guilt and shame of not knowing how to process the emotional hurt and sense of betrayal from my father's choices. That experience impacted my marriage; leaving me, like my mother, vulnerable to accept the subtle condescending treatment from my mother-in-law in order to protect the love of my husband and children for many years. Although the damage is irrevocable there has been forgiveness and God has healed the pain.

When people are young, they say what they won't do when they get older, how they won't tell their children "because I said so." The elders' response is, "Keep living." Be patient with people as they are in their stages. Those who are older, younger, or even your age want the same thing you do, and their stage of experience is important to them. They may be understanding life based on what they are going through, and you don't want to disrespect or belittle them because you have been able to get through something or have gained wisdom. Stay focused on what God says about you and His guidance about your life. Romans 12:2: "And be not conformed to this world but be ye transformed by the renewing of your mind, that you may prove what is that good, and acceptable and perfect will of God." (KJV) Ask the Lord for wisdom and discernment. Don't let the unsaved tell you how to love and live for Christ because they will try to deceive you for personal reasons. There will be people in your life that God tells you to let go. When God closes a door, do not break the window. Just because you are good for someone doesn't mean they are good for you. It is difficult to accept that because we want to be loved, and you have been loved, and you want to love. Don't dismiss what your family of believers tell you. Do not give or receive emotional opinions, and be cautious when saying or hearing "God told me to tell you." If it's from God it won't be confusion, it will be confirmation.

We have imagined what your future will be like as husbands and parents, but we have not talked about the strategies for navigating these relationships. Of course, it is not a one-size-fits-all. Marriage and parenting are no easy tasks, but they are choices. To be the best spouse and parent, you must choose to be your best self. This means addressing your shortcomings, traumas, or whatever negative character traits and habits you have picked up or suppressed. Take accountability for your actions in disagreements; what could you have done differently to find a solution? You can't master marriage, but you can manage it. You don't have to be the perfect parent, but you should be a present and prepared one. My parents grew up with both of their parents being married until a partner departed from their spouse in death, and the surviving spouse did not remarry. Your father and I have been married for nearly 30 years. People often ask us the secret to marriage and raising pretty good kids. Our answer to both is, "To God be the glory! That is a very simple answer to an ambiguous question. It's like telling someone to just "eat healthy" without explaining the variables of "healthy eating." It's easy to tell people the 4 principles of being a man that God gave to your father when you all were young:

1. Be a Man of God

2. Be a Man who can think for himself

3. Be a Man who knows right from wrong

4. Be a Man who is a leader, not a follower

However, taking them through the unpredictable life lessons that impact one's decision-making is complex. Parenting is a verb, and you must be intentional about it. I want you to be prepared to be a good husband and be blessed with a good wife. I have seen how God has blessed and delivered so far. The two most impactful situations in my life are praying for my parents to get a divorce and being obedient when God said I should stay at home to raise you all. I did not want to stay at home, but I clearly heard God and wanted to be obedient. How it turned out is more than I could have hoped, imagined, or expected. We always say we trust God but are surprised at what he does.

PARENTING:

Train up a child in the way he should go and when he is old he will not turn from it.

Proverbs 22:6 NIV

Home is the training ground where parents build a foundation of morals, beliefs, and behavioral attributes for their children. Your first relationship is with family. When you become a parent, be intentional about your vision for them. You are responsible for their emotional stability, communication, and healthy social interactions. Think about all the things that affected you as a child. There may be different preparations for their gender roles, but they should be taught to understand roles and changes. Use age-appropriate language; you don't have to tell it all, but you do have to make sure it does not get lost in translation. It is the responsibility of the parents to be intentional about connecting their children to family. I did with you all what I experienced with my parents; taking trips so you could be introduced and spend time with family. My parents agreed with that, although one may have been more intentional than the other; that's why you have two parents. It is the parent's responsibility to foster those relationships and make sure that they are positive. We all have our quirks. Don't speak ill of family, the truth will reveal itself.

When you become a parent, people will want to give you their opinions and advice; know the difference between the two. My great-uncle believed our cats were bad luck because cats suffocate babies while they slept. On the other hand, my doctors gave me the option of taking prenatal pills or adhering to a diet that would provide the necessary nutrients in place of taking medications. People mean well; sometimes, as a courtesy, it's best to just smile and nod. Still, there are those times when you will have to block a hand when someone wants to touch the baby or firmly tell people not to give your child a gift, a hug, or a kiss. If you are intentional about parenting, you will not have regrets or consider your efforts in vain when your child makes choices you disagree with or may cause them harm. Try to give them options and opportunities. You may be disappointed but you should not feel guilty or regret when you do it God's way.

As parents, we have tried to equip you with the tools to become great men of God. Preparing your children for marriage does not mean you become their first spouse in the sense that no one can do for your child like or better than you can. Nor does preparing your child to leave your home mean that you will no longer have a relationship. I cannot teach you (my sons) how to be a man, but I can guide you in understanding what it means to be a husband from a wife's perspective.

MARRIAGE:

My mantra has been "Leave and cleave," and I truly believe that. That mantra is not what I "feel" or my opinion; it is biblical guidance. Genesis 2:24 and Matthew 19:5-6 "Therefore shall a man leave his father and his mother, and shall cleave unto his wife: and they shall be one flesh." (KJV) What God has joined together, let NOBODY come between. When God has chosen your spouse, it is a unique relationship intended to reflect the exclusivity of God's love for us. If there is anything or a person that dishonors, tries to compete with, or threatens the security of your marriage (felt by you or your spouse), it is imperative that you seek a resolution. Marriage is wonderful especially when you choose to make it a priority! The covenant between you may be exclusive, but sharing the love of your relationship with others in a healthy community of friends and family gives glory to God. There are plenty of books that tell you the strategies of marriage, love languages, and how to keep the spark in your marriage. Everyone has their own marriage journey, like DNA. Suppose you both are putting God first, communicating clearly, making each other the priority, and appreciating each other's expression of love for one another. In that case, there will be more good days than conflicts.

Whenever you decide to get married, listen to God's voice so you can discern a true bond from a trauma bond, a red flag from someone just not being perfect. Whoever you connect yourself to, you both should want to engage with the community that influenced your lives and loves you. You are the initial bridge of introduction to both sides. How you describe (if you share positive or negative attributes and experiences) and introduce each to the other will impact first impressions and establish the foundation of the relationships in your circle of family and friends.

A girlfriend is not a wife and should not be treated as a wife before becoming one. The title of girlfriend is a caption that describes interests, availability, and potential. The elevated position of fiancée is the prelude to marriage, preparing for the commitment but not entitled to the benefits of a wife. You mustn't dilute the sanctity of marriage. Exercise restraint in the progression of each status (for you and her) so that you are not undermining God's blessings for your marriage.

CLOSING:

I didn't tell all of my stories because there's a lot to tell, and there are some things I do not want to tell. The experiences shape you, but you don't always have to live it to learn it. My experiences and hearing the testimonies of others have shaped me into the person I am and the mother I am for you all. I did my best to address my own insecurities and traumas. You learn from your traumas. When you have allowed God to heal you from the traumas, the memories do not trigger sorrow but joy, praise, and worship. As your nana would say, "Take my good and grow and my bad and throw [it out]. Let God grow something beautiful over that rough and tough time in your life. It is what I have asked the Lord to help me do as a parent. Don't be quick to judge or dismiss the unsolicited advice from those who love you. You each are gifted with talents from God and he has blessed you with one another. You are a trifecta of power. Learn how to tell and accept the truth in love from one another.

Love, Your Momma

About Jacinda

Jacinda Beason Corporate Anthropologist

Jacinda Beason began her career in human behavior and development while employed as a diversity trainer with World Vision's CityLinc program and then in community outreach and volunteer management with the American Red Cross of Greater Chicago.

Her experience at two of the world's largest non-profit humanitarian organizations was a catalyst for her passion to create cooperative community environments of human capital thru training and service as a Corporate Anthropologist.

Since 2006, J.L. Beason Consulting has been instrumental in developing strategies for diversity, professional development, organizational development, and community engagement for corporations, campaigns, churches, and non-profit organizations.

In addition to her entrepreneurial work as a Corporate Anthropologist, Jacinda Beason has also served on several boards, was a moderator and guest panelist for Emory's International Medical Volunteer Conference, moderated the debate for IL 2nd Congressional district, and has been a campaign consultant. Jacinda was featured on the Telly Award Winning Podcast "Speak Out World: Arts, Activism, & More to discuss her expertise in volunteer management and on NPR's report on Chicago Parents raising sons.

Finding My Delight
DIONTRISE BLAKE

I can remember vividly the challenges I experienced as a young girl. The early years of my childhood can be classified as bitter/ sweet. My life toggled between turmoil and excitement, moments of extreme happiness, as well as moments of desperation and agony. King David said it best in the book of Psalms (51:5- AMP) Behold, I was brought forth in a state of wickedness; In sin my mother conceived me [and from my beginning, I too was sinful}. I was the product of two teenage parents. My mom was a rising senior in high school at the time of my arrival. She went on to complete her studies, obtain her diploma, and make plans to pursue post-secondary education, which she completed successfully.

While my mom was finishing school and working, I spent a lot of time with my dad. He would work nights and get up in the mornings to make me breakfast and chauffeur me to school. He would also make appearances at my school to check in on me and make sure I was behaving correctly. I went everywhere with my dad. I would long to be around him and to be showered with his loving affection and attention. I looked forward to hanging around the neighborhood and having others adore me as he did.

As a growing girl, I had come to expect a lot of attention and affection. Because I was the only child between my two parents (or at least I initially thought), I was very spoiled and craved attention exclusively. I thought the key ingredient to a successful relationship was for one to pay me all the attention I desired and lace my palms with dollar bills. At times, I was very outspoken. I could spell very well, and I had a knack for flaunting my knowledge of an unfamiliar word stock to show off my intelligence to garner money and attention.

All this began to change when I was about eight years old. I don't remember my exact age; however, I am very cognizant of the sequence of events. As previously stated, I was very vocal. My maternal grandmother was very shy, but if you rubbed her the wrong way, getting on her last nerve, as she would say, she would not hesitate to lash out at you, and she did often with me. My grandmother was my primary caretaker while my mom worked and went to college. So oftentimes, I would be at my grandmother's house, although I lived with my parents.

I recall being stood up by my mom many times. I would wait anxiously for my mom to come and fetch me to take me home, but according to my grandmother, my mom would be working late or she would be hanging out at the clubs (most of the time with her sisters) and would not be coming to pick me up to carry me home. I was highly disturbed, disappointed, and agitated as a result. That's when my spoiled nature kicked in. I would say to my grandmother, "You need to call your daughter and tell her to come and get me because I am ready to go home." In the beginning, she would respond softly, "Baby, go to sleep, and I'll wake you up when your momma comes." So, I started attempting to go to bed but found that I could not sit still.

My anxiety would kick in, and before I knew it, I was back up in my grandmother's face again, pleading with her to call my mom so she could come and pick me up. By this time, she became agitated. I would plead and plead with her to call my mom and tell her to come and get me. She would insist that I go back and lie down. I refused. And that's when name-calling started. She would say things like girl, take your crazy self and go lay down. I would, in turn, say you're crazy. These moments became increasingly intense, and her words, along with my words, became increasingly damning. She would say your Demon a _ _. I think my great-grandmother, who was a religious churchgoer, explained my situation to her madam, and her madam told her that I had a demon. She, in turn, informed my grandmother (her daughter), who in turn informed me. Labeling me as such caused my behavior to become progressively worse. I was very problematic, to say the least. That is when I formed the perspective that I am just not right. I took on the identity of a possessed child – and man, did I walk it out.

This routine continued for years until, one day, my grandmother was fed up. She was just too tired to continue to contend with me. In her frustration, agitation, and irritation, she relented and called her mother, my great-grandmother. At the warning of my great–grandmother, my grandmother hastened to follow her directions, instructions, and advice and proceeded to order me to the backyard to retrieve a switch. I went to fetch the switch (which was in the backyard of the apartment building she resided in). Upon my return, she ordered me to prepare for the whipping she was about to administer. I did as instructed. When she finished whipping me, she ordered me to fetch a copy of her bible.

I also obliged. While tears were pouring down my eyes, she demanded I open the bible and read the 23rd Psalm. I, being upset, refused to read it initially. Huffing and puffing and refusing to obey her outright, I initially refused. She hollered again read the 23rd Psalm. So I did. I read it to myself. She then screamed, "Read it out loud". So I did. As I think back to this time, I realize it was a day that drastically changed the course of my life. What I noticed at the moment was that as I read the passage, my tears dried up. There was a level of comfort that quieted my soul. It fed my soul. It comforted me so that I felt the presence of a being (someone much higher than me) surrounding me, letting me know that everything would be alright. I did not have to want any more or look further. Love had shown up and rescued me out of the pit of despair.

This happened once or twice more at the admonition of my grandmother. Afterward, I would take the initiative and withdraw to the scriptures to comfort me when my soul was disturbed or in trouble. I discovered that my pity, hopelessness, and sorrow dissipated at hearing and reciting God's word. I was beginning to discover this God of All comfort; this Father and Sustainer. This became a practice in my life.

Although I continued to act out in school for several years, it eventually changed my behavior. I went from cussing out my neighbors and my teachers (or at least speaking in an intense manner of disrespect- I spat on my fifth-grade teacher) to becoming academically and behaviorally sound. I was expelled from school due to my insulting my teacher in such a degrading and disrespectful manner. In spite of this despicable act, something in me had changed. Now, all of a sudden, I could feel remorse, and I was aware of the damage my actions had caused to another human being. I was now saddened by my behavior, and because of this incident, I vowed not only never to assault my teachers again but to exalt them and honor and respect them for the work of guidance they were providing in my life. Socially and physiologically speaking, I had begun to experience the course of evolution in my life. My path had become illuminated by the light of my Heavenly Father sent through his word.

As I transitioned from childhood to adolescence, I noticed that this level of peace surpassed my understanding and started settling in over my life. Not that I was immediately healed of all my emotional traumas and scars, or even the iniquity that I was brought forth in, but there was just this peaceful calm that began to accompany me, almost like a guide assuring me that no matter what the journey ahead entailed, I would not be faced with more than I could bear, neither would I face the road ahead alone. My grades immediately begin to improve. I began to take school more seriously. I started to move with a more resolute purpose and identity of some sort. My attitude drastically changed. It was as if my frown was turned upside down. I became almost a natural optimist. I began to see the bright side of life instead of the hopeless darkness of my environment that I had been accustomed to experiencing. I moved with purpose and goals. I graduated with excellent honors and was at the head of my elementary school class. I was geared toward greater academic achievements and accomplishments at the high school level.

My high school years, of course, brought about the challenges of adolescence along with the consequences of the iniquities of my forefathers. As I mentioned earlier, I was brought forth in a state of wickedness; in sin, my mother conceived me {and from my beginning, I, too, was sinful. My father would sometimes refer to me as a child as a hot ass – meaning I liked to walk around and strut my stuff (whatever that means). As a child, I had no idea what he was referring to; however, during my teenage years, I discovered that it meant I longed to be the subject of one's undivided attention. It became a necessity during this stage of my life. I hungered for it. It was definitely a part of the fabric of my make-up.

I would entertain guys on the phone beginning in my eighth-grade year, although my mom told me I could not date until I was sixteen. I think she was afraid that I would become a teenage parent as she had done and slight myself of the chance to achieve any worthy goals in my life. She sort of "scared me straight." However, my fiery, passionate nature would not let me rest where boys or entertaining male company was concerned. So, I talked over the phone with boys and often conversed with them during the school day. Against my mother's wishes, I started courting semi-officially during my ninth-grade year. I would go to movies in the theatre and kiss, smooch, and the like. I guess one could say

I was definitely hot in the pants. However, I was careful enough not to cross the lines of sexual intercourse for fear of what might happen to me if I did. My oh my, I must say this was a difficult temptation to withstand.

During the summers of my high school career, I would visit my cousins on my dad's side. There would be a plethora of boys hanging around their house during this time. Needless to say, I became caught up with a few of the boys; however, by the grace of God, it did not escalate immediately into promiscuity. There was a whole lot of foreplay going on. I realized at this time, if nothing more, that I like to show romantic affection to the boys, kiss them, and smooch, but that was as far as I would go. I would play hide and seek and entice the boys to chase me, but all to no avail. Yet, at that moment, I was keen on not giving up the "panties," as they would say during that time.

I thought I had fallen in love during the summer of my tenth-grade year. I caught the eye of a guy who lived in a neighboring community down the street from my aunt. He was about five years older than me; he was twenty then, and I was fifteen. We would hang out and date, but with him, it was different. He had a car to pick me up, and we would ride around town in comfort and isolation. At the time, it was as though he consumed my world. We would talk every day for long hours and hang out until late in the evenings, often past midnight. We were all lovey-dovey until one day while having a public conversation with my cousins, he blurted out that I had given him a blow job, and we had had sex. With the onset of embarrassment and a slight impairment to my pristine nature, I refused to allow him to bring shame and deformation to my character, so I ended it there. I decided he would not have another chance to mispresent me to my family or anyone else. I was as done with him as done could be.

Shortly after dismissing him, school started again for the fall semester of my 10th-grade year. At this point in my life, I became an avid roller skater as my mom introduced the sporting art to me as a child (a toddler really). So it was on an October night in 1991 that I hung out with some cousins of mine and decided to go skating on Metropolitan Avenue. We had arrived at the skating rink by bus, and we were standing in a long line when all of a sudden, I heard a chant from someone in the crowd seeking to get my attention so they could inquire about my identity and lure me away from the line into his presence. I complied.

Nonetheless, we started talking, and before I knew it, he had whisked me away to go get something to eat. I didn't hesitate to follow. Once we grabbed something to eat, we left the scene of the skating rink and my cousins, for that matter, and off we went. At this particular age in my life, I had no clue what I was getting myself into. We went to a park, and soon we started talking, kissing, smooching, and the like, and I realized it had gotten very late into the night. Cell phones were not affordable at this time, so I could not reach any of my cousins or family members to assure them that I was safe and secure. I suggested to him that we better get a move on it so that I could arrive safely at my aunt's house without anyone being alarmed by my absence. He adhered and took me to my aunt's house.

He was in his second year of military college, which was a little over an hour away from the city. We would talk on the phone sparingly. I thought I was in love again, but this time, I thought it was more real than the first time. I was enamored with the idea of love and what it meant for someone to shower me with attention and affection. I thought I had arrived. He came to the city several weekends and would take me around his family. Although I thought I was madly in love, I didn't want to run the risk of getting pregnant as my mom had done with me. I am not sure if I was more afraid of the actual act of having sex or afraid that my image would be tarnished by becoming a teenage mom. What I do recall is that my mom drilled me to no end on the dangers of having kids before it was time. I saw the difficulty and challenges she experienced with me and how she often questioned whether she had made the right decision to have me.

The conflict she was experiencing caused me to reconsider my sexuality, at least for the time being. So, because of my mental and emotional inhibitions, needless to say, I decided I would wait for sex. I thought the way we felt about one another was very strong and that he thought I was worth waiting on. I wanted to believe that he cared enough for me to allow me to come into my own comfort and assurance where my sexuality was concerned. This was not the case. After about two to three months of seeing each other, it was Christmas time. I felt this warm, fuzzy holiday feeling that something magical was in the air where our love was concerned. We saw each other around the Christmas holidays, and afterward, the fire and passion I thought we shared began to subside. Once the new year arrived, I wrote him several letters but did not receive any letters in return. I took it as though that brief chapter of love had ended. I started to have thoughts of being hopeless in love.

As spring/summer approached the new year, my family was having an event in the park, and I met the brother of my best friend, who was my fleeting love. They attended the same school and knew each other very well. We seemed to have hit it off pretty well (the brother and I). We started talking on the phone, and before I knew it, he would meet me after school and I would meet him. I went to his house on several occasions. Again, sex was not really on my mind. I can't say the same thing about him. At this time, I was more interested in discovering what happened between his brother's best friend and me. Nonetheless, rumors got back to me that it had been said that he and I slept together, and this was not true. So again, it was time for me also to part ways with this encounter.

Shortly after, the end of my sophomore year of high school had come to an end. During the last few weeks of school, I was approached by a graduating senior. I thought myself very intelligent and felt honored to be pursued by such a shrewd individual. We talked and hung out because he was soaring his wild oats before leaving for college to attend Tennessee State University. We spent a considerable amount of time engaging in intellectual conversation with sexual under and overtones. I was hesitant with him because I didn't want to give away my cookies. However, he definitely wooed me intellectually and could have taken my cookies had that been his desire. So we courted periodically during the summer, and then he was off to Tennessee to begin the college years of his life. We would talk and keep in touch upon his return home.

The Fall of my Junior year in high school was fast approaching, and I had met yet another male suitor. He seemed to be the perfect gentleman. He was five years my senior and the most senior of the suitors pursuing me at this time. We often talked on the phone, and we would go out to eat and things like that. I started working earlier that summer at Checkers fast food restaurant. He would periodically pick me up from work and deliver me safely home. We spent countless nights talking on the phone with each other. He was really gentle to me. At the height of our courtship, we reached some heated moments where I was tempted to give in and have sex with him. I was older now, and he made me feel mature. I think I enjoyed that he didn't pressure me, although he let it be known that his attraction to me was very strong. I must say I enjoyed being around this guy. He caused me to feel, believe, and think that I was maturing into a decisive, strong-willed, confident young woman. We courted for the duration of my Junior year in high school, and that flame also dissipated. It was becoming apparent that if I weren't giving away the cookies, then there would not be any continual admiring of the cookies or the jar that housed them.

Finally, my junior year was ending, and I was becoming empowered by what lay ahead in my senior year of high school. As the school year ended, I focused my energy, efforts, and attention on getting a car, so I worked diligently towards that goal, saving my money and working as many hours as possible. Work assisted me with the feelings of loneliness and the realization that no one was actively courting me. I decided to walk the single path, being very happy and content with being to myself and by myself. This chapter of loneliness did not last very long. As fate would happen, I stumbled across another graduating senior who was also a basketball star. We hit it off also. I became very fond of him because he was silly and made me laugh. We talked often during the summer, and he, too, was off to college, which again left me feeling very unwanted and alone. This left room for me to focus on my senior year and dedicate myself to being in the top 10% of my class. I reached the goal. I graduated 10th in a class of roughly 400 graduating high school seniors. I was simply thrilled.

Once graduation night had passed, I found for the first time in my life that I was not only very lonely, but at this moment, anxiety had also crept into my mind and my emotions. I was very anxious about the approaching adult life and what lay ahead. I was about to start college, and most of all, I had made it through my high school career without getting pregnant. I felt somewhat accomplished but still very lonely. After graduation, I immediately threw myself into roller skating, where I continued to entertain male suitors. I fell in love with the idea of getting a full body exercise and garnering the attention of spectators. It was very exhilarating. So this summer was no different. There were several male fans noticing me, and I felt the need to entertain the attention they were giving.

I felt grown and free. I had purchased a car the summer before (starting my senior year of high school). So I was a young and inexperienced driver with a lot of gas on my chest and a lot of unchanneled energy to invest. I invested my energies in several male suitors in the skating atmosphere. This finally led to me losing my virginity. I felt depressed, violated, and discouraged. I would enter into the college chapter of my life no longer a virgin but also unsure about the road ahead. I felt like in this stage or season of my life; I had arrived in the middle of nowhere (a desert) with no promising direction of pursuit.

My college years were very revealing. Looking back, these years of my life have provided a lot of insight and knowledge concerning my womanhood. During this stage of my life, when I was able to make my own decisions, I began to realize that with the free will I had been given and nobody to really answer to, I became full of myself. As Paul said in Romans 7:15 (MES) – What I don't understand about myself is that I decide one way, but then I act another, doing things I absolutely despise. So I can't be trusted to figure out what is best for myself and then do it, it becomes obvious that God's command is necessary. It seemed to me during that period of my life, my sin meter was fast and out of control. I had begun to go down this path of sexual promiscuity, and nothing about it felt right. I was seeing someone whom my flesh suggested I loved, but my spirit said no way. Deep down in the pit of my soul, I could sense that even at this young age, he was not the one for me. About six months into dating him, I received a very disturbing, painful phone call one morning. It was my cousin informing me that he was married. I thought at that moment someone had taken a knife and shattered my heart into broken, fragmented, unrepairable pieces. He told me he loved me, yet I found that he had married someone else while dating me.

How could this be? My life had begun to spiral out of control. As months passed, I reluctantly forgave him and let him back into my world, all to my demise. I have realized that I get the wrong painstaking results when I do things my way. Nothing but heartache, agony, affliction, and torture came from this entanglement: lies, deceit, a lack of trust, and ultimate betrayal. There was no way I could establish a life of trust, love, and respect with someone who had no knowledge or understanding of the subject. The way of this relationship led straight down the path to destruction, for the wages of sin (doing my own thing and pursuing what pleases me) is surely death.

From this point forward, the fabric of my world has changed. I was plagued with guilt, shame, and condemnation for my actions. I was very sorry for my decisions, which led me to focus even more on my Heavenly Father and His word. I immersed myself in a self-led study of the bible. I made an outright effort to change my ways. I considered dropping out of college as I was dwindling in a state of pity and feeling sorry for myself for the things I had done. I was experiencing what my therapist would later refer to as "Learned Helplessness." I kept reminding myself that this wasn't me. It was probably somewhere at this point in my life that I realized the sin and iniquity I had been born into: A serious pattern of sexual sin and immorality. Because this vice was larger than me, I felt helpless and hopeless in defeating it and overcoming it. I did, however, discover that I had a Heavenly Father who did not put me here to be defeated by the wickedness that had plagued my antecedents before I had arrived on the scene; but had sent his only begotten Son to me to save me, to redeem me, to heal and restore me from the evil ways of my predecessors. Praise be unto the most High God. I did repent of my actions, and peace returned to me.

As time progressed, I began to refocus my energy on my studies, finishing school, and looking forward to the next chapter in my life. Later in the year, I received a phone call from one of my college classmates who asked me if I would do her a favor and attend the World Series with her stockbroker. She knew I was not interested in dating anyone and assured me that this was not a date but a fill-in for one of her other friends who would be dating him later in the week. I agreed. Shortly after, I received a phone call from a very articulate individual. He stated his name and told me he had been given my number by my college classmate and proceeded to give me the details of the date, which happened to be to 1996 Major League Baseball World Series. We discussed the details and arrangements for the day to follow. The next day, he arrived at my door and rang the doorbell. I peeped through the hole and opened the door.

As I opened the door, I noticed he had on very tight jeans. Before I knew it, I closed the door in laughter, and before I could open the door again, I heard a still, swift voice inside of me saying, "While you're laughing, this is going to be your husband!" I immediately wiped the smirk off my face, opened the door, greeted him properly, and attended the World Series game. On the way to the game, he played Celine Dion, and I thought, oh wow! This must really be meant to be. He likes what I like. We went on to enjoy a lovely evening at the World Series. Upon arriving at the game, he asked if I was hungry (and I thought to myself – yes, as a hostage). He proceeded to ask what I wanted to eat. I ordered a hot dog, a slice of pizza, a pack of M&M's, some potato chips, and a soda. He said, "I know you're not going to eat all that?" I was thinking to myself – just watch me. I ate the meal in totality and actually thought that it just teased me- I wanted more.

After the game, he invited me to another game the next day. I was overjoyed to go. I was like, I know I'm going to get a great meal if nothing else. He was very different to me, like no one I had dated before. For the first time, I wasn't madly in love with this man. However, I had a strong admiration and deep respect for him, probably because he respected me. Naturally, we started dating. We traveled some, and the next thing I knew, we were in a whole relationship. I got pregnant, gave birth to my son, and we were married several months later. We went on to attempt to build a life together. We were married for twenty years, together for twenty-three. We produced three wonderful children together, and I must say, looking back, I have no regrets.

There were several factors that led to the demise of my marriage. There was a lack of communication, a lack of trust, and overall, a level of respect that dissipated between the two of us. Also, during the end of our marriage, I was raped by a childhood acquaintance. I sought counseling, but it was difficult to move past this hurdle. I heard a sermon before, and the preacher said people don't divorce because they fall out of love with each other; they divorce because they do not know how to make the marriage work. Proverbs 24: 3 – 4 AMP reads- Through [skillful and godly] wisdom a house [a life, a home, family] is built, And by understanding it is established [on a sound and good foundation]. And by knowledge, its rooms are filled with all precious and pleasant riches.

Ultimately, I realized that my life journey had me traveling through the tunnel of darkness. I did not possess the wisdom {application], understanding [comprehension], and knowledge [information] to build, establish, or fill my house [life, marriage, and home] with precious and pleasant riches. This is currently the journey I am on, one where my life and virtue match my profession, and all glory and honor go to the Father, Son, and Holy Spirit. One that glorifies my Lord and Savior Jesus Christ.

About Diontrise

Diontrise Blake is an heiress on a journey to walk in the fullness of her divine inheritance. She is a devoted mother to three wonderful fellow heirs, finding immense joy in guiding and growing alongside them.

A passionate lover of God and life, Diontrise seeks daily to embody joy, strength, peace, kindness, laughter, and fun. Her unwavering faith is her foundation, rooted in the belief that one does not live by bread alone but by every word that proceeds from the mouth of God, the Creator.

Diontrise is committed to living with purpose, embracing the abundant life promised by her faith, and inspiring others to do the same.

From Pieces to Peace

Masiya Bomoni

"Amidst the Scattered fragments of my life lies a profound journey waiting to unfold. Join me on my transformative path from pieces to peace".

My life journey began in the summer of 1968. I can't say specifically who I was in previous lives. Yet I was told by several people that I was a fighter. One who would stand for right and justice even if that meant being a martyr. I can't say what DNA I was associated with before this life's path. But from what I can remember, my mom was also a fighter. It wasn't until I was forty-five that I found my dad's people through Ancestry.com. With both parents departing from this life, I have no clue as to the situation of my inception of pregnancy. However, this journey would be one of true transformation and elevation. Because of who I am and how I have always been a warrior when asked if I would go during this time of change to be a soldier and further my purpose, I said yes!

When conception took place between my mom and dad, it was to bring about an experience that would assist me in continuing my purpose of growth and transformation. "Like a puzzle coming together, this life journey is and has always been one of transition, progressing from scattered pieces to evolving into a masterpiece of peace and fulfilled purpose. "I am Masiya Tyone Bomoni born Contrina Tyone Walton in Atlanta Ga April 8, 1969. I was told by my mom at the time of my birth that things moved pretty fast during my delivery. She was told by the doctors to go home because it wasn't time for my arrival. However, while putting on her clothes, she felt an uncontrollable need to push. She did, and I was out. That should have been her awareness that I would be a force to be reckoned with. This was the beginning of the pieces that would come together to make my purpose-filled life eventually assemble into peace.

As explained to me by relatives, the first three months of my life were already starting to display pieces of my puzzle being scattered about. Being that my mother herself was conceived through rape, she too was in pieces and could only give to me what she was capable of. At the time of my beginnings, she couldn't provide a loving, nurturing, or stable environment. She always felt unloved, abandoned, and even hated by her own mother. This probably had to do with her conception. Because she was broken, she would leave me in the house alone for hours. Several times, my aunt, who was twelve then, or grandmother would find me alone, usually in a soiled diaper and hungry. Sometimes crying or playing and cooing as if someone was there watching over me.

What made the pieces start coming together was one day, I was left alone, and my aunt found me on the side of the bed, lying on the box spring between the wall and mattress. She said it was as if someone or something adjusted the mattress for me to lay safely. After that particular incident, my grandmother became concerned about my safety. She cried out to God for help. Immediately, the answer came to her to call her cousin Barbara to see if I could come for a couple of weeks until she could figure out a plan. She said yes. The next day, I was put in a taxi and taken to Barbara's house, and those three weeks turned into five years. The puzzle pieces were being arranged. Everything was happening just as it was supposed to. I didn't understand then, but my guardians and angels were always in place for my protection and provision.

During those five years of living with my cousin, there were positive and negative situations that helped build the necessities needed to fulfill my journey in this lifetime. No matter what, the right people and provisions were always in place. So many people were able to contribute to the beginnings of my life. Whether it was a roof over my head, food, clothes, or nurturing and love. I had all of that.

It wasn't until I turned six that life became complicated and discombobulated. The pieces of the puzzle were moved, tossed, and shuffled around. At this point, I felt unsure, unloved, and abandoned even by those whom I trusted the most. One day, after six years of living with my cousins, my mother called out of the blue and said she was moving to Florida and taking me with her. Instantly, my stomach dropped to the floor. I didn't even really know my mom. Those times I spent with her were very unpleasant. Three weeks later, she came to pick me up. I went from a loving, nurturing, stable home to a house that was lonely, abusive, and very unpredictable. Within six months of moving with my mother, I gained sixty-eight pounds. This was not only the beginning of the lessons I chose to come and learn, it was also [the beginning of a weight gain journey that would spiral so out of control. The pieces were being put into place. All I know is that the little girl, Tye, couldn't understand what was happening. In the meantime, my heart was being crushed, my mental and emotional state was devastated, and my body was being physically assaulted.

My mother was very abusive. Anyone at that age would feel the same. This phase of my journey or process was to move me from brokenness and discord (pieces) to being able to one day fulfill my purpose. I felt alone and isolated. Therefore, I went into survival mode. I became very angry and sometimes even aggressive; at that, I lost trust and was unable to see the world as just or fair. At this point, life wasn't loving, calming, or nurturing from my point of view. My world was a world filled with conflict, violence, and challenges. It was chaotic from where I was. What was going on inside was also showing up outside. "As within so without."

Gaining almost seventy pounds was my way of protecting myself, and food comforted me. At this point, food became my friend, and the weight I gained became my protection. It represented a false peace. Seven months after living in Florida, my two brothers (twins), whom I had never lived with, came to finish out the last two months of us living there. They didn't adjust too well because they had lived with their grandmother from birth, the same as I had lived with my cousin Barbara from three months of age.

None of us had ever lived with our mom permanently or constantly. We were all trying to adjust to each other and our new living conditions. The three of us were coping the best we knew how. Because my mom worked many hours, I became their mom. That was hard for me because they were used to being wild and free. And to keep them in the house was an unfair duty for me. But I had to unless I wanted to get a beating.

It wasn't long before we moved back to Atlanta, but the harm and detriment had already been done to my psyche and my body. In the meantime, all provisions were still being put in place for me. Moving back around some stability gave me a sense of hope.

After several years of back and forth living with my mom, the Department of Family and Children Services had to be called in to permanently remove me from my mother's custody. I was exhausted and becoming angrier. I was twelve years old and weighed about 400 pounds by this time. This was the beginning of the puzzle pieces being arranged where I could see the puzzle forming into a picture. In my heart, I could still feel some relief and hope.

Several months later, I started Douglass High School. This was a new beginning for me. I could now let my guard down. I felt there was hope for my life and future. Even though all this was happening to and through me, I now weigh over 400 pounds. But, regardless of my size, there was still a sense of knowing there was something special and unique about me. I still always felt the presence of God and protection around me. My sense of awareness became even more keen. I was always yearning for more, and I knew there was more than what the world displayed to me. I began seeing the world differently. This made me question everything and everybody. I even sometimes questioned God.

There was this sense inside that this world wasn't fair or just, and I questioned why this would be allowed by a loving God. Why I was born into a life of abuse. I was always in trouble with my mouth and my perception because I was taught you are to be seen and not heard. But because of my strong will and warrior spirit, I couldn't conform. Even though many blows had made me sometimes feel I wasn't enough when it came to the world. Even though my life was in pieces, I always had a sense of inner peace. I now had to learn how to maneuver through.

While at Douglass High, provision was still put into place. My homeroom teacher and others were placed on my path to help me develop and learn. What do I mean by that? Because of all I had experienced, I was very angry. Before the first quarter of school was over, I had already gotten into several fights and gotten suspended. My attitude was, I don't care! Even though I did, I wouldn't show that part of me. That would have made me feel weak. So, you could say something wrong or even look at me wrong, and I jumped. That was the fighter in me. And because my homeroom teacher and others could see something in me that I couldn't see for myself then, they were my angels and guardians.

It wasn't till my junior year that I started changing for the better. Before then, I would fight and get suspended. One day unexpectedly, my homeroom teacher came smoothly walking towards me and jacked me up on the wall, and said, "If you get in one more fight, I am going to beat your ass myself. Baby, that's what she wrote. I fell in love. That was all

I needed, a little tender yet tough love, and the true change began. The pieces were coming together. Yet, the true transformation or outlook on life didn't start until my senior year. Around December, everyone was excited about what school they had been accepted to. Before then I wasn't thinking about attending any post-secondary school. I wanted to be a singer.

One day, I auditioned for La Face Records and was told because of my size and the way the world viewed people, my music would not sell. Before Christmas break, I went to my counselor to inquire about college. My GPA was 1.5 then, and I hadn't taken the SAT or ACT. At the time, I was in the work program. I would go to school for half a day and work the other half. I worked at English Ave Elementary School. On my way to work one day, I asked God what I was supposed to do. I only had five more months till graduation. A quiet, still voice came to me and said, "I want you to teach." Ones you can touch and make a difference with. I went straight to my counselor and told her I wanted to go to try to apply for West Georgia. We did! A couple of weeks later, I received a call stating that because I had not prepared for college, it would be best for me to apply to a Junior college. That same day, I called Atlanta Jr College to ask what I needed to do. They told me, and I started the process. That was one of the best things that could have ever happened to me.

Once I applied and was accepted that fall quarter, the puzzle pieces were moving around in my favor. I had to start from the bottom because I didn't apply myself in school. My first two semesters were basic developmental courses. I didn't know much about reading, writing, or arithmetic. I didn't know anything. Looking back, I don't know how I graduated outside of my ancestors, angels and guardians looking out and moving puzzle pieces on my behalf. But again, this was the best thing that could have happened to me. I learned everything I didn't get in grade or high school. I met my reading teacher Ms. Hunter, and I worked under her for work-study. She helped mold me in so many ways. I love and appreciate her for that to this day.

In my second year at AJC, I ran for Ms. Photography Club and won. Many students inspired me to run for Ms. AMC in my last year. In my heart, I wanted to run. Yet, I was doubtful not because I didn't believe in myself but because the way of the world is and has been for a long time. This system discriminates against people for so many reasons because of class, race, color, disabilities, and, for me, my size. Even though I now weighed over 450 pounds, the student body could see I had it in me to represent the school. They saw my truth beyond weight.

They insisted, and eventually, I gave in and pursued. I started championing; we had the pageant and the talent show. It ended up being four of us running for queen. In my heart, I felt like I could win. No matter my size, I knew, and the students knew I was beautiful inside and out. I was still on edge and felt uneasy about everything because, intuitively, I knew there would be deceit and dishonesty.

I went to Ms. Hunter and expressed that I felt the person over the pageant would cheat to keep me from representing the school. She pulled me into her office and said, "What's for you is for you." The day came for the voting to occur. My intuition was so acute that on the day of the voting, I asked if I could be in the room when they counted the ballots. Of course, I was told no! When they came back and announced Moniqe as the winner, my heart dropped. I knew that would be the outcome. I went back to Ms. Hunter. and told her that they didn't allow the true results because of my size and didn't want me to represent the school at 450 pounds. She turned to me, held her finger, twisted it, and said again, "What is for you, Contrina, is for you." I took her on that and believed justice would prevail.

Fall came, and Monique chose the theme for the coronation. I kept playing back to what my professor had said. It bothered me, so I became sick. And I wanted to not face things because, in my heart, I felt they had cheated. After being out of school for a week, several people called and asked, "girl, when are you going to return to school."

The next day, when I was getting off the bus, people kept saying, "Hey, Ms. AJC." After class, we had to meet to start practice. When I entered the library, everyone was smiling. It wasn't until the dean came in and said due to unconditional circumstances, Monique could no longer be Ms. AMC. Everybody started clapping. I was in shock and disbelief. I thought to myself I already had my dress made for Ms. 1st attendant.

After practice, I couldn't wait to get to Ms. H. She just rolled her neck and smiled. I knew exactly what that look meant. It wasn't until later that I found out what had happened. Monique dropped a class, which made her a part-time student, and she couldn't represent the school with that status. The interesting part was that the dean tried to do everything he could to get her reinstated. The professors and student counsel at the school fought and said no. It belonged to Contrina; they had no choice. Their backs were against the wall.

You can't wiggle your way out when God puts things in place. The same man who cheated was the same man who had to give me the crown that was mine in the first place. The coronation was extraordinary, and my dress fit the part perfectly. It was Silver like royalty. That year, I graduated. I went from having a D average in high school to a C average in Junior college. It should have taken two years to complete my associate's degree, but it took three because I had to play catch up. AJC was the real foundation of my transformation. Even though I was always a fighter, the fighting began changing from a physical fight to a more mental and spiritual fight. I even learned about Islam, and that, in itself, took me down another path in my journey. I was becoming a more insightful thinker, gaining a sense of peace. I applied to Albany State to further my education and obtain my bachelor's degree and I was accepted.

August came so quickly, and I was off to Albany, Ga. I remember the day like it was yesterday. As soon as Momma and Daddy left, I went to get my schedule. Things didn't go as I was told. Classes I was told would be accepted where not. They added more classes, which would cause me to have to be there longer than I had anticipated. I was so upset that I reacted. I packed all my belongings and asked my new friend Michelle to take me to the Greyhound Station. I left! I didn't call Momma and Daddy until I was back downtown in Atlanta at the Greyhound station. Daddy came to the station, and I was standing there with my TV, footlocker, and pillows. He looked at me and took a deep breath and said," Do you think you jumped the gun and reacted too quickly, or do you think you thought about this and responded." He then chuckled and said, "You almost bet us back home." I couldn't hear what he was saying to me at that moment nor did I understand the implications of what he had just said to me.

I just decided to get a job and not go back to school. That was what I did. No one really said or guided me to go back and try again. After six months working at KinderCare and seeing those checks for $200.00 a week, I decided to go back and complete my education. The only thing I regret about my stay at Albany State was that I didn't gain the full fun college experience for those two years because I was headed home every weekend.

Two years later, I finished school with a B average. Every time I graduated from any institution, I visited my 6th-grade teacher to give her an invitation. I will never forget when she overlooked my acting out in school because something in my home life was off. She didn't pay attention to me wearing long-sleeved shirts in April because of bruises I was trying to cover up. I remember her standing in my face, and she told me I would never be anything or do anything with my life. So, each time I graduated, I made it my business to show her. Those words she spoke over me which could have broken me are the words that pushed and motivated me. And the pieces of the puzzle were still being put together.

After graduation, all of my friends were off applying for teaching positions. I interviewed and was hired for a teaching position with Atlanta Public Schools at the Emergency Shelter. They placed classes at the shelter for children who had been placed in DFCS custody. Depending on their situation, they did this so the children could continue receiving services while they were waiting to be placed with family members, in foster care or in a group home.

It was so ironic because I had to go through that same place when I was taken from my mom in 1982. And what a coincidence for me to end up working there. Those children had been in a situation similar to mine. I ended up working there for 10 years until it closed. Those were the best 10 years of my teaching experience. While working there, two of my relatives were removed from their homes, and I ended up fostering them. Doing what someone had done for me, giving back.

Several months after graduating, at the age of 23, I became a foster mother to a 12-year-old and a 5-year-old, who were my relatives. Quanna was 12, Boo was 5, and I was only 23. I was in school working on my Master's degree at the time. They went to school with me every week. After two years in school, I graduated Cum laude in my class with an A average. Who would have ever thought, being I was told, I would never be anything? For seven years, it was just the three of us. In 1998, I purchased a home that was built from the ground.

One day, I wasn't feeling my best. I had been feeling tired and sleepy for about a week or so. I went to the doctor for a sinus infection, I thought, but was told I was pregnant. I couldn't believe it because I now weighed nearly 500 pounds, and the doctors said it would be next to impossible for me to have children at that weight. Yet nine months later, my first biological son was born. Even though I waited, I had a career, a home, had completed several degrees, had a new car, and had given birth to my own child, my mind and my life were still unsettled. Something still felt incomplete.

There was no peace. I was still in pieces. Yes, I was learning lessons, growing and had several accomplishments, there was still a sense of unsettling in my soul. Yet, I could feel a tugging of my spirit that knew something wasn't right. I was still doing more but feeling less than. Being that I was now over 500 pounds, I decided to fight my insurance company in order to have gastric bypass surgery. Even though I was healthy at that weight, I could only think of leaving my children behind because of the long-term risk of being that overweight. I had the surgery and released over 300 pounds. I thought that would make me feel more at peace. I even received three more children in my home to foster. A 15-year-old who had a 9-month-old and her brother, who was 6 at the time. I thought the more I did and gave back, the better I would feel. In the process of doing so much, I wasn't taking care of myself. My spirit self, to be more precise. I was just doing and not learning to just BE!

After realizing my eleven years on and off relationship with my son's father was done, I finally terminated it. Yet, because I was still broken, I attracted another person that was even more toxic. I was still in pieces. I was attracted to who and where I was at that point in my journey. I met Jose. At first, I was excited. We had so much in common as far as business aspects were concerned. We both had ideas of buying and renovating houses to sell or rent. As my grandmother would say, I jumped the gun too fast and put the horse before the carriage. What was supposed to have been a bridge encounter turned into a lifetime experience.

It wasn't long before I became pregnant with my daughter. I began seeing the red flags. Yet, I chose to ignore them. My rationale at the time was we could make this work. We had a child on the way and some of the same aspirations. While I was pregnant, he went back to Mexico. He stayed for two years, and in the process, we got married in Mexico. Within the next four years, we created two more children. Once he returned, we were also married here in the USA, in Tuskegee, Al.

Tuskegee reminded him so much of his homeland and country life that he decided to relocate there to farm commercially. He had farmed most of his life and could no longer work in the flooring industry. He wanted to do something he was good at and make an income from that to provide for our family. Against my better judgment, I decided to follow and be the supportive wife. I went from living in a brick home and being a schoolteacher to living in a trailer, becoming a stay-at-home mom and farmer's wife. In the process of following his dream, I lost myself.

It got to a point where I felt like I was losing my mind. My soul was yearning for me to find my purpose, and I was in chaos mentally, spiritually, and emotionally. My life was spiraling out of control. Jon wasn't who I thought he was, and I was becoming someone I couldn't even recognize. But being who I was, I tried to stick it out. An opportunity presented itself where we could work with Walmart and Tuskegee University. Tuskegee University experimented with minority farmers on a project to supposedly help farmers get their feet in the industry of growing commercially. This project was just another Tuskegee study. Different times, different people, same sinister outcome.

We and other minority farmers lost everything. What kept me sane during this time was I got to stay home with my children full-time. I learned farming, became GAP certified, cooked, cleaned, washed, and whole nine yards. I was a full-time homemaker, making soap, toothpaste, butter, and all kinds of natural remedies. In the process of all of this, I was losing my sense of self. Turmoil was taking place inside and out of me.

Around this time, I felt so defeated and depleted. I started searching for what I thought I had lost, my soul, my spirit man. One day, I went out in the field and cried out for help, and the help was right there waiting for me to ask. And the answers came. Just at that moment, I could feel peace coming upon me. I began to seek my higher self. I began to knock and the door was opened onto me. I found Christ, the Christ within. For so long, I had been searching, seeking, church hopping, looking for the Christ, I was taught about. The one outside me, not the Christ consciousness inside of me. Even though I was finding peace within, hell was about to break in my home in my marriage. My newfound findings caused a shift in me. I was no longer willing to sit and accept what was happening around me. I was truly beginning to see with my spiritual eye. I was no longer wandering around in darkness. I was moving and taking back charge of my life. I was now understanding and learning what was meant to seek ye first the kingdom of god and his righteousness. The more I learned, the more I wanted to learn. The pieces were finally coming together. I was finally feeling some sense of true peace.

I decided to stand straight with my head high, looking to the hills from which cometh my help. In doing so, I realized I wasn't who I was supposed to be or wanted to be. And Jose wasn't what or who I wanted to be with. I knew I deserved better for myself and my children. I was no longer willing to settle. The pieces were coming together. One of my regrets was by this time, I had subjected my children to my mess, and they, too, were in pieces. At the time, I didn't realize how much damage had taken place. But they too were on their journey having their life experiences.

With this newfound realization, things could only get worse before they got better, and they did. I was learning my truth, but my truth wasn't His truth. I was willing to take back what was rightfully mine in the first place. My life, my freedom, my joy, my peace. For most of my life, I had been existing and not living. The pieces finally aligned with my truth and my purpose. But I knew it wasn't going to be easy. I had to pick up the pieces and intentionally place them. I had to create the reality I wanted. Yet, I had to be strategic with it.

Out of nowhere, a quiet voice told me to reach out to Lei-Ann, a girlfriend who went to high school with me, and I did! I explained where I was spiritually and expressed where I was seeking to go. I told her I wished I could contact Iyanla Vanzant and be on her show to have my life fixed. She then told me about Inner Visions, a program Ms. Vanzant had developed. A program where you learn through spiritual self-development.

I applied to the program and was accepted to summer intensive. I went for a week of intense spiritual learning at Omega. This was the beginning of my rebirth. I learned so much and was exposed to so much knowledge and wisdom in that short time. There was a peace within I had never felt. My soul was hungering after righteousness. But at home, things were only becoming more tense. I was no longer sitting at the table I had allowed to be prepared. I was standing at the table I was now preparing. And Jon wasn't hearing that!

After attending a week at Omega, I knew I wanted more of what I had learned and experienced. I felt emotions and feelings in my heart and soul that I had never experienced before. My soul opened. I knew this was what I needed and this was what I wanted. Yet, I didn't know how I could afford the two-year program where we would have to travel to Maryland once a month. I wasn't working at the time. Right before I left for Omega, I applied to start teaching again. I had to believe this was for me and everything would work out. On my way home, I received a call from the elementary school principal and was offered a position to teach 1st grade. Things were beginning to look up for me.

Once back, I started working as a teacher at Carver, and the school at Inner Visions began the following month. I traveled every month to Maryland. The homework and the dedication to my spiritual growth were not on the front burner as it should have been. There were so many ..rods and distractions, but I kept going. I was learning and growing. I would go to school every month to learn and gain a sense of peace. Yet, before I could get back to Alabama, the conflict would continue until the following month, which continued for the next year and a half. Even though I was in school, my spirit was still unsettled. I couldn't hear the quiet, still voice inside. There was so much noise.

I was told I should seek a higher form of spirituality during this time. I was told about Ayahuasca. I had never heard of that, but I researched it and somehow ended up in Peru, seeking what was already inside me. After my experience, I was told by the Shaman I needed to learn to be still, meditate, and seek within. Your answers are already there.

In the meantime, I could see and feel the resentment and hostility brewing between Jon and me. It was getting scary; I knew it, and he knew it. It wasn't until I cried out and asked for help to end this madness.

One Sunday morning, I prayed and expressed how tired I was and that I had no consistent peace. I was beaten, and my soul was worn. I prayed and repeated a verse from Psalms in the bible several times. And I heard a small voice that said everything was already alright. By Wednesday, my prayer had been answered. Jon left the house to go out of town for business and never again set foot on that property. There was a gentle peace, yet a fear that came over me. Because for eight years, he had provided for the house, and now all responsibility would be on me. I had to be accountable for myself and my children, including Boon, who still was with me. Both of my mom's had transitioned. I had no one to lean on or confide in. I continued working and going to school. It was rough, but we did it. I did it!

I made it all the way to two weeks before Graduation, yet I didn't get a chance to complete the graduation requirements. Even though I didn't complete the graduation process, there was still peace in the whole situation. Over those two years, so much was going on that I didn't come full circle and get everything I should have from Inner Visions and Momma Iya. The pieces were still being arranged. Being honest with myself, I can truly say I wasn't ready to graduate. I am just now, after six years, choosing to put into practice what I learned and walk this path to my purpose and my destiny.

Since then, I sold the farm to repay a $50,000.00 loan we had taken out for the farm. I changed my perspective on life. I even changed my name to Masiya Bomoni. Masiya, which could be pronounced Massiah, means that I am the creator of my reality. Bomoni means warrior, and I am and have always been a warrior. I get the opportunity to create my reality. Once we moved from the farm, the children and I downgraded to an even smaller house. But the downgrade made me see I had to take that leap of faith to upgrade and move into my purpose.

For a long time, I suffered from Lymphedema in my legs. Legs carry us forward in life; lymph systems or problems represent the mind needing to be reentered on the essentials of life. And that's what I did and am doing! A year ago, everyone (my four children and I) stepped out on faith and moved to Florida. We didn't know anyone in Florida. That was a big leap of faith for us and especially for me. Even though we didn't know anyone here, I am so happy we took that leap of faith.

We never know how what we ask for will come to actualization. But our heart desires manifest when we see it, say it, believe it, and take action to do the work. I have always dreamed and spoken of owning my own school. I recently accepted a position working at a Waldorf charter school. After teaching for over 20 years in regular school systems, I am finally learning a curriculum intended to develop little scholars' intellectual, artistic, and practical skills and a curriculum that focuses on their imagination and creativity. In other words, they believe, let children be children. This was not how I was educated, nor was it the way I was taught. Even though I was a teacher, I always believed the system and the ways of the system were not for the betterment of the students. Therefore, in most schools where I taught, I would be rebuked by those in authority. I didn't blame them for their responses to my way of handling my class. Because people only do what they know and/or understand. Now, I get to teach according to my personality and the students who are attracted to my frequency or vibration.

Don't get me wrong, academics are important in this curriculum. However, cultivating substantial relationships and developing social skills and moral character is just as important, if not more. I will take what I have learned and what I am learning to create a school that is not just holistic but one of truth, justice, equality, equity, responsibility, accountability, understanding, willingness, and forgiveness. The ultimate goal is harmony, growth, transformation, resolution, and endearment. And for me, that's peace within and peace without. The peace that surpasses understanding. The peace the bible speaks of. A new world order of things. And this change begins with me.

At this point in my life, I can truly say I am not where I used to be, broken and shattered into so many pieces. I am growing, learning, and transitioning from pieces to peace! There have been lessons learned, obstacles, and challenges I have faced. I have had some achievements and successes. I have persevered and have shown resilience time and time again. I am on my way to total reconciliation with myself and achieving a sense of balance and well-being. I once was lost, but now I'm found. I was blind, but now I see. I was once told my purpose for being here in this lifetime was to gain peace. I know and interact with her (peace) frequently, but not on a constant yet! With me now knowing my purpose and standing in my power, I can truly say those things that could have broken me, made me! The more I embrace my truth, the more I love myself, my mom, and life itself. My ultimate goal is to gain an unchanging peace! And I am on my way.

About Masiya

Masiya Bomoni is a proud mother of four biological children and a nurturing "mom to many." Her journey through life has been marked by significant challenges and obstacles, all of which she has faced with determination and unwavering perseverance. At 55 years young, Masiya brings a unique perspective to life, having achieved remarkable successes despite being told she would never accomplish anything. She stands as a living testament to resilience, self-awareness, and the power of perseverance.

A lifelong advocate for justice and fairness, Masiya is an educator and motivational speaker who inspires others to pursue their dreams and embrace their authentic selves. Her passion for learning, reading, and research fuels her ability to ignite change and growth in those around her. She also finds joy in cooking and dancing, hobbies that reflect her vibrant and dynamic personality.

Masiya thrives on intuition and individuality, living life boldly on her own terms. Having endured moments of brokenness, she is now at a point in her life where her focus is on love, joy, happiness, and a peace that surpasses all understanding. She hopes to inspire others to embark on their own journeys toward this kind of profound peace and fulfillment.

The Impact of Prayer From Childhood to Adulthood

GWENDOLYN BRADLEY

Purpose: To enhance reflection on one's childhood and recount the numerous encounters with the voice of God and prayer.

There are numerous examples in scripture of how God revealed himself to children, but the most notable passage to me is 1 Samuel 3: 4-20:

"Then the Lord called Samuel.

Samuel answered, "Here I am." And he ran to Eli and said, "Here I am; you called me." But Eli said, "I did not call; go back and lie down." So, he went and lay down.

Again, the Lord called, "Samuel!" And Samuel got up and went to Eli and said, "Here I am; you called me."

"My son," Eli said, "I did not call; go back and lie down."

Now Samuel did not yet know the Lord; the word of the Lord had not yet been revealed to him. A third time, the Lord called, "Samuel!" And Samuel got up and went to Eli and said, "Here I am; you called me."

Then Eli realized that the Lord was calling the boy. So, Eli told Samuel, "Go and lie down, and if he calls you, say, 'Speak, Lord, for your servant is listening." "So, Samuel went and lay down in his place.

The Lord came and stood there, calling as at the other times, "Samuel! Samuel!" Then Samuel said, "Speak, for your servant is listening."

And the Lord said to Samuel: "See, I am about to do something in Israel that will make the ears of everyone who hears about it tingle. At that time, I will carry out against Eli everything I spoke against his family—from beginning to end.

For I told him that I would judge his family forever because of the sin he knew about; his sons blasphemed God, [a] and he failed to restrain them. Therefore, I swore to the house of Eli, 'The guilt of Eli's house will never be atoned for by sacrifice or offering.'"

Samuel lay down until morning and then opened the doors of the house of the Lord. He was afraid to tell Eli the vision, but Eli called him and said, "Samuel, my son." Samuel answered, "Here I am."

What was it he said to you?" Eli asked. "Do not hide it from me. May God deal with you, be it ever so severely, if you hide from me anything he told you." So, Samuel told him everything, hiding nothing from him. Then Eli said, "He is the Lord; let him do what is good in his eyes."

The Lord was with Samuel as he grew up, and he let none of Samuel's words fall to the ground. And all Israel from Dan to Beersheba recognized that Samuel was attested as a prophet of the Lord." (New International Version).

In the above passage, three times the Lord called out to Samuel, and three times Samuel went to Eli the priest, confusing the voice of God with the voice of Eli (vv. 4–9). Over the years of maturing in God, I have learned that sometimes the Voice of God will sound like your parent, teacher, or spiritual mentor in your inner ear. At Eli's direction, the young boy asked to hear from God the fourth time the Lord called to him.

Jesus's love for children is evident throughout the Bible, where he protects them and welcomes them into his kingdom.

Prayer has always been a spiritual discipline in my life since childhood.

Just as God used Eli to teach Prophet Samuel how to recognize and hear His voice, God used my grandparents to teach me the rhythm, necessity, and power of having a conversation with God and listening for divine instructions.

According to the American Association of Marriage and Family Therapy, Grandparents raise their grandchildren for various reasons. Most of these reasons reflect difficulties experienced by the grandchild's parents, which prevent the parents from caring for their children.

In my situation, my grandmother volunteered to raise me as my mother after accomplishing the awesome milestone of graduating from high school as a teenage mom planned to move out of Alabama into New York

For better job opportunities. As an African American woman living through the 1960s during the Jim Crow era, her moving plans would have been considered courageous and wise.

Many grandparents in the South would volunteer to raise their children's children so that they could pursue career opportunities out north, such as in states like Michigan, Ohio, and New York, that were not afforded to them.

God was working through this divine situation of teenage pregnancy in my mother's life to bring me to an expected end. He was preparing me to be a global prayer warrior! God also taught me how to travel, as I grew up taking many flights to New York, beginning at age Five!

I had a 16-year-old cousin, Pat, whose mother also moved to New York for better employment. Pat would chaperone her sister Pam and me as we took many summer flights to New York City to visit our mothers.

Preparing To Travel

The day before leaving on the trip to New York, I spent my evening on my grandparents' front porch, getting my hair hot combed. I used to hate this because I knew I would get burned at least once! Immediately after the hair straightening process, the community braider, Ms. King, tightly cornrowed my hair in tiny portions for a two-week sustainment. I was always thankful and overjoyed to complete this process!

My grandmother would prepare a care package that included fried chicken sandwiches, banana and mayonnaise sandwiches, crackers, and peppermint candy. She also wrapped money in a handkerchief for unexpected expenses along the way.

I visited New York for the first time when I was 7 -8 years old. Traveling by Plane was the scariest and most exciting experience ever! I remember sitting by the window and seeing the beautiful white clouds as the airplane glided through the sky. The ability to view the skyline above the clouds was worth any fear of flying that I had to overcome.

New York City had unending tall buildings and numerous cultures of people I had never dreamed of experiencing. It was great to see how my mother lived and spent time with her and other family members who had also migrated to New York. Sometimes, I wondered how my life would have been if I had grown up in New York instead of rural Alabama. I believe I would have missed valuable character development that I could only receive by being reared by my grandparents.

My Grandparents were very protective and selective of my surroundings and friends. The few friends that I had were mainly from the community that I grew up in and the Church that I attended. My Grandmother knew and had relationships with all of my friend's parents. She would allow me to visit their homes for a quick game of hopscotch, Red Rover, Jacks, or playing with paper dolls. I was barely allowed to participate in extracurricular activities other than youth choir, usher board, and Baptist Training Union until my high school years. My grandmother taught me valuable life skills like cooking, canning, cleaning, farming, painting, saving for a rainy day, and how to work for a living. I always thought that she was mean to not allow me to participate in a lot of things, but now that I am an adult, I realize that she was trying to protect me. She did not want my destiny in life to be thwarted. She did not want me to be abused, molested, or misused. She did not want me to be a teenage mom.

When I visited My Mother during the summer months, she allowed me more freedom. She taught me how to travel on the subway, train system, and bus. The streets were much safer than they are now. I learned that we live in a big world with many types of people. She took me to the movies and amusement parks and allowed me to visit the neighborhood corner store alone. Life was fast and busy!

As an adult, I travel frequently across America and Internationally on Ministry Assignments. I will always be thankful to God for preparing me as a child to be adventurous and willing to experience new cultures, territories, and people.

I am a firm believer in God's providence. Jeremiah 29:11 in the Passion Translation states, "Here's what YAHWEH says to you: "I know all about the marvelous destiny I have in store for you, a future planned out in detail. My intention is not to harm you but to surround you with peace and prosperity and to give you a beautiful future glistening with hope."

God had already planned for me to be grandparents by Rosie and Robert Mitchell. It was in their home that I learned about the love of God and the power of Prayer.

Rosie and Robert Mitchell served faithfully as deacons and deaconesses in the New Jericho Missionary Baptist Church. One of their responsibilities was hosting weekly Monday Night Prayer gatherings for the deacons and deaconesses within their home for New Jericho Baptist Church.

I had to turn off the television each Monday night while watching "The Gilligan Island Show" as prayer time began.

I was always amazed at the spirit-filled sounds that filled our home each Monday Night. Just the idea of the ability to commune with God interested me. Not only were the women talking to God, but the men as well.

My Grandmother only had a second-grade education but taught me how to pray, read my Bible, and speak in front of an audience. God used all these skills to raise me as the prayer warrior I am today.

One night, while we were traveling to my great grandparents, David and Betty Smith's home, who lived in the country, I felt compelled and drawn to gaze into the beautiful moonlit skies and have a conversation with God.

Prayer was, in some ways, mystical. That night, I pondered the honor of having the great opportunity to communicate with God.

When we talk to God, we must pause and allow God to talk back to us. Prayer is two-way communication.

Many would have the opinion that the most honorable appointment in the world would be an appointment with the President of America or another nation. The greatest appointment in the world is an appointment with God. He is never too busy to meet with those who seek time with Him!

My favorite scripture is and will always be, "Call to me, and I will answer you. I'll tell you marvelous and wondrous things that you could never figure out on your own." Jeremiah 33:3.

Supernatural Encounter

I can remember numerous supernatural encounters with God as early as six years old. I loved attending Church and serving in the Church. I participated in Sunday School, the Youth Choir, the Usher Board, and Youth Revivals. As a child, I had several dreams about future events. I remember waking up one night to see angels standing over me.

I would share all of these encounters with my grandmother, who was always eager to hear. As I reflect on my childhood, I now realize that God used my grandmother to teach me how to discern the spiritual realm and hear God's voice in my dreams. She had always shared her salvation experience with the family, which included, according to her, an angelic visitation at age eight.

My grandmother was very receptive as I shared my experiences with Angels, as she had had similar encounters.

Growing in Prayer

My transition from childhood to adulthood was filled with opportunities to learn more about Prayer and Seeking God in times of suffering and disappointment. One of my greatest life challenges was low self-esteem. I was overweight as an adolescent and often felt overlooked.

I suffered greatly emotionally and was often depressed. I began looking for love in all the wrong places. I allowed people in my heart who should have never been allowed there as I was taught to be giving, supportive, gentle, and to Always speak life. Treat people as you want to be treated. I received the opposite in some situations.

All of us experience trials and tribulations in life. Life's triumphs are not based on what happens to you but on how you react to or handle what happens to you.

Usually, we pray more when we encounter a hardship or difficulty in life.

David once said in Psalm 119:71, "It was good for me to be afflicted so that I might learn your decrees." We must remember that God controls the affairs of our lives. He has the master plan. Only what He allows to happen in our lives will occur. "And we know that in all things God works for the good of those who love him, who[a] have been called according to his purpose." Romans 8:28.

We gain insight and wisdom concerning our current plights when we pray to God about life's struggles.

Unless we encounter setbacks, struggles, and disappointments, our prayer life will not grow. Jesus learned obedience through the things that he suffered (Hebrews 5:8).

Inspired to Pray

Marriage was a tool that God used in my life to teach me how to release situations that I could not control. As a matter of fact, meeting my husband was an answer to prayer. I met him in my junior year of college after asking God to send me someone

To date. I prayed in my dorm room and asked specifically for the type of guy that I wanted. I loved watching western television shows like Bonanza and Big Valley, so I asked God to send me a cowboy! I laugh every time I reflect upon it. I did not want to take anything for granted. I had heard too many stories concerning dating woes and wounds from my college friends.

One Saturday Night, my college friends and I decided to attend a homecoming dance after a college football game. I met my husband at this dance. He shared with me his love for horses. At that moment, I knew He was sent by God, and my prayers had been answered.

Shortly after marriage, my husband was assigned to duty in Germany. I had never traveled outside of the country, so I had to learn how to trust God at a new level. Six months after moving to Germany, my husband was assigned to the Persian Gulf War. I had prayed and asked God not to send him, but God said, "No." I had to submit to the plan. The safest place to be is in God's will.

The Lord used my husband's deployment to teach me how to pray through uncertain and difficult times. I was not sure if he would ever return from the war. My relationship with God sustained and guided me through these uncertain times, helping me cultivate faith that everything would work together for good.

In Germany, I matured in my faith, spiritual disciplines, and prayer life. Some of my greatest spiritual growth and development were during difficult seasons.

Established in prayer

Matriculating through the School of Prayer has become my greatest asset in life. Learning how to pray more fervently and effectively requires submitting to seasons of adversity, suffering, and disappointment from childhood to adulthood.

Just because something that you go through in life is hard doesn't mean it isn't beneficial. Simply come to God with your whole heart; He'll heal and teach you how to take life's lemons and turn them into lemonade for His Glory. If you did not have a problem, how would you know that God is able to solve them? Prayer is definitely the vehicle to release those Problems to God. You grow through what you go through.

God uses those seasons of testing to draw us closer to Him, to refine and mold us, to strip away what isn't needed, and largely to shape us into the prayer warriors we need to be. The reward is so much greater than the suffering, which is an anointing on your prayer life.

About Gwendolyn

Dr. Gwendolyn Bradley is recognized as a Global Strategic Intercessor, Third Generation Pastor, Teacher, Media Influencer and International Prophetic Voice. She has traveled and ministered to over 30 Nations with boots on the ground In over 20 inclusive of Israel, Ghana, Sierra Leone, Liberia, Germany, Belgium, Spain, South Korea, The Netherlands, Poland, United Kingdom, Czech Republic and others.

Gwen Bradley serves on the Staff of National Day of Prayer Task Force and she is the National Liaison For Prayer Mobilization and Partnerships. She also serves as the National Area Leader of the Southeast Area (AL, FL, GA, MS, SC, Puerto Rico and Virgin Islands. Gwen diligently serves alongside her husband, Bishop Dr. Willie Bradley as Pastors and Founders of Anointed Remnant International Ministry in Prattville, Alabama.

The ecclesiastical couple also founded Anointed Remnant Global Assemblies, a global Fellowship providing mentorship to leaders in North America, the Caribbean, Australia, Asia,

Europe, Liberia (Gwen Bradley Girls School of Excellence) and Kenya (Orphanage).

Gwen's passion and heart is to connect, build and strengthen prayer warriors globally and to mobilize unified, public Prayer for America. The Bradley's have three beautiful children: Adrian (Vander), Andreas and Andria. They are proud grandparents of Aiden, Adrian II, Arden and Atlas.

Social Media:
Facebook: https://www.facebook.com/gwendolyn.bradley.96?mibextid=LQQJ4d

Instagram: https://www.linkedin.com/in/gwendolyn-bradley-271a5043?utm_source=share&utm_campaign=share_via&utm_content=profile&utm_medium=ios_app

YouTube: https://youtube.com/@gwendolynbradley8841?si=mfru-p_EwEqiOQl6

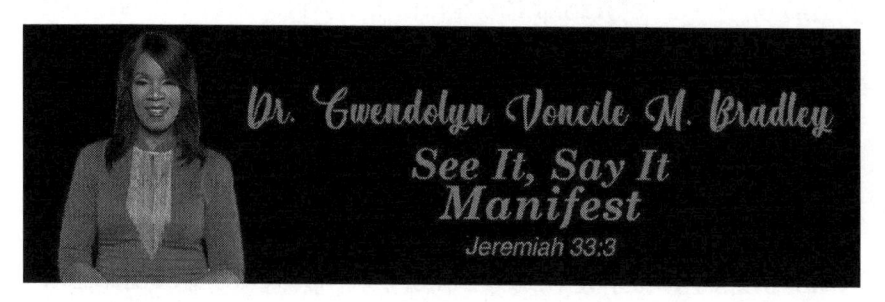

LinkedIn: https://www.linkedin.com/in/gwendolyn-bradley-271a5043?utm_source=share&utm_campaign=share_via&utm_content=profile&utm_medium=ios_app

Guess What? I Grew Up!

Carolyn Coleman

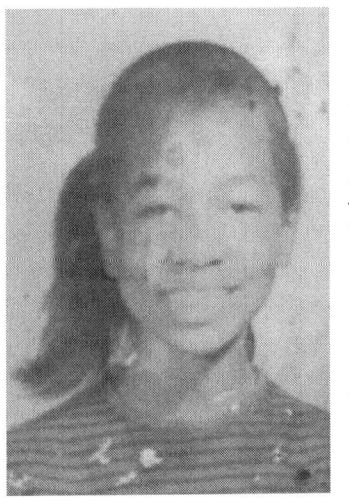

My journey to grow up seemed endless, and at the same time, it went quickly. Let us talk about my journey from girlhood to womanhood. Being a child was not so bad, the growing pains made it no walk in the park.! It is more like a wild ride on a bumpy road, filled with all kinds of bumps and detours. You have roadblocks, potholes, and sometimes, those one-way streets that make you feel like you are going in circles. Well, let me tell you, I hit that "U" turn and got outta there as quickly as possible, I had places to go and things to do.

Growing up, family was my anchor. My brothers and cousins—oh Lord, the love was real! We laughed until we cried, and those memories are Priceless! But then, as you start to grow up, you find your own friends, and suddenly, things shift. You can feel the air change around you, like a warm breeze on a summer day. It is like, "Whoa, what's going on here?" We are growing up.

I am sure every child has thoughts of one day being a big girl or guy and thoughts and aspirations of what they will do once they become adults. "When I become a parent, I will not do this, or I will do that. I am not going to treat my children like my parents treat me. Wow, our thoughts were far from the truth. Growing up is more than your age changing it is making decisions about your future. What will I be when I grow up? One thing I know is that talk is cheap. It came at a time when we realized our parents did the best they could. My cousins together were mischievous, not troublemakers. We covered for one another. We speak on these things now and laugh. The difference is that now we have jobs and responsibilities. Who saw that coming? We thought our parents' rules were to hold us captive; in actuality, they were to lead us on a path of freedom and self-respect.

One parent was bragging about her children to our parents. When she left, our parents instructed us to act more like them. We were teenagers at the time, and we all started laughing. She does not know her children. We have been keeping them out of trouble. My parents were speechless. Their rules worked well for us. No, we did not like the rules, but we enjoyed living, so we obeyed them.

When it comes to negativity, I must ignore the naysayers; the negative talk and criticism are draining. As I grew older, I realized if they would talk about them, they would talk about you. That is all about them! It took me a minute to figure that out, but once I did, I said to myself, "This disease of hate doesn't belong to me!" It is a heavy burden, but you must let those toxic folks go, even if they are family. Life's too short to hang around people who throw shade instead of love. As the saying goes, there are three places you can go when it comes to me: Out of my way, over there, and out of my lane.

WOW, can you believe it? We used to party together and had each other's backs, or so I thought, and now you hear that disdain creeping into your voices. Your little car, are you sure he is the one for you? Why did you wear that skirt? "Girl, are you for real? You would not be out here if it were not for me!" Marvin had it right, "What in the world is going on?"

Now, let us have a conversation regarding jealousy! It is an evil thing that can lead you down a road of trouble. You gotta watch out for those who do not have your back. Sometimes, you do not realize it until it is too late. You see a smirk on their face or frown; I was laughing, because I thought you were joking, then I felt your eyes cut. I realize you are laughing at me. Trust is everything. I know I cannot trust you as Johnny Guitar Watson would say, "That is a real Mother for You? I later would grow to realize God had my back the entire time.

Let us rewind my childhood, where life was simple and sweet. We were just kids, making mud pies and having a blast! Neighbors looked out for each other, and it felt like a big family. At one point, I felt kindergarten was not for me. I was not a fan! I came home with scratches from those sticky bushes. My legs would hurt, and mom would put that red liquid on me. My legs looked like polka dots; what a sight! Those bushes might have been roses, but to me, they felt like a trap because they only stuck me.

And Miss Sister Gant, bless her heart! My mama said we could not call her both names, and I was confused. I had to pick one—either Ms. or Sister. But now, it is all about titles; Heaven forbid you get it wrong! Times really do change.

My dad was out there working hard while my mom was at home, cheering us on at every event. I thought that was just the way it was. But now, looking back, I see how those moments shaped me into the woman I am today. It is a journey, and I am proud of every step!

Let me break it down for you! Do you know how, looking back at the past, you want to wrap yourself in a cozy blanket? It is like everything shines a little brighter when we remember those sweet times. We tend to focus on the good stuff—the laughter, the joy, and all those warm memories—while the not-so-great moments fade into the background. It is like we are seeing everything through a sparkly lens that makes it all look fabulous!

Those memories come packed with emotions! It is like when you hear a song from way back, and suddenly, you are hit with all those feelings that take you right back to that moment. Those emotions can make those experiences feel even more significant as if they are woven into the very fabric of who we are.

As we reminisce, we also get to piece together our identities. It is a little like putting together a puzzle, seeing how each memory fits into the bigger picture of our lives. You realize how far you have come and how those experiences have helped shape you into the amazing person you are today.

Realistically speaking, when life throws challenges our way, thinking back can be a real comfort. It is like a little escape to a time when things felt simpler and happier. Those cherished memories give us strength and remind us that there were moments of pure joy, and we all need that sometimes!

And let us not forget that this reflection is not just a solo ride. It is a community affair! Sharing those memories with family and friends creates bonds that tie us together. Those shared moments help us feel connected to our roots and each other, which is a beautiful thing.

But here is the kicker: sometimes, we might look back and think everything was perfect, even when it was not. That can make it tough to appreciate the present or feel satisfied with where we are right now.

Yet, despite all that, remembering those good times inspires us to create new experiences! It sparks the desire to reach out to loved ones, revisit those special places, dive into activities that remind us of the good old days, or make new memories.

Reflecting on our past fills those memories with emotions, the highs and lows, the happy and sad. We must take the bitter with the sweet. All this guides us as we navigate this beautiful journey of life. It is all about embracing where we have been while keeping our eyes on where we are headed. We all should learn from the past.

Life is about stages:

- Childhood.
- Teenage years.
- Learning to drive.
- Having my first real job.
- Shopping by myself.
- Asking my dad to go half with me on my prom dress.

It was simple but beautiful. My cousin adored it so much that she asked to borrow it after my prom; it looked as good on her as it did on me. College was different; I learned how to hitchhike, and one of my college friends taught me the ropes:

1. Never get in a car with two men and just you.
2. Look them in their eyes.
3. Make sure you have a travel buddy.

We survived! There were no issues whatsoever. Praise God. I am laughing now. Okay, ladies, no hitchhiking in today's world. Being a young adult living on my own was scary and liberating at the same time. That is when you become more independent, a real adult. That is when I first realized I was on my journey from being a girl to becoming a woman.

Nursing school had me leaning on my roots, getting back on my knees, and praying I would pass. After navigating the prerequisites and degrees, nursing stuck. It was not on my radar, so I knew it was heaven-sent. I often said I knew He did not bring me this far to leave me, and He did not. I am now more than 38 years in and still counting.

All these reflections have shaped my journey from a girl to a woman! As I look back on those days of laughter and love and even the bumps in the road, I see how they have all played a part in making me the strong, determined woman I am today. Each memory, each lesson learned, has been like a steppingstone, guiding me forward and helping me stand tall in the face of life's challenges. Once you become a woman, there is no turning back.

Growing up, I learned to embrace my identity and stand up for myself. Those moments of joy with family and friends taught me the importance of connection and support, while the tougher times showed me how to rise above negativity. Every experience has been a brushstroke on the canvas of my life, and together, they have created a masterpiece of which I am proud!

Now, if I could share a little advice with the next person on this journey, I would say: do not shy away from your past; embrace it! Learn from it, grow from it, and let it fuel your fire. Remember, as Phylicia Rashad beautifully said, "The only way to deal with change is to embrace it." So, lean into those changes, celebrate your growth, and do not forget to lift others as you rise for those who cannot or will not go; do not let them deter your growth. Do not be afraid to leave them behind. You will see them again; be the inspiration they just might need to go and grow.

Thoughts to consider... everyone is not for you. They walk with you to keep you back or distract you from your purpose; they do not want you to get ahead of them. You can be intimidating to others, unaware of their true feelings about you. You are walking your own path, and authentically, you are moving in your own way. You are independent and doing what you do best, being you.

Once the snake bites and gets sick from your glory, do not embrace them again; they will try it again. Do not let anyone disrespect you more than once; I overlooked the disrespect, for I felt I was mistaken; when I truly listened to God's voice, I realized I had to protect myself by letting them go. Remember, they were a snake when you met them, even when you did not expect it. Once they show you, move away accordingly. If you are not appreciated, do not give more of your support and love. Why? They do not want it, or you, because it came from you.

So, here is to every girl on her path to womanhood! Embrace your journey, cherish those memories, and do not be afraid to shine! You are on your way to something beautiful, and I cannot wait to see how bright you will glow!

About Carolyn

Carolyn Pickens Coleman MHSA, BSN RN

Carolyn Pickens Coleman is a daughter, wife, mother, sister, cousin, friend, and co-worker from Alabama. She has a B.S. in Nursing from Samford University and an M.A. in Health Service Administration from Strayer University. Carolyn is a Lifetime member of the National Black Nurses Association, an active member of the Birmingham Black Nurses Association, Inc., and served as the Chairperson of the Outreach committee for two years and is the Past President of the Bessemer Public Library Trustee Board, She is also a Board Member of C.H.L.M.S. Medi-Helpz Foundation whose mission is Patient Engagement, Empowerment as well as education for the patient and community. ForbesBLK Member and a recipient of the Presidential Lifetime Achievement Award.

Carolyn has more than 35 years of experience as a critical care nurse and presently a nurse case manager. She worked with hospital administrators to establish plans regarding complex patient cases, concentrating on outcome management, utilizing best practices, advocating for patients. She is also an adjunct instructor.

Carolyn is the author of a five-book series. The title character is Gentry who faces her life choices, as we all do, For Carolyn, writing is cathartic. She enjoys reading and staying active by line dancing, walking, and spending time with her family and friends. She is an international podcaster.

Carolyn has co-authored six #1 Best-selling anthologies, three of which are international best sellers.
Carolyn Is an award-winning author and motivational speaker, an international podcast host

You can connect with Carolyn via:
Website: CPWbookshelf.com, Instagram: Carolyn_author,
FB: Carolyn Coleman
Stationhead.com-gentryjourney1,
Podcast: Gentry's Journey
http://www.linkedin.com/in/carolyn-coleman

The Me You See

JACQUILINE COX

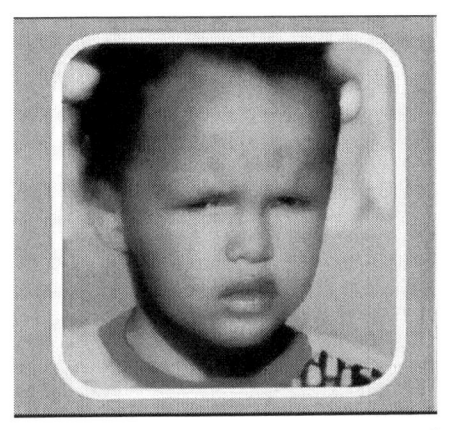

Coming from a broken home and landing in foster care—was tough. As a little girl, I was faced with mountains that felt insurmountable. I experienced things that no child should ever have to endure, things that left scars deep in my soul. I was taken advantage of and sexually assaulted by people I thought I could trust—family, friends, relatives, and even those who claimed to care for me. It all started when I was just five years old.

And let me tell you, I heard it all. Folks told me that my accomplishments were just due to my skin color and that I was just a pretty face. They said if I weren't beautiful, nobody would care about me. Can you imagine? That pressure weighed heavy on me. But life, life had other plans.

Fast-forward, and after climbing those mountains shaped by the earthquakes of my past, I found out I was a diamond in the rough. I met someone special—my husband, partner, and best friend. But I came into that relationship carrying a whole lot of baggage, like trust issues, insecurities from experiences of domestic violence, and emotional turmoil. It wasn't easy. I was desperate to prove my worth, always saying yes to please others, even when it drained me.

I had a son, too, and I wanted to protect him and create a loving home for both of us. I thought if I just did everything right, I'd be accepted. When my husband and I started discussing marriage, we knew we needed to live together first. We had to see how we fit together daily and how we handled life behind closed doors.

When we finally shared our plans for marriage, I felt the shift in the air. Suddenly, people started bringing up my past— those old wounds they thought would destroy us. They tried to dig up dirt, talking to those who had hurt me, trying to find something to use against us. But they didn't know that there were no secrets between us. He was my best friend, and we faced those demons together.

My husband is a man of God and wasn't easily swayed. He saw through the tricks and manipulations. But even as I noticed those things, I still thought I could win them over, that if I just gave in, I'd be accepted. I was so used to keeping the peace and pleasing others that I tried to dress down to fit into the shadows. But that vibrant spirit of mine? It was hard to contain.

I brought my husband peace. I used positive affirmations to lift him so he would see himself as a king and demand respect. We learned to set boundaries together, which wasn't easy for those around us. Suddenly, we were "acting funny" because we no longer let disrespect slide.

Then, he told me something that hit me hard: "It's one thing to be a Queen; it's another thing to own it." Those words resonated with me. I started demanding respect, and oh boy, did that stir the pot. Arguments erupted, old wounds reopened, but we stood our ground. We were one and made it clear that disrespect had no place in our lives.

Our love and the word of God bound us. I faced humiliation and games designed to hurt me, but I refused to let that define me. I learned to say no to disrespect and to love myself enough to walk away from anyone who didn't treat me right. That was the moment I knew I had evolved into a woman of strength.

Once my husband saw that growth, our connection deepened. We became more than just a couple; we became partners, united against the world. I earned and owned my place and wasn't sorry about it.

I didn't just survive; I thrived. I walked through the fire and came out stronger. Real love is about respect and the courage to stand together against all odds. We shaped our destiny together, and I found my voice and power in that journey. In the process, I found myself!

Life, honey, is a winding road full of unexpected turns, and every step we take shapes who we become. When I look back on my journey, I see a tapestry woven from both heartache and strength. Growing up in a broken home taught me that love can be complicated, sometimes a balm and other times a blade. I craved warmth and connection but often faced betrayal and neglect, navigating a harsh and uninviting world.

Foster care was supposed to be a safe haven, but it reminded me of everything I'd lost. There, I confronted my deepest fears and learned the hard truth about trust. The trauma I faced from those I should have relied on left me cautious, building walls around my heart, believing that showing vulnerability made me weak.

But in that darkness, I discovered a strength I didn't know was there. I began to understand that my past was a chapter in my story, not the whole book. That's when my journey led me to my husband—a light in my turbulent life. He didn't just see my scars; he saw the woman I could be.

Our relationship became a healing process. We learned to communicate, share our fears and dreams openly, and support one another in real ways. His love was a refuge, and together, we built a partnership grounded in trust and respect. It wasn't always smooth sailing; we had our challenges, but we faced each one together, growing stronger with every hurdle.

As I embraced my role as a partner and a mother, it hit me that my son wasn't just an extension of me; he was his own person. I wanted to create a loving home for him, free from the shadows of my past. That drive pushed me to set boundaries—not just for me but for our family. I realized that nurturing love meant fiercely protecting it.

Whenever someone tried to undermine what we had, I reminded myself of who I was and what I stood for. I learned to harness my voice and stand firm against any negativity. The more I asserted myself, the more empowered I felt. I became a woman who demanded respect, not just for myself but for my family. I understood that love should never come at the expense of my dignity.

In those moments of confrontation, I discovered my power. I learned to say no to toxic relationships and unnecessary drama. I found a community in those who lifted me up and distanced myself from those who sought to bring me down. My husband was my rock, believing in me even when I struggled to believe in myself.

As we built our lives together, we didn't just create a house; we built a sanctuary. Our home was filled with laughter, love, and the kind of respect that was often missing from my childhood. We became a united front against the world—two souls intertwined, committed to each other, and guided by our faith.

My journey hasn't been without its trials, but every challenge has taught me about resilience and grace. I learned that owning my story means embracing every part of it—the pain, the joy, the growth. It means acknowledging my past while stepping boldly into my future.

Today, I stand tall, proud of the woman I've become. I advocate for myself and my loved ones, using my voice to uplift others who may feel unheard. I share my story to reflect on my past and inspire those who may be climbing their own mountains.

In the end, love isn't just about what we receive; it's about what we give and how we stand for one another. It's about creating a legacy of strength and resilience for those who come after us. Through it all, I've learned that the most beautiful transformation happens when we learn to love ourselves fiercely and authentically.

As I reflect on my journey from girlhood to womanhood, I see it as a powerful transformation that's not just about me—it's about the legacy I'm creating for my children. Growing up, I faced challenges that could have broken me, but they instead became the very fabric of my strength. I learned early on what it meant to navigate a world that wasn't always kind, and through that struggle, I found resilience.

As I transitioned into womanhood, I embraced the lessons that came with my experiences. I realized that every tear, heartbreak, and moment of doubt shaped me into a woman who knows her worth. I learned that true strength lies in fighting through adversity, owning my story, and using it to uplift others, especially my children.

I want my kids to see a mother who stands tall and demands respect and love for herself and them. I want them to understand that a supportive home is a sanctuary where they can flourish. I strive to create an environment where they feel safe expressing themselves and sharing their dreams and fears without hesitation. I want them to know that vulnerability is not a weakness but a strength that connects us all.

In this journey, I've learned the importance of communication. I want to model for my children to express their feelings openly, listen with compassion, and resolve conflicts gracefully. I want them to grow up understanding that relationships are about mutual respect, empathy, and support. When they see me standing up for what I believe in, I hope they'll carry that spirit into their lives, knowing they deserve nothing less.

I want my children to have the confidence to expect support in their relationships, just as I learned to expect it for myself. I want them to know that they are worthy of kind and respectful love and should never settle for anything less. I want to teach them about resilience—the ability to face challenges head-on and emerge even stronger, knowing that they have a solid foundation to lean on.
As I embrace my role as a mother, I reflect on the dynamics I want to instill in our home. I want them to see a family rooted in love, where we celebrate each other's victories and support one another through hardships. I want to create a cycle of positivity and strength that they can carry into their futures.

So, this journey from girl to woman is not just about my growth; it's about the seeds I'm planting for my children. It's about empowering them to become the best versions of themselves, embrace their own stories, and know they hold the power to shape their own lives. I hope that as they grow, they'll carry forward the lessons of love, resilience, and respect I'm instilling in them. That's the true impact of my journey—creating a legacy of strength and love for the next generation.

About Jacquiline

Jacquiline Cox is a dynamic Chicago native, Co-Founder and CEO of Listen Linda Brand & Marketing Firm and YoungSavedLeaders. She is the visionary behind the impactful anthology and devotional, "Women of the Waiting Room: Surgery for Your Soul." With a commitment to making a positive difference in the world, Jacquiline graduated Cum Laude with a bachelor's degree in business administration from the University of Arizona Global Campus.

As a prolific writer, Jacquiline has authored seven books and serves as the Founder and Editor in Chief of Listen Linda Magazine. A 10x International Best-Selling author, she is also a motivational speaker, engaging with audiences at schools and nonprofit organizations alongside her husband, a retired decorated military veteran, best-selling author, and lifetime achievement award winner. Together, they inspire empowerment within diverse communities. Their two sons have followed in their footsteps as accomplished authors, recognized for their literary contributions and community service with multiple prestigious awards including the MLK Service Above Self Award, Mayor's Award of Excellence, and Presidential Volunteer Service Awards.

Jacquiline's influence extends beyond writing; she is a branding strategist and hosts the global radio podcast "Listen Linda!", where she motivates and inspires her audience. A passionate advocate for autism and lupus, she is also a certified Business Coach, reflecting her dedication to causes close to her heart.

In 2017, Jacquiline launched Class E Defined, offering CryoSkin Services, which earned accolades as the Best New Business in Oswego, IL. During the pandemic, she successfully rebranded her business to Listen Linda Brand & Marketing Firm, expanding her services to include marketing, branding sessions, podcast production, content creation, and life coaching.

Recognized as a World Record Holder, Jacquiline has received numerous accolades including Presidential Lifetime Achievement Award, being named one of NYC Journal's 40 Under 40 Innovators and a Forbes Blk Member. Her entrepreneurial journey exemplifies resilience, determination, and an unwavering commitment to uplifting others. Join Jacquiline in her mission to connect with and empower a vibrant community of entrepreneurial voices, as she continues to transform the podcasting landscape and support aspiring podcasters in achieving their dreams.

Trauma Tried To Kill Me

SHANITA DAWSON-UGWUOKE

As a little three-year-old girl, I wanted a pet; it did not matter what kind. So, one day, my mom's boyfriend surprised me with a white rabbit. I was so happy to have something I could play with that was real. Only having had Bunny for a few months, who would have thought it would come to an end? Late one night, I heard a loud voice coming from downstairs. I walked downstairs to see what was going on. There, I saw my mom and her boyfriend arguing. The closer I got to them, the more I began to cry. He then snatched Bunny from me and threw Bunny on the ground. Bunny stopped moving, and all I could see was red. The room went silent. As I reached to pick Bunny up, my mom's boyfriend picked him up and started apologizing for what he did.

He promised me another bunny that I never got. Reflecting on this moment now as an adult, I realize I had my first trauma experience.

Around nine years old, my mom and a co-worker went out to a club. My siblings and I, along with her co-worker's children, were left at the co-worker's house. The co-worker's sister was in charge of watching us. In the middle of the night, I felt someone touching me inappropriately in my private area. When I opened my eyes, I could see my mom's co-worker's husband standing over me, and then he put his hand over my mouth, keeping me from making a sound. It was like my mind went blank. The only thing I could remember was when my mom returned, I ran to her and told her what had happened. She immediately called the police, but the man had already left. I went to counseling, but at my age, I can honestly say I do not remember a thing that helped me. From that moment, all I could think about was where is my dad and why bad things happen to me.

I loved both of my parents, but the love for my dad was stronger than the love for my mom at the time. I love my dad most because I was the only child he had. We would have special weekends together as he would take me to his house to cook breakfast on the B-B-Q grill. On the way home, sometimes, he would get me special treats. If I had to go home early in the morning, he would get me pig-in-the-blankets from Mrs. Winners. If I went home in the evenings, he would stop me at Wendy's and Dunkin' Donuts. It was not often that my dad and mom would say they loved me, but I could tell by their actions that they did love me. Never feeling genuinely loved by my parents or family had left me confused. I frequently questioned what real love is and if I would ever get the chance to feel it.

My paternal grandparents did not have much, but there was never a doubt about their love for me. It did not matter how many cigarettes they smoked or how much alcohol they drank. Their doors were always open for me. During my preteen years, I was so confused. My father was not around because he was incarcerated. My mom was so overwhelmed by my oldest sister's behaviors that she neglected her priorities for me and my brother. My mom began working two jobs, so my brother and I spent more time at home alone. During this time, my oldest sister had a baby and lost custody of her child. The state then gave my mom custody of my niece. Because I was a girl and always followed the rules, my mom placed a lot of responsibility on me. Taking care of the house and helping with my niece made me think I could make my own family since I had already taken on adult responsibilities as a child.

Shortly after, I connected with a long-lost childhood friend. He was going through a similar situation. After a few months of communicating, we decided we wanted to be better than our parents. We planned to make our own perfect little family. One day, at my grandparents' house, my granny asked me about the boy because she knew I liked him a lot. I denied the question because I did not want anyone to know what we had planned. Then my granny said, "What goes on in the dark will come to light. "At the time, I thought if we had a baby, we could live a good life, but I had no clue what was about to take place. I became pregnant at the age of 14.

My mom was so mad at me when she found out I was pregnant. She beat me and tried to force me to have an abortion, but I refused. My grandparents were upset, and to be honest, I do not know what my daddy's thoughts were. During the pregnancy, my child's father came to appointments with me. Thinking I was living my best life, the unexpected happened. His family sent money for him to purchase all the things that were needed for our daughter.

After getting the money, he took my brother and his new girlfriend on a shopping spree. A child on the way, complications with my pregnancy, and, to top it off, nothing for my child; I was stuck looking stupid. Not knowing what to do, I could only think about giving up.

Just when I was about to give up, my niece's aunt stepped in to help me with the basic stuff I needed for my baby. I felt like time was moving fast when I came home from the hospital. I knew I would have to return to school in a few weeks. My child was allowed to attend with me. My baby girl was growing, the need for pampers was crazy, no money, no help. One day, I asked my dad if he could help me because my mom was not giving me money, and he said no. Yes, I was upset that he said no; I was upset because my mom was collecting money from welfare for my child and child support from my dad for me, and she never gave me a dime.

I felt like my dad could have offered some stuff for the baby, even if he did not want to give me cash. That is when the lightbulb came on in my head, letting me know I had brought all this on myself and had to fix it. When I turned 15, I got my first job at McDonald's. I knew there was hope for me. I told the manager I had a child and asked if she could come to work with me during my interview. Yes, they looked at me like I was crazy, and then I told them I like to clean up and that I would be the best for the position if they gave me a chance. The manager told me that it was impossible, but they would see if they could work around my schedule. On the first day of work, I showed up with my baby in her carrier. I told them no one would help me and that I needed the job and money, so the assistant manager told the manager she would sit with my baby so I could work.

This was the moment I knew what church people meant when they said God will show up and show out. Philippians 4:19 (KJV) states, "But my God shall supply all your needs according to his riches in glory by Christ." Showing up for work and not being sent back home reminded me of how good God is.

We only went to church with my mom on Easter, Mother's Day, and Christmas Eve. I used to walk to church by myself at the age of six, and I never missed vacation bible school. My most fun memories of church were when Easter came, and I would go with my stepmother. She would take me to Easter Egg Hunts. My life started to become meaningful to me when I saw how loving the lord and reading his word can make life better. Like a timer, something must stop. Just when I thought I was on top of the world, I got pregnant again. My mom told me I had to get out.

I had nowhere to go. The guy I was pregnant by lived with his family, so I was not welcomed there because I already had a child. Stress had taken its toll on me. The next thing you know, I went into early labor, and the baby did not survive. My father came to visit me in the hospital, and as we talked, I remember he said, "God make no mistakes." I was mad about what he said but I knew he was telling the truth. Can you imagine how and what I would have endured with two babies at the age of 16? Depression had kicked in. I slowly began to give up again. That is when I met my new friend with low self-esteem.

I stopped going to school and started tricking men out of their money. One day, my brother said, "You better stop playing games with these men before someone hurts you." At this time in my life, I had an I do not care attitude and was trying to find someone who would take care of me and my daughter. One day, I went to Wendy's to get food. As we sat down to eat, a man came up to me smiling, being nice to my daughter. Before I left, we swapped numbers. He must have assumed I was grown because I had a child. After a few conversations, I invited him to meet my mom. It took him three times before he showed up, and when he did, he came with his best friend. Somehow, his best friend began to call me and talk to me. After some time had passed, he began to tell me I was too smart and that I should go back to school.

He paid for my child to go to daycare, and I enrolled back in school. After a few months, I dropped out again because I found out I was not going to graduate on time. I then went and registered myself for the General Education Diploma. During this time, my sister called me while I was out and said my mom told her to tell me I could not return home. I called the guy and asked if I could live with him, and he said yes. Remember, he had no idea I was a teenager because I had a child and a job when we met. I moved in with him and his mother. After a couple of weeks, I took him to meet my maternal grandmother, and she immediately said, "Shanita, he is a devil. You need to go back home to your mother." I did not listen; I continued with him because, at the time, he seemed like an angel sent from heaven.

We lived together a year before engaging in sexual activity, so I knew for sure he was a winner. He cared for my daughter and me without a blink of an eye and was always nice and gentle. Little did I know what was ahead, the old saying, "Everything that glitters ain't gold." We moved out of his mom's house and got our first apartment. By this time, I was about 17 1/2 years old. One day, he came home and asked me if I was 18. I lied and said yes because I knew he would break up with me if he found out. I didn't want to be homeless, nor did I want to go back to my mother's house.

His anger grew stronger towards me because he knew I was lying. This was the first day that he put his hands on me. The slap to my face was harder than the one my mom had ever given me. Later that night, he apologized and said it would never happen again. I do not know if he apologized because he was sorry or if it was because I was turning 18 soon and it would be okay for us to continue the relationship. A few weeks later, he came home and proposed to me. I was so excited knowing that I would finally have the life I had imagined with my first child's father. We were all set the date for our wedding was supposed to be September 12, because he wanted to marry on his birthday. The night before, he did not come home; I thought something had happened to him. After a few hours of paging him with no response, he showed up to the house. I asked him where he had been, and that is when he began to grab me, shake me, then put a pillow over my face and told me, "Don't question me." One would have thought to walk away and never look back. But I was willing to give him a second chance; I did not want to be alone and wanted him to keep his promise of marriage to me. I began questioning myself: How do you walk away and determine if enough is enough?

We had finally married, and a couple of years went by without any abuse. I got pregnant again with my third child, and that is when the abuse started again. One time, he poured Surge soda on my hair in front of my mother while I was pregnant. That is when I knew I had to fight back because I was so embarrassed. I picked up my cast iron skillet and hit him in the head with it as hard as I could. He called the police on me. He must have been scared of me because he had never tried it again, and shortly after, we went our separate ways. Ten years passed, we dated other people and became better at parenting our son.

One day, he came to the house to drop our son off and said he wanted his family back, that he had changed, and would prove it to me. I decided to give him another chance because I was not dating seriously and wanted my kids to have a real family. We remarried and had two kids within two years. By this time, I had finished my associate's degree and started working on my bachelor's degree. While we were preparing to celebrate my graduation, he decided to degrade me in front of family and friends.

One of the happiest moments of my life became another sad and traumatizing moment. The only difference is it was not physical, so again, I overlooked it. Everything was going well until he went outside our marriage and began to disrespect our home. During this time, my mother passed. I overlooked the cheating because I was grieving the loss of my mother. During this time, I became pregnant again and lost the babies. That is when the mental abuse started; he started telling me I was not going to amount to anything and that no one would want me. I decided to get an easy job that could be performed with my eyes closed. I filed for divorce and began dating again.

After dating for a couple of months, I knew I finally had a chance at a healthy relationship. The man was respectful, loved my kids, and encouraged me to be my best despite my past. Soon, my ex-husband started harassing us. I was careful about doing things for our safety. One night, I was leaving the guy's house, and I got a call saying to come back because it was not safe for me to go home. I immediately returned to his house. When I arrived, I noticed the door was kicked in, and multiple police were there. Then I was questioned about who I knew would do this because this was the second time something had happened while I was at his house.

Later that night, my ex-husband was arrested for the crimes that were committed. The man later decided he no longer wanted a relationship with me. My oldest son asked me if I had ever loved his dad because I would not let them see him. Guilt entered my mind, and like before, I took him back. I convinced myself that their dad would change for sure this time. I wanted my kids to have a family. I made myself believe he was meant for me, which is why every man I met before left. After I took my ex-husband back, a good friend of mines said, "Girl, that man isn't going to change; you're wasting your time." Again, I did not listen. After four years of being back together, the old became the new. I became tired, and my thoughts became demonic. After we reconciled, he decided to move out of town and become a better man for his children.

God did say there would be a warning before destruction. My stepmother once told me if you keep finding yourself in the same situation, you need to re-evaluate yourself. This was the first time I decided to take her advice. Looking back on how she would tell me things, I saw that her actions aligned with how she lived her life. I then started dating a guy I had known for a year. He knew what I had gone through. He encouraged me to go back to church. On the weekends, I would drive the children to see their father. In the beginning, he was okay with the agreement. He became angrier than usual. I know in my mind that he was jealous of my /9ew relationship. He began to call more than normal, asking questions unrelated to the*-+ children. Then, he began to show his old side. I stopped taking the kids to visit.

I knew this was the last chance for me to break away from this abusive relationship. As I began to attend church faithfully. I saw that the church was different for me in an effective way. I stopped seeing things in the physical. I began to see the spiritual aspect to the fullest. I started asking God why he kept keeping me and thanking God for protecting me even when I did not know I needed it and/or deserved it. One day, I was putting together some furniture, and God showed me I would be shot by my ex-husband and told me I would be okay. It scared me so bad that I left home and went to my maternal grandmother's house. I told her if they did not hear from me that, they should know my ex-husband killed me. She did not believe me and told me to stop saying that. I called my dad and told him the same thing. The first thing he did was pray for me and then ask if I was okay. The following week, my ex-husband called me and told me if he could not have me, no one could. The same day, I went to the courthouse to file for a restraining order. From that moment, fear came along because it wanted to be my friend, and being scared, I accepted the friendship.

March 2018 changed my life forever. Genesis 50:20 (KJV) states, "But as for you, ye thought evil against me; but God meant it unto good, to bring to pass, as it is this day, to save many people alive." On March 19, 2018, I went to school that night, and a bad storm came, so they released us for class early. I told my classmate what God showed and told me earlier in the week. We talked about getting a hotel room. When we went on break, I realized I had left my clothes, so I told her that was a sign from God that I should trust his word when he told me I would be okay. As I was getting ready to leave school, she stopped me, prayed for me, and begged me not to go home. I told her I had to go home and be obedient. On March 20, 2018, I woke up to being shot multiple times. I knew it was nothing but God. I was able to call the police for myself. That day was the true testimony of how good God is. It is not because he saved my life but because of his love, grace, and mercy. When I first opened my eyes after the shooting, the doctors were staring at me and whispering. I could not speak because there was a tube in my throat, and I could not move.

The look on their face was as if they expected me to die. When I began speaking again, there were four chaplains and three psychiatrists who came to visit me at separate times. I did not understand why different people came to talk to me, asking the same questions. After speaking with me, they finally decided I was not crazy and that I did not cause harm to myself. I remember the last chaplain quoted, NLT, Ephesians 2:8 states, "God saved you by his grace when you believed." When my dad came to the hospital, he asked me what I wanted for my birthday; I told him I wanted a bible study book like the ones he used to send me when I was a child. The smile on his face was priceless, and then I told him I did not just want it; I needed it. I knew I needed to relearn the bible because it would supply all my needs.

Once I was released from the hospital, I had follow-up appointments. During one visit, I was told I would not walk again for at least a year or longer. Knowing what I had been through in the past and present situation, I was sure depression would show up because I was used to mishaps when things did not go as planned. This time, I started telling myself that I had nothing to lose and that I had to keep my faith. James 2:17 (KJV) states, "Even so faith, if it hath not works, is dead, being alone." From the moment negativity tried to come back into my life, I started to fight it with scriptures. I told myself, "It is your time to win. You have the tools; now use them." Anyone who knows that from the moment you give it to God, the enemy attacks immediately. I began to have some complications. I took on a new perspective of life. I started by asking God to show me the way instead of asking for what I wanted, not knowing if that was God's will. Everyone has experienced some type of trauma in their life. Trauma is not the controller over your life. If you want to defeat trauma, you must first recognize it exists, set reachable goals to overcome it, find a safe place to communicate your feelings, be willing to receive positive feedback, and, most importantly, PRAY!

During my most traumatic experience, I discovered where my problems started, and then I began to work from there. I realized my first trauma started as a toddler. From there, I began attracting men who displayed negative traits that I had been exposed to. One, I was missing that father figure I loved so much. Two, I did not love myself enough. Third, any attention was good because I did not want to be alone. I learned to pray more instead of trying to fix it by myself. We should all know that God told us we will experience pain, but our faith in Him helps us through. James 1:2-4 (KJV) states, "Consider it pure joy, my brothers, sisters, whenever you face trials of many kinds, because you know that the testing of your faith produces perseverance to finish its work so that you may be mature and complete, not lacking anything." Going to church as a child was normal; I took it as something to do on the weekends. During that time, I had no clue about the importance of church and how important it is to know God. When I tell people my story, they always look at me and say I am a miracle. No, I give God all the glory. I know some are wondering why I kept going into dark places. My answer is that today, God used me for His good so that I can share His greatness with others. God never told me the day or time; he just told me about the encounter.

Sometimes, we get too comfortable and refuse to move, so we must be pushed out of our comfort zone to grow and become better. I had so many dreams, but at that moment, I settled because I let the devil tell me I was okay. The week leading up to the shooting, we were fasting at church. I had never fasted for the lord. The night before the shooting, I wanted to break my fast, but my partner at the time said "no, you have made it this far, a few more hours will not hurt you." I wanted food so bad that the taste of the food was stuck in my mouth; within moments, I could hear the song "You Deserve It." It was like a ball of excitement entered my body, and the thought of food escaped my mind, and then I went to sleep. I am alive today because I chose God and I heard Him tell me I am good enough.

Life is hard, but only hard when you do not have God. Yes, some days, I fell short, but I did not give up. Psalm 37:4 (KJV) states, "Delight thyself also in the LORD: and he shall give Thee the desires of thine heart." When I stopped trying to do things on my own, I could see the good works of God. All the things I had wanted started to flow like water to me. I was seeking my bachelor's degree. God provided me with a master's degree. God sent me a Godly husband who unconditionally loves me, my children, and my grandchildren. He took away my depression and anxiety. He restored my relationship with my father. He taught me how to love and trust again. Trusting in God to fight your battles is the best thing you can do, you should just remain still and let God tell you your next move. 1 Peter 5:6-10 (ESV) states, "Humble yourselves therefore under the mighty hand of God, so that at the proper time he may exalt you, casting all your anxieties on him, because he cares for you. Be sober-minded; be watchful. Your adversary, the devil, prowls around like a roaring lion, seeking someone to devour. Resist him, firm in your faith knowing that the same kinds of suffering are being experienced by your brotherhood throughout the world. And after you have suffered a little while, God of all grace who has called to his eternal glory in Christ, will Himself restore, confirm, strengthen, and establish you."

Today, I am grateful to know God. I love God, and God loves me.

About Shanita

Shanita Dawson-Ugwuoke, a native of Atlanta, Georgia, currently resides in Tennessee with her husband, Hillary Ugwuoke. She is the proud mother of five beautiful children—Ashley, Terrell Jr., Autumn, Ka'Maria, and Matthew—and the loving grandmother of five wonderful grandchildren: Winter, Olando, Cortez, Kameron, and Travis.

A dedicated housewife and former educator with over a decade of teaching experience, Shanita finds joy in traveling and spending quality time with her family. Her hobbies include singing and dancing, and she remains active in her church, serving in the youth ministry and singing in the choir.

Shanita's life is deeply rooted in her faith. Her favorite Bible verse, Psalms 46:5 (KJV), reminds her that *"God is in the midst of her; she shall not be moved; God will help her when the morning dawns."* Her favorite song, *"Second Chance"* by Hezekiah Walker, has been a source of comfort and strength through life's challenges.

A survivor of domestic violence, Shanita is passionate about making a difference for others by sharing her story and offering hope. Her chapter, *"Trauma Tried to Kill Me,"* highlights her resilience and determination to inspire and uplift those facing similar struggles. Her favorite saying, *"Never Give Up,"* embodies the strength and perseverance that define her journey.

Surviving Her Cancer
LaMonique

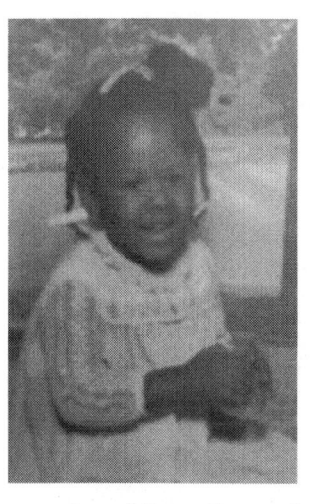

I'm smiling, so that means I'm happy….. right? I'm smiling so that you feel more comfortable and at ease. You already have a lot on your plate, and I'm not nearly as important as this life-altering situation! I won't add to our problems, so I'll stay out of the way and not take up too much space. I'll always be there when you need me. We could die tomorrow, so I have to make sure you feel comfortable today. It's my job to make your load lighter. I have to show you that it's okay so that you can be. When I'm feeling dismissed, it's only because you are going through so much, it's okay…….. really, it's OK. These are some of the private thoughts of a young only-child daughter, born to a single mother, learning to survive multiple bouts of breast cancer with the first occurrence at the tender age of 27. Yes, multiple bouts!

She was diagnosed with cancer a total of three times over 30 years, and she fought with her everything every single time! I reference her as a single mother as she was not married to my father. I had a father in the home for the first couple of years, and they split; she dated and shared space with another; they split, and she shared space with a third. He stuck around, but they were on again and off again through it all, so we'll stick with a single mom for the sake of protecting others. My mom is no longer with the living, but with a 30-plus-year battle of surviving cancer, I will always refer to her as a cancer survivor! I mean, how much more have we learned about breast cancer since the mid-70s? Think about it.

Over the years, I grew up to become somewhat of a protector, a mama bear, and a "fixer," I never really questioned where that stemmed from until now. I believed going through so much at such an early age was unfair. Anything I can do to help, I will. I learned to be flexible and always be available in times of crisis. I learned to tread lightly and never take up too much space while getting things done like no other! I learned to be there and stay there, no matter what. How could I hold someone accountable for how they respond to me when they are going through so much? She can't help it, right? Surviving the remanence of a breast cancer diagnosis to a young woman in the prime of her young adult years is not an easy feat. She would say things like, "That's a bitter pill to swallow!" My 27-year-old first-time mom had a mastectomy and was told she could never have more children. I'm the only child because the doctors told her breast cancer would not allow more kids. Now, who has to be the perfect kid?

The pressure to show that I am worth it. I became her purpose, and knowing how important my success was to her became my purpose. Learning to navigate the world and discovering your own way while carrying the weight and aspirations of another, some may rightfully describe that job simply as "being a mom," but her story paints a different picture. Don't misunderstand; my mom had a village like no other, yet that support doesn't omit carrying the weight she carried and managing the daily struggles of this new normal. Her new normal, raising a child while battling breast cancer. Who will take care of the kid when I'm gone? She worried about that. I could see the anguish in her face when I walked into the hospital room. She had developed an infection in her body from one of her many surgeries. The machines made all types of weird noises, and the smell of sanitizer was overwhelming. I remember feeling afraid of seeing her in the hospital room, but when I saw her, all fear went away. I knew we could get through it; it would be okay; even though she had a different look in her eyes, she assured me it would be okay. As I smiled at her, she smiled back but looked a little disappointed, almost guilty. She looked at me like she was the reason she was in the hospital. I immediately comforted her and began to report all my accomplishments. She's smiling now, and that made me feel better, I did my job!

The timing, the choices, the relationships, and the chronological order of events all carved a path and added colorful character to this life I'm living. I'm proud of the woman I am today; with all the bumps and bruises, there is love and laughter sprinkled with the grace of God. I have been shaped by the intensity and power of adversity, the struggle to try again, and the sheer will to simply exist today and maybe tomorrow. My journey from girl to woman has been molded, rooted, and grounded in the aftermath of HER cancer.

I recognize that we are products of our environment, our culture, our traditions, and our disciplines, and we gain perspective from our experiences. My likes and dislikes, dreams and desires, and tenacious ability to compartmentalize all stem from this place. My perspective over the years has undoubtedly shifted and developed to welcome my spiritual gifts and my God. I've embraced that the foundation of "me, the person" is heavily rooted in surviving. At the early age of 3, my survival journey began. As I learned to navigate life, my mother would give me noteworthy nuggets. She taught me critical thinking, with phrases like "figure it out," because she won't always be there for me. She gave me advice to help me persevere and learn to survive while believing I may survive alone! I learned to recognize when something has to be done and just do it. Take the initiative because it's the right thing to do. Tomorrow is not promised; I heard that one A LOT! When we put things off without viable reasoning, we assume we have time when we truly have no clue. She would say, "I need you to learn how to do this." Whatever "this" was, I tried with my everything!

As a kid, I learned basic life skills from my mom: simple chores like doing laundry, sweeping, mopping, and vacuuming floors early. Just keep the house tidy, that's all. Early on, I learned to be a self-sufficient kid! I smile when I say "kid" because I can hear her voice in real-time calling me her "kid!" right now. I learned to do a lot a little earlier than some. I learned to read and write early. I even started kindergarten early. Well, there is a little more to the reason for that. In Michigan, age five solidified your eligibility to start kindergarten, and I missed the start cut-off. With my mother's persistence, of course, I was afforded the opportunity to take a test to prove I was capable of an early kindergarten start, and I did it. My birthday was late in the year, and there was no way I was staying out of school a full year because I was born 3 months too late; after all, we could die tomorrow. We could die tomorrow; that was the perspective. As a little girl, I may have viewed my experiences as a bit of a handicap, a little bit of, dare I say...." victim."

Learning to comfort myself and focus on only what I can control. The tough love and the constant pressure of getting it right was not easy, and I failed at it quite a few times, but I couldn't show them that we were down, so suck it up and get over it. My self-talk had a little more of her tone than I realized. As I continue my journey to womanhood and gain more confidence and respect for my journey, I see that my lessons were the cornerstone to my success, my own parenting, my work ethic, and my drive to "be better."

If I felt I wasn't quite the best at something, I sought after formal instruction. I studied, researched, and learned where I was able. I would take a course or seminar and read a peer-reviewed article or something. I am my own competition to be better than I was yesterday. I now understand the value of tough love, it's a trust thing. I trust those that I love to accomplish great things. People will rise to your level of expectations when they believe it's coming from a place of love, and people will fall to them. There was a lot of love for me growing up! My mom was a social butterfly, she was born on New Year's Day, and she let everyone know. She threw epic parties every year! At least, that's what the photographs presented. As soon as I grew old enough to attend her parties, they were no more! I have to giggle because it was honestly a bucket list item for me to attend one of my mom's epic parties. I had to settle for regular holiday celebrations, which were still a great time spent.

With all the love I received, I was exposed to many types of love: motherly love, best friend love, sisterly love, sensual love, and "toxic love." The toxic love showed up for me emotionally, physically, and mentally. I saw real trauma in the form of domestic violence. This is the part I'm not supposed to talk about. I was raised, what happens in this house, stays in this house! When there is exposure to domestic violence in any capacity, at such an early age, there are bound to be some battered bricks in that retaining wall called my life. She would yell, he would yell, he would hit, she would hit, he would hit, she would stab, and I would clean up the blood. Yes, knives, shotguns, pistols, and screwdrivers or hammers were in corners for those "just in case" moments.

There was some suffering, some inappropriate touching, and diabolical words used. Yes, there were some experiences that shaped how I defined what love looks like. It's taken countless years to understand how these events truly shaped my understanding of love, how to give and receive love, and how to recognize a healthy love or behaviors that are not love at all. The first step of the program is to acknowledge what it is, identifying that it is, in fact, domestic violence. Domestic violence is not always a slap in the face. Sometimes, it shows up as control, manipulation, gaslighting, projected unnecessary fears, lies, or elaborate partial truths. They all create a scar.

Awareness leads to the path of acceptance, and then I am free to choose if I want to repeat what I learned or learn from it and do something different. The line is fine for what that actually looks like. I just knew I was doing something different, only to discover I was somehow repeating what I learned. Quick temper, zero patience, too high expectations of myself, and low expectations of others. Unintentionally creating scars. These less-than-desirable personality traits show up when there are triggers or scarred vulnerability. I'm human, and I have recognized these in myself, and when I looked in a mirror, I did not like the reflection looking back at me during those times. How do I address it? I change my environment and my focus. I love deeply with great passion, with no bounds, but at a cost of no real room for error.

I tend to give all until there is inflicted pain or betrayal and then I give nearly nothing. I can't control how people actually treat me, but I can control the space and air around me. Because I love so deeply, once betrayed, it's not a space I freely visit again. Once a person chooses to inflict pain upon me, I believe that is the space I will always reside in their heart. Now, if and when I decide to truly love, that love never goes away; however, the time and space given for that love is substantially reduced and forever changed. I'm confident these words will trigger someone, but that is not my intention. I'm only sharing the fragility of my heart and how I've trained myself to guard it. I'm a true work in progress.

As I continue to fall asleep and wake up each day, I gain a new perspective and learn something new about myself. My thoughts and feelings as a 20-year-old are vastly different from my current older woman's thoughts. I value my time and the time of others. If I don't feel like I'm adding value to others, I tend to distance myself and just go learn something new. How that distance translates to others may not align with my intentions, and I'm learning to better recognize the ramifications of my choices. My isolation is a tool in my toolbox that prevents me from speaking to others solely out of emotions because emotions change. On the flip side, I do have an insatiable need to feel like I am ready for anything and everything, which prevents me from planning a lot of vacations. How can I commit to attending an event or long-term vacation when I have to be ready for the next crisis? Living in a constant state of fight or flight is normal for everyone...right?

I've learned that it isn't, and that was a me thing. I am a fixer! When others lean on me to fix it, guess what? I show up to fix it and struggle with what comes next when I'm no longer needed to fix it. My purpose, my motivation, and my drive are now planted in being a resource to serve. I once heard that what you focus on is what becomes bigger in your life. My focus relies on the success of others and being supportive. Using my joys and struggles to help others be better than they were before they met me. Now, I'm not saying I'm the reason people choose to be better; there is always a choice, and I would never want to see someone worse off because they met me. If you know me, you'll know I'm not great with accepting; that's just how it is; I have a deep-rooted passion for research, learning the reasoning behind the behavior, the motive, and the decisions.

The toxic love experiences intrigue me and leave me wondering.... why? Why did it get here? How did it get this far? God graced us all with free will, He didn't skip one of us for giggles, He graced us all with free will. I believe there is always a choice and a decision to make. Doing nothing is, after all, a decision. Why people make the decisions they make adds to my perspectives and journey to understand more. It's really easy to blame life, and it's true life can be tough, but I believe there is always a choice in there, options. Thinking back to my younger years, I wasn't very confident in options or choices. When I was about 12 or so, I mustered the strength to ask my mom a really tough question.

I asked my mom why she continued to let him back in after the storm before the bruises healed and the wall still needed repair. She told me she wasn't tired yet, and when she got tired, she would do something different. The toxic love somehow weighed more heavily on me because it was presented as a true decision. In my adult life, I have made decisions that others may see as poor or sacrificial, but that's the foundation of me. I am trusting my Heavenly Father to guide me and cover me. Sometimes, we just need to trust, do the work, and be still. Pray that God's grace allows you to take from the life experience given and learn and grow from the experience so that you are free from repeating the same lesson He has for you. I watched my mom fight in her relationships, fight with her closest family and friends, and fight for her life. She made decisions, and when she was tired, she did something different.

Knowledge breeds confidence, and I thrive on feeling more confident about anything I do or say. It doesn't mean it's always right, but I'll get as close as possible from effort. I am a lifelong learner seeking to understand from both scientific and spiritual perspectives. My early years presented love, laughter, and trying to just survive. I decided I wanted to learn more about the reasons people behave the way they do, why they stay in toxic relationships, and why some people smoke cigarettes and others don't. Why do some people get addicted to drugs after one try and others don't? I am just really curious about why! My first college internship was in crisis management at a domestic violence shelter. Turns out my choices in a career path were rooted in her cancer.

My desire to understand my life experiences became my life experience. Rather than choosing a path for things I thought would source a ton of money, I opted to discover the why for my early years. Discovering human behavior and potential reasons for the path they picked. When I focus on others, I spend less time focusing on myself. I can remember her vocalizing her pain and stating, God will take away the things you love the most. She felt punished in a sense. She felt her low-cut blouses somehow caused the mastectomy. Fear of loving too much and staying below the radar was now my normal. If I don't take up too much space, then I'm safe. I'm working to improve that part of me. To take up space and live boldly! If I get hurt, I'll live another day, only the next day I will have the experience of knowing a bold love. It's really okay to shine and no longer dim my light for safety or fear. I'm making a better effort to shine and not be afraid. There is enough light for everyone, and we can all shine brightly.

My mom wanted me to be better, and she believed I could be! She gave me every opportunity within her reach, and it was up to me to make the best of it! She planned my high school years when I was in elementary school. Her village and her hustle were like no other. Although she was "legally" disabled, she set a goal for me to attend private school, and I did. I became her future. I attended and graduated from 2 private schools and two universities. Given the hand she was dealt, I believe my journey has been full of blessings, lessons, and unwavering grace from my Heavenly Father. I mean, I was the youngest person to work my way to hold the title of Director at a thriving non-profit institution. Living each day with the thoughts of death chasing you, now that's a different way of existing; it humbles you, it changes you. My journey from girl to woman is a journey of vulnerability and discovery. Honestly, I'm still trying to figure it all out. I often refer to today as my third life; who knows how many I'll have(Smile). We grow up thinking we know everything, only to get older and realize we know nothing at all! My journey has taught me to love others from where they are, not where they or the world think they should be. I believe that's my superpower.

Now, if I can just figure out how to consistently let myself benefit from my own superpower, who knows where my next journey will lead? I've learned that even the toughest times can work out for your good. I have grown to be a more patient person because I have faced and overcome adversity. My scars remind me that I'm also a survivor. Praying for my next journey to be a blessing to others and truly thrive in this life. This chapter is a part of that process, and I hope the nuggets my mom shared resonate with you and add positivity to your own journey to your next chapter.

About LaMonique

LaMonique is the only child born to a courageous cancer fighter, a journey that shaped her resilience and perspective on life. Throughout her childhood, she experienced different family dynamics, taking on the roles of the oldest and middle child at various stages.

Now married and a proud boy mom, LaMonique is a self-proclaimed empath who finds fulfillment in being the friend others call when they need a listening ear. She has a natural gift for creating a safe space for those around her.

In her free time, LaMonique enjoys walking in nature, a practice that helps her find balance and clarity. She also loves watching movies and listening to music, finding joy and relaxation in these simple pleasures.

The Beauty God Made Me In

SHELIA HARDISON

I recall one of the very few conversations that I would have with my mother regarding childbirth, and specifically what she went through on the very day she gave birth to me. She spoke of the most painful birth that she had experienced since having six babies before me. I remembered how she thought she would die on my birth date. Hearing this from my momma as a young girl made me sad. But as I reflected on this incident as an adult, on what my mother had to overcome, I saw her strength, resilience, and faith so much clearer. She was built differently, and so was I!

I grew up in rural South Carolina, feeling the soil under my feet and the sun on my face as we tended to the farm. That's right, I'm a country girl at heart. As the youngest of seven, with an age gap of five years between myself and the next sibling before me, I essentially grew up as a lone child. My second cousins were my playmates, and we enjoyed the great adventures of play house, making mud pies, hide n-seek, red light, green light, and so many more. Being the youngest in the family also had its perks. I was showered with beautiful clothes, toys, and much love from my parents and siblings. Life was good! However, I learned that even with all the good, we never know what things in life, big or small, will impact our views, sometimes for a lifetime, if you allow it.

Although I was happy, there were things that society made me take notice of. That thing for me, although subtle in nature, was being a dark-skinned black girl. For as long as I could remember, I had an awareness of how the world saw little dark-skinned black girls. These subtleties tended to show up whenever people got upset. Whether it was friends, cousins, or coworkers, young or old, the one thing they tended to say to cut into my emotional wounds revolved around skin color. Ugly names like blackie, darkie, and any demeaning insults would spew from their mouths. There were even times when dating a "light-skinned" guy would cause others to whisper, "How did she get him?" or even go as far as to say, "She's too black to be with him." So, even with all the joys of life as a young girl, these were the moments when I recognized the voices around me could and did have an impact on me. The voices...The voices were strong and loud, holding within them intent to pierce deep.

As life challenges come and go, I'm reminded of the scripture Psalms 37:1-4 where the servant David tells us, "Do not fret because of evildoers, Nor be envious of the workers of iniquity...Delight yourself also in the Lord, And He shall give you the desires of your heart." So, despite the cutting words of others, I never stopped being involved in activities, sports, Girl Scouts, church activities, and leadership. I was active! Not only was I active, but I was also good, although I simultaneously harbored internal thoughts on how I felt others saw me.

Interestingly, it would take years for me to recognize that although it was great to be active, my experiences, along with the opinions of others, affected how I showed up to places and spaces. I often shied away from the spotlight and being in the "In" crowd to avoid criticism or heavy opinions that could dictate my actions. In many ways, this separation helped me develop independent thinking skills. Ironically, this very character trait would be useful when the time came for me to have a mental shift.

The shift was near! The change in how I showed up as a young black lady, as well as restructuring how I thought everyone viewed dark-skinned women, was now! This new outlook came with going to college. I was in a new place, with new people with varying backgrounds, cultures, and world views. College would undoubtedly become the perfect hub for candid conversations about all kinds of subject matters; race, sex, politics, gossip, and trends. Having this freedom to meet people who would become my friends when I needed support, encouragement, laughter, and eye-opening revelations would be priceless.

I remember one day seeing a beautiful dark-complected young lady and a light-complected guy embracing and enjoying each other. Just seeing them instantly took me back to the memories of my own experiences. However, at that moment, a light bulb went off, and I had a revelation that those who scrutinize skin color had their own issues. These experiences, including having friends from all walks of life and people genuinely complimenting me for who I was, helped me see that the narrative I had developed and internalized over time because of others was false. I was smart, bold, and beautiful... Black and all!

As I began to walk in this newfound confidence, I realized that I had the blueprint all along for how to operate in this world as a black woman in my mother. Although we didn't talk much early in life about the beauty versus struggle of life growing up as a black woman, I still was able to glean from her active examples. She was always poised and respectful and treated people well despite how they treated her. One of my fondest quotes that she said whenever one would do you wrong was, "Feed Them with A Long Handle Spoon." She was a class act indeed!

As I had conversations with my mother, she always led with scripture and love. Her stories and faith never fell on deaf ears. Eventually, I began to become who she said I was, through the affirming word of God. Simply put, the word has a way of molding you, developing you, and releasing you from people's expectations. One thing I have grown to know is that people like to oppress others when they have gifts that they don't have. This realization only furthered my belief that who I was in Christ was true; therefore, what others think no longer affects me as it once did.

The more I believed God's word, the more people began to recognize my light and wanted me to be involved in their programs. This led me to be part of several groups where I directly encouraged and was a positive resource for other young ladies. I was part of the Girl Scout Organization for 30-plus years, leader of the Teen Youth Sunday School, Teen

Clinic Nutritionist for Grady Hospital, and President of the college Afro-American Choir.

Now, as a seasoned woman who has truly experienced life, I make it a point to pour into others, to let them know they are valuable and never alone. I tell them, "Don't let the noise of other people's opinions, limiting beliefs, and fears drown out the inner voice God has given you." In other words, we must recognize that the enemy works through people to prey on what they deem to be weaknesses in us. Fortunately, these tactics only work if you allow them to. So get up girl, Woman of God, look in the mirror every day and tell yourself I am a child of God, and because he is a King, I am royalty entitled to all my Father has to offer!

The commitment to pouring goodness into young women would also transfer into motherhood. One of my greatest desires as a mother was to always instill confidence in my children. I intentionally spoke wisdom (Proverbs 2:6-7) over my children, including showing them how having self-respect, honesty, and confidence would carry them a long way. Inferiority did not exist in any shape or fashion because they walked in the Psalms 139:14 declaration of being fearfully and wonderfully made by God. This would become one of my proudest accomplishments.

This one thing I leave with you that I would also tell my younger self is, "Love you for who you are. Don't lose yourself trying to please others. You are far greater because God has a plan for you! Why? Because YOU are built differently, and so am I!"

About Sheila

Shelia Hardison retired with over 30 years' experience as a Dietary Supervisor and Mental Health Assistant within the Grady Healthcare System. For most of her career she was in management positions where she strived to be people focused and displayed a servants' approach to helping others. This would be evident during her time counseling individuals dealing with mental health, as well as spearheading community outreach activities, and nutrition education in Grady's Teen Clinic.

Her strong ability to encourage, lead, and manage others would expand beyond the workplace and into the community; where she took up a renewed love for the Girl Scout Organization as a troop leader for over 30years.

Born and raised on a farm in South Carolina she developed core values of putting God first, being honest, treating others right, and hard work. These core values stuck with her throughout her life, even as she took the leap to move to the big city of Atlanta. She soon found a church home, got married, and raised two beautiful children.

Life would not be without its fair share of obstacles to overcome. However, Shelia has managed to stand triumphant through them all. Whenever there were times life was hard she would remind herself through scripture (Philippians 3:14) I press toward the mark for the prize of the high calling of God in Christ Jesus.

Today you can find her enjoying the outdoors as she nurtures an array of beautiful flowers, magnifying the Lord with her voice in the Golden Eagles praise team at Light of Joy, and continuing to love on her friends and family who she holds dear. If there was one piece of advice that she lives by, it would be to Keep God First in All that You Do!

Our Journey From Girls to Women

Young Girls

JEWEL L. HOWARD

Young girls, young girls
The precious beauties of the world
Who will teach them that being a
woman goes beyond dressing up
in Mama's high heels and pearls
Who will teach them that their
womanhood is a precious thing
not to be taken...by force or
for granted
Who will teach them to cultivate
all their innate treasures of femininity
and nurturing
Who will teach them their womanhood does not
lie between the sheets of a man child
but within their own hearts and minds
Who will teach them to be confident, strong
and brilliant in handling all that they do
Who will teach them that their bodies are not to
be used to negotiate prices and receive free items
Who will teach them that their arms should not be
black and blue from violence or tracked with

needle marks
Who will teach them a woman is to bring forth life
by the deeds of her hands and the words of her mouth
Who will teach them?
We will teach them, women who are daily overcoming the
challenges of life
Women who are a success in their own right
Mothers who raised their children with the fear
of God, wisdom, and loving care
Grandparents who tell them of our rich history
And speak of days that used to be
And tell these young girls
they have greater opportunities
and choices in this world
Fathers who are there, working setting an
example of a real man
Giving them the protection and support
they need
We, We, the community, will teach them
so young girls are feeding from someplace
strong, a place where people care
We care young girls, the future of our world
We will teach you all the positive things you need
to be strong, to survive, to be free
and you young girls, must be eager to learn.

What's in a name?

Before I was born, my mother always knew that her firstborn daughter would be named "Jewel," after her oldest sister, Jewel Lee. My Auntie Jewel was fifteen years older and my mother affectionately loved as a surrogate parent. When my mother told my aunt she was pregnant, my aunt asked if the baby was a girl, she would like to give her a name as well, to which my mom agreed. Upon my birth, my mother told my aunt my first name would be Jewel. Believe it or not, my aunt wasn't thrilled at the idea. My Aunt told my mother, we already had a Jewel. Their brother Jimmy named his firstborn daughter Jewel as well. I later discovered that my Auntie Jewel was named after her Aunt Jewel, but she was always called by her nickname, "Aunt Doll." My mom knew she was not going to give me the middle name Lee and happily accepted an additional name from my aunt. She also knew she did not want me to be known as Little Jewel my entire life. My Auntie Jewel named me LaTonya, and my mother liked that name. My family and friends affectionately called me Tonya, even today. And that is how I got my name, another "Jewel L" in the family.

When I was about five, my father's brother said, "Hey, Jewel!" No one called me by my first name and the thought of being called Jewel became fighting words. I remember I told him with all the anger a 5-year-old could muster, "Don't call me that name, I hate that name!" Now, I loved my Auntie Jewel, the issue was the name that seemed old and outdated. The original name Jewel in my little life was more than just the name of my aunt, it was the name of businesses too. My parents once owned a tavern when I was a toddler called "Jewel's Playhouse," it was a coincidence the original owner was Mr. Jewel. Then there is the major grocery store chain in Illinois, Jewel's Food Store. I did not want to be associated with the name at all. I wanted to make sure he knew it. But once the words left my mouth and hit my mother's ears, I saw in her face that I hurt her feelings. She never said anything to me about it and we never had a discussion, but I knew my words hurt her.

I would have never wanted my Auntie Jewel or my grandmother to hear me say that I "hated that name." I made a promise to myself at that moment that I would make it up to my mother, I did not know how, but I would reclaim the name Jewel as my own. It would take me till I was nine, but I reclaimed the name. LaTonya had been my name from kindergarten through third grade. On the first day of school in fourth grade, the teacher began taking attendance, and she called me Jewel. She then asked if there was another name I preferred. Trust me, I thought about it, but I knew this was my opportunity to make it up to my mother for my childish outburst years prior. I recall taking a deep breath and responding no. I cannot tell you the endless Jewel Food Store jokes and commercial jingles I got throughout the years. I even joined in the joke in 4th grade using the orange "Jewel" stickers from the stores and putting them on my school papers. Even my first job was at Kroger's Grocery Store, and customers would read my name tag and say,

"Your name is Jewel, and you work at Kroger." Despite the jokes surrounding the grocery store chain, I learned that I am a Jewel, and I embraced the name. This name has been the true definition of my journey from girl to womanhood.

My role models? I loved and admired the women in my family. There was a wealth of femininity and wisdom I received from my grandmothers, aunts, cousins, and mostly my mother. I thought she was the most beautiful and talented woman I knew, and I wanted to be just like her. At an early age I saw my mother as an artist. She could paint, sew, write, and loved to dance. I can remember as a toddler, my mother having a lead role as the only Black actor in community theater. I was so excited, she could hear me tell folks in the audience, "that's my momma." And at the end of the play, I could not wait to tell her how good she was. I watched her sew my flower girl dress, make flower arrangements, and coordinate her sister Linda's wedding and was an HGTV queen long before it was a thing, and she loved cars. But the other thing about my mother I admired was her love for her family. I thought nothing was more beautiful than seeing my mother and her siblings (and their spouses) hanging out on the weekends. When my mother's first cousins visited Chicago from Cincinnati and Detroit, the swag, beauty, food, dancing, and laughter from these three cities under one roof was amazing!

One cousin who lit the room with her beauty, smile, and fashion was my mom's first cousin Joyce from Detroit. Joyce had a style and swag of her own. She even had nails painted multicolored before it was even a trend. Joyce was the only female who did not follow the tradition of getting married and having children. She travelled the world and always made sure she visited the cousins in Illinois. During one of her visits, my mom forgot to pick me up from school on my first day of kindergarten. As I watched my mother pull up to the school on two wheels, I was standing there like a big girl, and when I got in the car, I told my mother, "Oh, I know you were talking to Joyce." To my mother's defense, she worked midnights at the time, so my father got me dressed and dropped me off, and my mother completely forgot I had started school. As much as I loved my mother, and wanted to be like her, it was the life Joyce had that I wanted.

How do you define womanhood and what makes you a woman? Unlike my little sister, who expressed she wanted to be a mother at the age of four, claiming she was going to have 100 kids. I never spoke about wanting or longing to be a mother. It is not that I did not think about playing with my baby dolls. I just felt I wanted to experience being free and having fun like when I was with my older cousins and hanging with teenage aunts. My definition of womanhood at age four or five was being happy, wearing a bra, and having a *good* man. Please note that I said a good man, not necessarily a husband, because most women I knew with husbands, including my mother, were not happy, free, or fulfilled. I saw a difference between my aunts once they married after finishing high school. I had witnessed women suffering one way or another from having a husband, perhaps except for my grandparents and their generation. I did not want that for myself. I wanted the freedom Joyce had. I wanted the freedom to pursue my dreams like the 1970s shows "That Girl" and "Mary Tyler Moore," living in the big city and living on their own. As for Joyce, living on her own was the one thing she did not seem to have the freedom to do.

Setting an example as the oldest. It's funny growing up, I often overheard adults saying about my parents, "they only have the two girls." I guess because families in my parent's generation were much larger. My mother is the 5th child of eight children. She experienced living Chicago with her older siblings and at age13 felt uprooted to relocated 60 miles south to a rural area. She did not like going from living in the city to the country, but she was the oldest in the household and had to set an example. My father is the 3rd child of seven children, but the eldest son in his household and lived on a farm. He was a high school athlete, but still had the responsibilities of the farm before and after school. But both my parents knew the responsibilities of setting an example as the oldest. Both my parents shared living with a two-parent household. I did not hear them discuss a girl's or a boy's job when it came to doing chores. Sometimes, a parent or a child had to do what was necessary for the family. I saw my father cook, iron, and on occasion or two, comb my hair. As far as a father-daughter relationship is concerned, both my mother and my maternal grandmother experienced a father who protected, provided, and went to the ends of the earth for them, which included nursing them if a child was sick. So, it was a team effort, and my mother expected this in her marriage for her daughters.

Being the eldest of two girls, it was my responsibility to set an example for my younger sister and even my cousins. Not having any brothers, taking out the garbage, helping with the furnace, and cutting the grass were some of my daily chores. One day, I asked my father if he wanted me to be a boy. He looked perplexed at my question, and he asked why? I said, "Well, why do you work me like one?" He responded, "I don't want you to have to depend on a man for anything." When I got older, both parents shared that my father never made a big deal about having a son to continue with the family name, especially with me as his firstborn. He only said he just wanted a healthy baby and was proud to tell his friends he had a baby girl.

What marriage looked like in my household. My parents appeared to be on the same page when it came to parenting my sister and me. They stood for education and character and had a united front. They made sure my sister and I had every opportunity given to other children despite race or gender. My sister and I never lacked anything. Honestly, I never heard my parents say, "We can't afford that." Together they were experiencing a life their parents never had or a number of Black families at that time. For example, when my parents bought a boat, we would go to the park and ride the river. I recall when they sold the boat and got their first antique car, a 1933 Black Nash. I enjoyed riding in it to Chicago and the Pembroke Parade. Once we drove out to the country, and my father drove slowly down the road, I got to hang on the outside like an old Chicago gangster.

One of the best times in my parent's marriage was Christmas. It was truly a day of peace and happiness in our home. But from the time I can remember being able to ask what I wanted for Christmas, my parents always limited it to two gifts. When I was young, I remember I wanted a kitchen play set, and a race car set since my older male cousins never let me play with theirs. So, I told my mother I wanted a kitchen play set, and her response was, "No, you're not getting a kitchen set." My mother was fighting indirectly for me not to get caught up in a stereotypical role. I told my father I wanted a race car set, and he said, "Isn't that for boys? I thought to myself, but this is about what I want. I did not get either of those things but opted for my third request, a beautiful Black Baby Alive. Just a side note my mother was intentional that all my dolls were Black. When I got older, I laughed with my family about my two Christmas presents because I realized I should have told my mother I wanted the race car set and my father the kitchen set. This is the only time I can remember they got caught up in gender roles. But after that, I learned to carefully choose my two Christmas items. We got other gifts, too, but literally until the last Christmas of their marriage, you got two items on your Christmas list.

My parents did not just think about the material opportunities, they made sure we had other opportunities, like every magnet program offered in our district, private tennis lessons, piano lessons, and summer vacations visiting my Auntie Dorothy in California. We came back that summer, showing my mother how we learned sign language and what we learned in ballet class. Some of those activities we did not continue pursue, but we were exposed to a world outside our small town south of Chicago. Even though my parents could afford to give us things, they made sure they were not raising spoiled, ungrateful kids. Trust me, they knew how to say "no" to keep us balanced. My parents wanted us not to live in lack, and they didn't want us to be tempted by someone giving us something we never had.

Life is a chess match. Every decision that you make has a consequence to it, a quote from P.K. Subban. One unique skill we learned from our father was the game of chess. I was about seven, and my sister was four when we started playing around with pieces. Only the men in our family played chess, and they could play for hours. By the time my sister was seven, and I was ten, we knew how to play, and it was a part of the daily rotation of toys we had in our playroom, along with dolls, board games, and our chalkboard. It felt like our secret because we did not know any other kids, especially black or white girls, who played chess. We never played with any of our friends or cousins. My sister was part of the first chess club at her elementary school, even taking a chess book in 2nd grade for "Show & Tell."

I never joined the Chess Club in school. I figured I already knew that, so why join? But as teenagers, my sister and I played chess with older men, who often lost the first game to us because they thought we were "so cute." My parents never put emphasis on our looks as a avenue to get through life. They would say they were not raising us to be silly women. My sister and I did not understand what that meant at the time, we just thought it meant because we laughed all the time. My mother would often say, "Think for yourself." My parents believed they would rather us to be a leader and alone than in the crowd following a fool. But despite all my parents' efforts to give us the best, a happy marriage was not one of those things. My sister and I learned to function in the dysfunction of domestic violence and infidelity. As the oldest, I felt a sense of responsibility to protect my mother and sister, something I had to relinquish within myself once my mother remarried and my sister married. I discovered that in my parents' marriage, money could not buy happiness, and beauty did not guarantee a man's commitment.

A prayer answered. When I was thirteen, my parents divorced. This was an answered prayer and a true turning point in my life. A month or so before the divorce, I remember crying and praying to God that I could not take it anymore. I thought of calling my aunt in California to ask if I could come live with her. I did not want to leave my mother and sister, but I could no longer stay in that environment. By this time in their marriage, my mother was living in her dream house, a mini-mansion Victorian home. My parents had more additional cars and property, but there was no peace. One day, my father told my mother he wanted a divorce. I remember my father wasn't home when my mom called my sister and me into their bedroom. We sat on the floor, and my mom sat in her favorite chair; she began to tell us they were getting a divorce. The three of us sat in silence.

Now, my sister and I have heard this before. We were already accustomed to breaking down our wood and metal canopy beds, learning to pack the essential items we thought were important to us, and moving clothes. As we sat there, all three of us trying to look sad, I thought, how long I got to sit here? I'm ready to go back to watch my TV show. We had all come to the end of our rope, but no-one spoke it aloud. My mother had one week to find a place and move out. In her search for a new apartment, she hesitated at first to inquiry about a vacancy for a 3-bedroom apartment in the neighboring all white town. She was surprised to discover an apartment was available but only a 2-bedroom and she would have to wait a couple of months for the 3-bedrooms. My mother accepted the 2-bedroom apartment and all that was required was $100 deposit. This was truly a blessing because my mother kept $100 in her Bible for such a time as this. The only furniture we had when we moved in was the bedroom set that belonged to my sister and me and two black chairs. In a week, we just left a 4-bedroom two story Victorian house on a corner lot for a 2-bedroom, 1 bathroom apartment with no furniture. But we had peace. And as my grandmother would often say, you cannot buy that. I remember when my mother picked us up from school, we walked into the apartment, and the entire place was furnished, including a bedroom set for my mom. I knew this time there was no going back. We lived on Gettysburg Street, which was symbolic. The Battle of Gettysburg is known as the turning point of the Civil War, which the Union won.

Divorce and Death. The divorce took place at the end of November, and it was a turning point in all our lives. Everything I had come to love in my youth changed, even for my mother, who grew up in her own womanhood or was at least learning what it meant. Meanwhile, another divorce happened in the church family I grew up in. So, the three of us were alone, and the paternal family and church family were no longer there. There was a major division in the church I grew up in, and my entire family left. I felt abandoned. However, within weeks of the divorce, my Auntie Jewel, Cousin Joyce, and my Aunt Curlie visited to offer emotional support to my mother. It was amazing once again to see this sisterhood in my family.

I cannot begin to describe what that first year of divorce was like, but I will tell you how it ended. In August of the following year, my mother organized one of the best family reunions to-date. Relatives from Detroit and Cincinnati came to Illinois, and we all had a wonderful time. Those who attended included my cousin Joyce and my Auntie Jewel. We were excited Joyce had an opportunity to spend time with us before her big trip to Japan. On August 31, 1983, tragedy struck our family. Korean Air Lines flight 007 was shot down by Soviet air-to-air missiles, killing all 269 passengers, including our beloved Joyce, at the age of 34. The memorial service held the following month in Detroit was full of press and unanswered questions. On the van ride home to Illinois, I remember laying my head in my Auntie Jewel's lap and falling asleep. In November, before Thanksgiving, my Auntie Jewel also passed away from an aneurysm. And just the previous year, these two women were there for a major turning point in our lives. I watched how my grandmother and her younger sister had to comfort each other because they both lost a daughter and a niece within a month of each other. These deaths changed my family, especially during the holidays. It was also during this time after my parents' divorce that my nails began to grow.

Jewel of a Woman. As I became a young woman, I am glad that I took all the pieces of the woman I admired and lived out the many dreams I hoped for when I was a girl. Like my cousin Joyce, I have traveled outside the United States, lived independently, and even bought my own house. When I moved into my first apartment, my maternal grandmother said, "Why don't you wait until you get married?" And I said, "Grandma, what if I don't ever get married?" I think they were just worried about the traps a young woman living on her own could get into. And though I was dating a steady boyfriend, my grandmother was so proud when I graduated from college. She would say she was proud I "did four years of college and with no babies and how you can live on your own, "Look, Tonya did it." It goes back to the expectation of setting an example.

Time has been able to heal old wounds. I was so proud to be the Maid of Honor for my mother and sister. At the time of this publication, my mother, artistically known as Annice, has been happily married for 36 years to a man who cherishes her with all the love gives and deserves. Dean has been a dad to my sister and me. My sister, Jacinda celebrated 29 years of marriage with her college sweetheart Dave. August 31st has brought our family a new reason to celebrate, it is the birth date of my eldest nephew. I enjoy being the only aunt and godmother to my sister's three beautiful and successful sons. And the new additions of my niece-in-law, and a new great niece. The relationship with my father may have been complicated over the years, but I am grateful he and I have been able to talk and reconcile the issues from childhood. There is forgiveness, acceptance, and love. I have been blessed to pursue careers in the arts like my mother and doing things I dreamt of as a girl. This includes working in the television industry and receiving several Emmy awards and a Telly and fighting for social justice.

Some lessons I have learned over time in my journey are:

*I must be who God created me to be, not defined by family, church, or society.

*I've learned to trust my instincts and not second-guess myself.

*Never attach yourself to an insecure person.

*Learn to discern the difference between imperfection and red flags.

*Remember to love yourself enough to keep growing so you don't become a grown woman stuck in an 8th-grade mean-girl mentality.

When I turned 50, I was grateful to have lived this long. My womanhood is not defined by my marital status or lack of being a mother. My cousin Joyce passed in her 30s, dying doing what she loved; my Auntie Jewel died in her 40s from the weariness of life; my Auntie Linda died in her 40s, yes from breast cancer, but mainly a broken heart at the end of 25 years of marriage. I have learned over the years that the journey from becoming a girl to a woman goes beyond the length of your hair and body measurements. There is a jewel inside all of us. The woman who has lost her hair to cancer or alopecia still rocks her crown with a bald head. The woman who suffered a mastectomy. The woman told she would never be able to conceive. Regardless of the circumstance, every woman still can be confident in her beauty, her resilience, and her strength. I still believe in love, and one day, I will meet a jewel of a man...but even if I do not, I know who I am. I am a jewel of a woman.

Our Journey From Girls to Women

Jewel of a Woman

I am the Daughter of the Dust
kissed by the sun
I've been tried in the fire
turning my trials into victories won
Oh, my womanhood has been challenged
even raped, bruised, and scorned
But God has given me beauty for ashes
A jewel of a woman to be adored

Yes, when the world tried to crush my soul
tears of weeping and wailing
only made me stronger, coming out as pure gold
I've been called to greatness from the time I was born
A precious, unique beauty
A jewel of a woman to be adorned

So don't judge my femininity based on my breasts, butt, and thighs
Don't place my value on the brand of purse
my marital status, my hairstyle, my ride
Should I only be defined by birthing a child or being somebody's wife

Why does it matter
When I'm glowing, living my best life
I recall Adam was asleep when God brought Eve into her womanhood
So there's only the Master who truly understands
the way a Jewel of a woman was created for good

Because I'm more than a conqueror
there's no need to compare
the richness of my beauty and the fire of my stare
my gray hair is but a silver lining,
every wrinkle is a line of wisdom
A life of purpose, and my light is shining
Yes, fire and tears
made this gem
Jewel of a woman

About Jewel

Jewel L. Howard is a writer, activist, poet, multi-Emmy nominated television producer, and Award-winning Bronze Telly Award recipient as a co-host/producer for her podcast, "Speak Out World!" dedicated to artists and activism. She has performed as a spoken-word artist in Chicago and Atlanta, performing in the Atlanta Jazz Fest.

In addition to her work in the arts and love for travel, Jewel has been an activist in civic engagement work in Georgia since 2015. She is a graduate of Roosevelt University from Chicago, IL with a Bachelor of Science in Business Administration.

From Scaredy Cat to all That...Almost

Mz. Inez

This is supposed to be about little ol' me going from girl to woman. It had to start somewhere, and it did, or should I say, I did. Born at Travis AFB in California early in the morning in May to a couple whose father was in the Air Force and was fortunate to have a mother be a stay-at-home mom - Mr. and Mrs. Manuel Brown. I was the fourth of five children. I will praise thee; for I am fearfully and wonderfully made: marvelous are thy works; and that my soul knoweth right well. (Psalm 139:14 - KJV)

Born on Monday, from the traditional nursery rhyme, "Monday's child is fair of face," which identifies me with attractive beauty, yet current interpretations portray me as shallow, selfish, and impulsive. Thou art fairer than the children of men: grace is poured into thy lips: therefore God hath blessed thee forever. (Psalm 45:2 - KJV) This rhyme is a traditional English superstition that attributes certain characteristics to children based on the day of the week they were born.

I don't believe the second part, but that is what the definition turns out to be, and I MIGHT have a wee little bit of some of those qualities. Monday-born individuals are highly intuitive and sensitive to the feelings and emotions of others. I was born with gray eyes, light skin, and a big ol' smile. That is why I don't believe the second part about being shallow, selfish, or impulsive. (HAHA!) This is what they said. I was a happy child. I was a good child. I was a butterball. A fat little girl with roly-poly legs like that of the skin of a Shar Pei dog.

As Monday-born people possess the calm nature of the Moon, their aura represents the delicate brightness of the Moon. Even if they are quiet, their eyes tell a lot about them.

No one can care for their life partner as they do with their warm and caring nature. I am giving you all of this information and background because these characteristics are important in my life growing from a girl to a woman.

From what I remember as a child, I was such a scaredy cat, and I don't even like cats. But come to find out, as a spirit animal; the cat teaches us to embrace our sensitivity to trust our instincts and intuitive perceptions. It encourages us not to be afraid of exposing ourselves to the world, even if this sometimes means experiencing intense emotions or uncomfortable energies. I wish I had known that as a child. I may not have been so afraid of everything and those around me.

I remember that, in kindergarten, there was a day I was late for school, and my mother had to drive me to school. She dropped me off early enough to go to school, but guess what I did? I was so afraid to go into the classroom I waited outside on the steps until I had to go to the bathroom so badly that I almost wet myself. I finally entered in, and about that time, it was time for Art Class, and my other classmates were already painting. I made sure I got paint on my shirt, so it appeared like I had been in school all day, but as you can see, I hadn't. I don't know why I was so afraid to enter in, but fear had me at the door. YOU may know that "For God hath not given us the spirit of fear; but of power, and of love, and of a sound mind" (2 Timothy 1:7- KJV), but didn't nobody tell me that during that time in my life.

As I grew up, I still was an old scaredy cat. I would stay under my mom because, being the fourth child, my older siblings were six, four, and three years older than I, and my younger brother was seven years under me. I guess you can call me somewhat of a loner, in essence. I did things by myself. I remember the older kids were playing softball, and I got hit in the head by the ball and received a big ol' juicy knot. I just wanted to hang around Mom and the other mothers, but my mother told me to go play. I had to obey.

Since my dad was in the Air Force, we got the opportunity to travel to Zaragoza Air Force Base in Spain as one of his tours of duty, and I enjoyed myself. Spain is a place I would love to visit again as a check-off on my bucket list. The family spent two and a half years there. The base was called a "closed base" because we didn't have all the luxuries or amenities other bases had, and there weren't many families stationed there either. Everything was very limited.

The base consisted of a gym, bowling, a movie theater, a BX (Base Exchange), a school located in the church, and a commissary. The commissary had hardly any items, so we had to journey to Torrejon Air Force Base near Madrid. It was about a four-and-a-half-hour drive. When someone did make that long trip, other families would ask around to see if anyone needed any groceries to be picked up as a kind gesture. We had this 1969 Red and White Catalina Pontiac Station Wagon; if you had ever seen one, you know it was huge. Then, to have black people with a family of seven passengers in it AND driving it made an even bigger scene.

When we would drive down the tiny streets of Zaragoza, everyone else had to back up their vehicles to let us through. Driving in the country one day, this lady put down her groceries, waved, and yelled, "Que Bonita!", which means "How pretty or Beautiful."

There weren't a lot of kids on base, and school was held in the church from kindergarten through eighth grade. All the grades were in one room. At that time, I was in the third grade. I must have gotten some stored-up courage from somewhere as I taught some of the sixth graders spelling and math. My brothers and sister had to be sent off to a boarding school in Torrejon one year, and my sister was sent to Rhoda Air Force Base in Sevilla our last year. We learned Spanish, and I picked it up quickly because we had a Spanish maid named Pilar. She was kind. There was also the "Gardner," whose name was Eduardo. He tended the sheep he herded through the base, and I remember always walking through sheep piddles on the way home from school. They would stick to my shoes. My little brother and Eduardo would hang out, and my little brother, who wasn't very old then, would come home with wine down his shirt. I think that is why he likes to drink a lot now. The Gardner got him hooked at an early age.

Mom and I would go downtown to pick a few items like material during our time in Spain. Mom made our clothes for special occasions. I remember her making my sister's New Year's dress. It was beautiful—a light mint green with a black embroidered flower on the left shoulder. Mom and I were downtown at one time. She wasn't much taller than I was. This Spanish lady passed by us, and she was short as well. She wore these thick, black-rimmed, Coke-bottled glasses and was wearing a black coat. She got so close to me that she scared me. I ducked behind Mom, of course.

The Spaniards would ask in Spanish, "Are you American?" Mom would say, "No, Africano!" Then, a little later that same day, someone would ask, "Are you Africano?" Mom at that time answered, "No, Americano!" I just laughed at that and still laugh about that today. Now, some people call us, WHAT - African Americans. I think Mom was just ahead of her time. I was a little mischievous as well as a scaredy cat. But I wasn't the only bad one. I don't remember right off why, but some of the kids got into a rocks-throwing match, and one of the girls got hit in the top of her head by a rock BY ME. Why did this girl have to be the Commander's daughter? Yes, and of course, I was scared of the consequences, but hey, things happen. I didn't get into too much trouble, but she did have to have stitches in the top of her head.

My dad was in Civil Engineering in the service. He made things from wood. One of those things was a paddle with holes, so it was less wind-resistant when you swung it to spank someone. He gave that paddle to the principal at school, Mr. Green. Why was I the first to get a spanking by the paddle my dad made? I told you I was mischievous. What had happened was... I had sharpened this pencil oh so sharp and set it on this boy's chair. (In my Steve Erkle voice) "Did I do that?" Yep, I did. I don't know what possessed me to do so, but I did. I was sent to Mr. Green's office. I even remember the dress I had on because it was a short blue dress, and I think when I bent over to receive my spanking from that wind-resistant paddle, my panties showed. I knew I was busted then, and yes, I was scared to go home because I already knew what was waiting for me there—another spanking. The base was small, so as I traveled home, the news traveled and got there before I did, and I was somewhat prepared, but dang it, anyhow, I got what was coming to me. As I WAS born on Monday, that is where that impulsiveness came into play-acting or done without forethought. I didn't think about the consequences of my impulsiveness. I wish I had. Hindsight WAS 20-20 on my hiney...

You know when you get that crush on someone, but you don't want to let the world know? There was this boy named Fred on base, and I liked him. He had red hair and freckles. I thought he was cute, but I couldn't let him know I liked him. I turned eleven in Spain, and on this particular birthday, because there weren't that many kids on base, I asked Fred and others to come to my birthday party. There were a few of us. I wanted to ask Fred to dance, but I was a scaredy cat. To this day, I don't think Fred knew I liked him. Then there was this boy named Stanley, and he liked me, but I didn't like him. I was scared to tell him I didn't like him. (LOL!) I was scared either way.

We returned to the states after that two-and-a-half-year stint. Time passed, and my father had to go to Vietnam. He was stationed in Da Nang for approximately one year.

Oh boy, what a long year. He would communicate with us not through letters but through reel-to-reel tapes. I was young. Mom and the five kids would sit around and listen to his voice with bombs going off in the background. Mom would jump every time she heard a bomb explode. Prayers were most definitely going up for him. Yes, we were all scared for Dad's safety during that long year. He was supposed to have returned by Thanksgiving, but he didn't. We waited for him to return before we had our Thanksgiving dinner. We had something to be grateful for by his return.

I was in Home Economics in the Eighth Grade during junior high school. I wanted to sew like my mother did for us. She would make and place our clothes at the bottom of our beds. I was so naive. I just knew a cloth fairy had put those clothes on our beds during the night. Er Duh!!! No, boo boo. I found out that Mom would stay up late at night as we slept and slumbered to create these fabulous clothing items for us.

I specifically remember this blue robe with a long candle on it. I wore the heck out of that robe. We had to pick what we wanted to make for our sewing project in class. I picked out one of the hardest patterns you could imagine. It was a Butterick 2-piece Tennis outfit. It consisted of a thigh-length top with splits in the front down the front legs and a pair of shorts. I can still see the material I made the outfit from. It was a light brownish color with small flowers on it, and it had a ZIPPER down the back of the top and elastic waist shorts. Oh lordy. I told you I picked a hard one. I was scared to put the zipper in, but with Mom's assistance, I accomplished my feat. Yesssss!!!! We had to do a little fashion show, and the wonderful thing was that the garment fit. I didn't have any crushes in Junior High. I didn't have to worry about liking anybody, but I don't know if anybody liked me or, should I say, had a crush on me. There weren't that many blacks in my Junior High. They could be counted on one hand.

I made it to High School, and oh, what a time I had. That was one of the best times in my life, as I remember. Of course, when you get to High School, you are already scared.

Why? Because you are a freshman and freshmen get picked on. I was lucky to have one brother as a Senior when I entered High School. Did that matter? Kind of. He was one of those Jocks, as we used to call them back in the day. You know, a Football player and a Wrestler. But I still had my scaredy-cat moments. You know, when you enter unchartered territory, you don't know what to and what not to expect. Even though Monday's child is fair of face, I never considered myself attractive or pretty. I would call myself Average Annie. That was where the lack of self-esteem played a part. Even in High School, there weren't many "US" to choose from to like or be liked by. We were a total of about 10-12. But that didn't make a difference. If someone were to like you, they would like you no matter what.

As a freshman, I joined almost every sport and got into everything I could. I immersed myself in gymnastics, volleyball, basketball, track, and even Red Feathers (a marching group performing at the games and parades). I was excited to be a part of my high school. I became friends with just about any and everyone. I used to be impulsive and did some of the most craziest things ever. I would hide in my locker and yell out people's names. They would look around and didn't know where I was calling from. That was the best prank ever. I garnered a ton of friends, and we went to the games and hung out afterward. I became part of the Rowdy Squad.

Now you know you can't have High School without High School Dances. There was this one dance called "The Sadie Hawkins Dance," where the girls would ask the guys, and we would have to pay, and so on. Well, as well as I know my friends, fellows, guys, buddies, whatever you want to call them, I wanted to ask one guy to the dance. I just couldn't muster up the courage to ask him. Every time I saw him, and he was by himself, I froze up like a chocolate popsicle. I couldn't open my mouth to form the words to ask him. Funny thing is, he already knew I wanted to ask him.

He gave me plenty of opportunities to make my request known, but those words just didn't flow. Until it was the final hour to ask, I did it and was proud of myself. Thank God he said, "Yes". I don't know what I would have done if he didn't. Probably I would have cried like teenagers do when somebody breaks our hearts. I even had a great time.

It got easier to do the bidding until it was Senior Prom time. Again, fear rose in me. I had to ask someone from out of town to be on my arm and escort me the evening of my Prom. This young man was so handsome and talked about a serious crush. OOOOOOOWEEEEE!! His grandmother introduced us at church, and, OH MY Jesus! I just knew I was in love. Or at least I guess I was. What do we know at that age? Heartthrob maybe? I didn't have to do this one face-to-face as he was out of town, but I had to call him and talk about an uneasy conversation. He, too, knew I wanted to ask him. His grandmother had wanted us to go.

She and I attended the same church. I had to find that deep-down courage to part my lips to ask. Once we got through the pleasantries and I fumbled my way through the conversation, it came out. I asked him. My heart wanted to sink, but I got through it.

In my junior year of High School, I tried out to be a cheerleader. Now, that was funny. Why do I get so nervous or scared when you know these people? It wasn't so much as that. It was a routine to have to remember and then perform. Yep, I was scared, and no, I didn't get chosen, but that's ok. If I had been chosen, the outgoing cheerleaders would swoop you up or kinda kidnap you at night while you are sleeping and take you out, and you would have to perform some of the cheers. I wasn't swooped or kidnapped. Some of the girls were disappointed, but that is just part of life. There were a lot of factors in the making of the finalists for cheerleading. I didn't meet them.

Senior year was the bomb dot com. I had the best time of my life. That year, I did pretty well in gymnastics and was not too bad in track. I guess being a Monday child has its benefits. In the town I lived in, there were Lilac Princesses chosen from each school, and then from the Princesses, a Lilac Queen was chosen for the Royal Court. I happen to be asked to run for Lilac Princess at my school. Now, mind you, I told you I always thought of myself as an Average Annie. There were beautiful classmates chosen to run for this prestigious honor. We didn't have to do any talent of any sort. Just speeches and answering questions the judges posed to us. I don't remember any of those questions, but I do remember the title of my speech. It was entitled, "The Long and Winding Road". I was scared yet and again to get out in front of all those people and family members in the auditorium, but I did it. Back then, there weren't the best options for black makeup and not many choices. Plus, I didn't know how to apply makeup because I didn't wear makeup in school. I was barefaced during school, and maybe barefaced is how I should have gone out on stage. I felt like I looked ghostly. But, hey, I thought highly enough of myself to go out and do my best. That, to me, was part of becoming a strong and positive woman.

Maybe my face didn't look too bad in High School as I was voted the "Most Popular Girl" in school. My Monday Fair of Face mug was plastered on just about every page it could be plastered on in my yearbook. Everyone wanted me to sign their yearbook. I didn't have a boyfriend, per se, in high school. Just male friends. We all just gathered and hung out together as a group, which was fine by me. The impulsiveness came out again one night after a football game. Our group went out to Taco Time, and again, I was feeling myself. I put packages of hot sauce in one guy's back pocket, and they busted open. Here I go again with the Erkle voice - "Did I do that?"

Some of the strangest guys asked me out on dates. Strange in the way I was shocked to be asked out by anybody. The only thing was, they had to pass the Oldest Brother Test. I was so embarrassed by my brother. He would stop them before coming up the steps to the house and ask them all kinds of crazy questions and statements. Where do your parents work? How much do they make? Let me see your teeth. Let me check your muscles. You better treat my sister right or you'll have to answer to me. Things wouldn't have changed even today if I were still living in the same town as he does. He still tries to interrogate my male intendeds.

I graduated High School and enrolled in the Community College, where I was fortunate enough to get a full scholarship for gymnastics and track. Yippee Skippee!! I was shocked to shout. Our team didn't do too bad the two years I attended to get my AA in Legal Secretary. I had a great time on the gymnastics team during my Community College years. I was a vaulter and bar girl. (Uneven bars, that is.) Why was I scared to do anything and had to go backward? I tried to do a backflip but couldn't pull it off. There was a gymnast there who weighed 30 pounds more than I did, and she did the floor routines, front flips, back flips, all types of tumbling moves and everything in between. She was really good. I attempted this one move on the bars called a belly whip full and didn't make a full rotation all the way around. I landed on my left thigh and now I have a nice reminder in the form of a lump middle side of my thigh.

At the end of gymnastics season, there was an indoor pool at the college we were able to swim in. Even though I was a gymnast, why did I body shame myself? I was scared and didn't want anyone to see me. I thought I was too thick to be in a swimsuit, but how could I still be in a gymnastics leotard? If that wasn't a confusing thought. As we went to get into the pool, how is it that I dove into five feet of water and busted my front teeth out? Didn't bust the lips, just the teeth. I just felt like I was too fat (body shaming) and wasn't paying attention. I dove right in as if I was smiling and happy to see the bottom of the pool. Why did I have to be the first casualty in the pool? Blame it on the black girl. Me, of course. I like being first in some things, but that was not one of them.

Yes, ma'am. Yes, sir. I said it, and I did it. Talk about pain. I had to go to my dentist, have a root canal and have my two top teeth filed down and cast for crowns. My two bottom teeth were busted a little, but not like the top. Not too long after I had become a casualty, we had to take pictures for our Legal Secretary team. They were taken not long after I had my two top teeth with temporaries on. For some reason, it looked like I had Bell's palsy on my face with rabbit teeth. Bell's palsy is a neurological disorder that causes temporary weakness or paralysis on one side of the face. It's the most common cause of facial paralysis. I was not feeling those pictures that day. I was not a Monday Fair of Face child that day. A myriad of events happened after that. I grew up into a woman. I fell in love a few times and got heartbroken once or twice. I got engaged. The first time I fell deeply in love, I met this one at church. He was a PK (Preacher's Kid), and his father was the Pastor of the church. This young man would call the house with his deep voice and say, "Deacon Brown, may I speak with your daughter?" We would talk for hours. My mom called him a mandarin because he wasn't quite a man yet, but he had captured my heart. Our love grew, and he was my first at 20.

Talk about someone being scared for the first time. Someone needs to teach a class on letting someone know the "ins and outs" of getting involved with a man for the first time. You know, the birds and the bees. This is a time I was really scared. I mean, scared to death. I had no idea what the pain being the first time would cause. Ouch!! No more cherry pie. We thought we were going to get married, but the moon, stars, earth, or none of the other planets aligned. He was not there, and then I got married. I got divorced, and then he was in the mix of getting married. I'm still the daughter-in-law by proxy (they say I should have been).

Guess what? After I attended the community college to be a legal secretary and received my AA degree, I didn't want to be one. HAHA!! I wanted to be a fashion designer and move to New York. I didn't want to sit at a desk for eight hours and work for someone. I wasn't afraid to move to New York, which struck me as strange, but it was something I wanted to do. I wanted to live in a brownstone or warehouse with half living quarters and have a designer area. Talk about a dream douser. You wouldn't believe where I ended up with my first job—International Business Machines, which we call for short IBM. My sister-in-law told me to apply as a switchboard operator and receptionist. Didn't I tell you I didn't want to sit at a desk for eight hours and work for someone or anyone? That's exactly what I did anyway for 16.5 years.

During those 16.5 years, I moved out of my folks' home, got my first apartment, and bought a house. I had gotten engaged to another young man, and that is a story as well. We were supposed to be married one August, and plans were made, and the announcement was in the local paper. As we were approaching closer to the wedding day, my mom had had a slight stroke, and I was scared as well as I didn't think she was going to be able to attend the wedding. My mom meant the world to me; if she could not attend, there would not be a wedding. I explained to my fiancée I wanted to postpone the wedding until my mother felt better. He was totally against it. I was like, oh heck no.

I took off my engagement ring and left it on the pillow at the apartment. He was working and was using my car. I wanted to check on my mom. I walked, mind you, 11 miles to go check on my mother. I wasn't playing. By the time I got there, there were church members around her. I got there, and everyone thought I was crazy. I think I was about to have a nervous breakdown due to the situation with my mother and then breaking up with the fiancée. I was scared I was going to lose her. Instead of going back to the apartment, I stayed with some friends on the Air Force Base for about a week. How could he get on the Air Force Base and find where I was staying? First off, who vouched him on and then how did he know where I was staying? Things that make you go HMMMMM????

Things had calmed down some, and I wanted to get my car back. He was staying with his mom after that episode. He tried to give the ring back. I didn't want it. He jumped on the hood of my car and held on as I was driving down the street. Finally, he got off, and I went back to the apartment. I put him out. He had given me another ring from one of the elderly patients he had been caring for where he was working. She told him to give it to the woman you are going to marry. Why do I still have that ring today? Earlier in our relationship, we were preparing for a show. I was supposed to be doing a backflip, and he was supposed to be spotting me. Why is it that he didn't spot me and I fell on my face and busted the same two teeth I had busted in the pool?
Those crowns busted, and I had to get another set of crowns. The dentist and I became real good buddies. Oh yah, and by the way, we didn't get married.

A couple of years later, I became engaged to an Air Force man and the ring was beautiful. He had a tour of duty over in Germany for a little minute. While there, he "got busy" with another young lady, and they had a child. Somehow, the child ran into a coffee table and hit the top of its head on the corner, and it died. He came back to the states trying to make it up to me, but I wasn't having it. Then in June of 1984, another Air Force man who had just arrived in town from Kadena Air Force Base, Japan, stepped up at an all-nighter dance and asked me to dance. We started dancing until we got married six months later that December. If all of these events don't make a woman out a person, I don't know what's happening. We had a daughter in January of 1986. We were married for nine years and nine days. We divorced, and he got married two weeks later. Is something wrong with me, or am I too hard on a man? We had gone to counseling with two different counselors. I told the second counselor I didn't love him anymore. He had no backbone. Monday's Child - Am I shallow or selfish? They called me, "The Maneater". I can do bad and good all by myself.

I had to put on my Big Girl Panties and "WO"manned up. And I did. I became a single mom and the man and woman of the house. In March of 1994, I lost my job with IBM and was unemployed. I was clueless as to how I was going to make ends meet. I took a moment to think long and hard as I was collecting unemployment. During all this time, I had been sewing in the basement of my house as it was my actual passion. I spoke with my dad, and he added a 24'x24' addition to my existing house. Dads are great for taking care of their little girls. I just knew I was going to become the next haute and top fashion designer. In my mind, I can do anything, but as it states in the Bible, what? I can do all things through Christ which strengtheneth me. (Philippians 4:13 - KJV) That is one of my favorite Bible verses. As is this one as well because of what God has given unto me - A man's gift maketh room for him, and bringeth him before great men. (Proverbs 18:16 - KJV) I was unemployed for seven months, and there I go again, working for somebody else instead of just for myself. I was employed by the Medical Service Corporation, which became the Premera Blue Cross.

I was an employee there for 10 years until I got married on January 1, 2005. Many of my fears had been removed as I took that leap of faith or something and moved to Tampa, Florida, across the country from where I had lived for over 40 years. Now, I knew I could do just about anything. But that marriage didn't last long at all—only about two and a half years. I tried. Some people you can't trust. He told untruths. How can you fix your mouth to say you have children and don't have any? RED FLAG. I love red, too. I kept my guard up. Usually, it is the other way around. As a man, you normally try and hide the fact you have children. After the fact we were married, his mother told me he was a habitual liar. I tried to give a person the benefit of the doubt, but this would not work.

Remember earlier about the cat. As a spirit animal, the cat teaches us to embrace our sensitivity, to trust our instincts and intuitive perceptions. It encourages us not to be afraid of exposing ourselves to the world, even if this sometimes means experiencing intense emotions or uncomfortable energies. I got uncomfortable, alright. I had refinanced my house so we could have some cash in Florida. After the dollars got down from nil to none, I was told I had to go to work. So I did. I worked for the same security company he worked for. I worked 16-hour shifts so I could get out of the marriage. He wanted to retire in five years, and I asked him, "What would I be doing?" "Taking care of you?" You see what had happened was, again, he told the whole church at our wedding, I didn't have to work as I was going to be doing my fashion designing and be bringing money in.

Taking another leap of faith as an "Up and Coming" Fashion Designer in Tampa was quite interesting. That's a story for another book. Since I was new in Tampa, I had to start from the bottom, and I didn't get anywhere. I would sometimes do two fashion shows a weekend. For my first fashion, my parents tried to surprise me. But I surprised them instead. They tried to sneak into town. My mom kept calling and asking me questions about the show because she was "trying to send me flowers", etc. They had arrived in Tampa, and Mom was on the phone. I heard the car door beeping and knew my dad's car doors didn't beep. It was nice to see them at the show. I get my determination from my parents.

In February of 2011, I was getting ready to do a fashion practice, and I received a call from my brother above me; I had to come home. Mom had to be revived three times. The doctors made her comfortable until I could get home. That was on a Friday. I made it home on the following Tuesday. They weren't sure how much longer she could hold on. She held on for another 27 hours after I got there. Death is a funny thing sometimes. The choir sang songs to her as she was one of the Church Mothers. The hospital didn't mind. Every time she took one of those deep breaths, everyone else held their breath. She said she was tired and ready to go. She had diverticulitis and sarcoidosis. Mom had a colostomy bag attached, and necrosis started settling in. The doctor said he had never had a case like that before. He felt so bad. A friend of mine stopped by to visit Mom and see me. Why was it that as soon as I stepped out of the room, my mom took her final breath? My brother came out and told me mom just passed. I was selfish. I said, "Mom,

Really?" She was 78 when she passed away in February 2011.

Before all of this, my sister passed away on April 1, 2000, in her sleep. I asked Dad if it was a joke. I knew better. My dad doesn't play like that. She passed away in her sleep at the age of 47. Things had not gone right with her ever since someone spiked her drink at a club she and her girlfriend were at. I am saying this because I want to keep my sisters safe. If you leave your table and go to the restroom or on the dance floor, DO NOT COME BACK TO THAT DRINK and partake. You just never know who may have handled your drink. She had to be placed in a psych ward, and she did things unlike her. She chased Mom with a knife and ran across the highway in her robe. My sister always thought her boys would be taken away from her. She knocked Mom down the stairs and tried to start a fight with her. The neighbor saw it happen and came to Mom's defense.

When my sister was living in a care facility, she would start fights with the other residents and have to be put out.

I brought my sister's story up for a couple of reasons.

(1) Ladies and Gents, be safe when you are out and about, and you have an unfinished drink. Get a new one. (2) Sis was always telling me how pretty I was. She used to be around 100 pounds, but with all the meds she was taking, she

blossomed up to over 250, and she was shorter than I was. When she passed, her ex-husband couldn't believe all the weight she had gained. I loved my sister. She was ALL THAT to me.

I didn't know all my gifts, talents, and acquisitions until I took that leap. Still growing into my womanhood, yes, I was scared. But that was the human side taking over. I worked at a restaurant as a busgirl because I was too scared to be a waitress. One day, a customer asked me if I was a Christian, and I answered, "Yes. Why do you ask?" She said there was an aura around me that was showing. I used to be in plays, and my mom told me, "Every time you entered the room, there was a light around you." While journeying on our Damascus roads, we need to be the light. "And as he journeyed, he came near Damascus: and suddenly there shined round about him a light from heaven:" (Acts 9:3 - KJV) This little light of mine, I'm gonna let it shine. I am a church girl, a Christian, and a Child of God.

Whatever you want to call me. I know what I am. I was still a scaredy cat. I sang in the choir, and every time I led a solo, why would my lips go numb from being so nervous or scared? Crowds scare me. I was asked to speak at church while I was back home, taking care of my father while he was going through stage four stomach cancer. I was so quick to say "No," I forgot who I served for just a moment, and I quickly rescinded my "NO" and said a resounding "YES". I am so glad I did. That was the only time my father got to hear me speak. My topic was "God's Got Your Back". Dad cried, and my Pastor was proud of me as well. Pastor asked for my little sermonette. I was happy to give him a copy. Dad was diagnosed in May 2019 and passed away on September 8 at 9:08 p.m. I got to call his time of death even though I had just laid down to take a nap, and Dad slipped away on me. God knows when to pick his flowers for his heavenly vase.

One last thing from me being a Scaredy Cat to All That (Almost). My eyes. They change colors. Earlier, I gave you information about the eyes. "Even if they are quiet, their eyes tell a lot about them." One day, I was at a restaurant having a nice conversation with a friend, and then we started talking about someone I didn't care too much about. The person said, "Mz. Inez, Are you ok? Your eyes are turning red." I told this person I didn't particularly care for the person we were talking about. My eyes are hazel - green, brown, orange. I am never sure what color my eyes are; the person looking at or speaking with me must tell me. My eyes speak volumes about me. You can say I have Cat Eyes from being a Scaredy Cat, but the longer you are involved with me or get to know me, you'll know I am ALL THAT - (Almost). I am ALL THAT God wants me to be.

Everybody's journey from girl to woman is different. None of us have the same story to tell. Some are complicated. Some are dark. Some have secrets. Some are scary. Some have scars. Some have wisdom. Some have mysteries or are mysterious. Some are page-turners. Nail biters. Hair raisers. Clutch your pearls. Suspenseful. But still, they are our stories to tell. Your story to tell. Each woman is her own book or should I say each person. Everybody has a story, and "EVERYBODY" has a story. You be your own book and tell your own interesting and inspiring story.

Mz. Inez

About Mz. Inez

Mz. Inez, creator of Anaise Valcour Designs, believes everyone has their own fashion style and it belongs to them. **Fashion is Yours. It Belongs to YOU!** is her motto. She has over 50 years of experience as a seamstress and designer and now is CEO of her company.

It started with her mother's homemade clothes for her five children and a passion from watching her design extraordinary pieces with limited materials. She spent time in Spain, as a youngster, crafting her skills and techniques, while her father served in the military. She uses an old age style and incorporates new trends into the design with custom pattern pieces.

This method of design gives her the ability to give her clients a high-quality finish or haute' couture fashion look. This approach to design has been her trademark style and made her one of the go to designers. Mz. Inez calls herself "The Material Murderer" as she kills her creations of men's and women's attire.

Visit www.anaisevalcour.com to see her stylish garments.

Hello Food

JACQUELINE L. JACKSON-HOMER

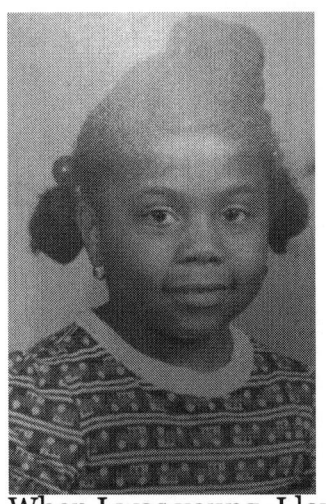

Hello, food. We all know you, we all need you, and you are welcome to come here....

One thing is very true, food makes a party. It's a conversation; it sets the atmosphere at a meeting, a conference, or a date, depending on the situation. It can make you feel good or sick if you eat it at the wrong time. Food is good, like medicine.

When I was young, I loved Chinese jump rope and snacks, not sweets but salty snacks like potato chips and pickles. I would overindulge. Food was always available in our home. It was never hidden; anyone who came to our house always left with food. My mom always delivered unexpected food to friends and family; when they heard her horn blowing, they knew it was my mom bringing goodies, and it was healthy. Oh, and they didn't have to pay. This was a thing she did cause it made her feel good. I believe it was her worship.

While helping give families this happy food, I would see her deliver this same food to people on the street. While heading home, I would often ask for McDonald's since it was the only fast-food restaurant at the time. She did this only because it was my request. I believe she did it because it made me happy; she wanted me to feel that same happiness the friends, families, and strangers felt. Well, at the table it was good food..... good, good, good food. Collard greens, okra, and string beans, but snacks took control of me. When I got home, I would eat at least two bags of Fritos. This was on top of what I'd already had in school. Some days, it was chips; I loved dill pickles.

The intake of these snacks added up, and someone called me fat. I didn't know I was fat until someone called me fat, let me be very transparent, I even suffered bulimia as kid, which damaged my esophagus but weight sneaked up on me. Although I love jump rope, it wasn't enough to keep my weight down. I enjoyed playing sports in school. Soccer, kickball, and basketball were some of my favorites. I noticed I would be out of breath sometimes, especially while jogging, which is one sport I was intimidated by. But Ms. Garber, my gym teacher, stayed with me for success, and I got the hang of it. My health teachers, Mr. Cutter and Ms. Green, taught me a lot about food, but I learned more about food values from Nancy, Kathleen, Phyllis, Melissa and Kia.

While caring for My brother Willie, who had lupus and kidney failure, I had to refocus. He was in Connecticut while I lived in Atlanta. Being his administrative assistant, his sister, and his spiritual strength were difficult but emotionally fulfilling. While talking to my brother on the phone one evening while he was in a rehabilitation center, I heard a staff member say, "Willie, what did you have for dinner?" Willie said, "Pizza, corn, mashed potatoes, and cake for dessert." Although I didn't say anything, my mind was screaming, and my stomach was saying, "OUCH!" I thought this was food abuse! All lack of nutrition. All in my mind, I'm saying I don't like this. How can I fix this with us living so far apart? The thoughts lingered as I went through my daily tasks.

One day, after coming home late from traveling from Alpharetta to Marietta, I realized there was nothing to prepare to eat but cabbage. I had gone straight home and walked my dog Paris without stopping. I thought I would just go to the Kroger grocery store and buy some fried chicken from the hot bar, but then another thought came to mind; just eat the cabbage and be okay with it. And that's just what I did, but because I didn't have meat, I added value to the cabbage by stir-frying onions, bell peppers, and various seasonings. I thought, wow, this was really good, so good that I took the cabbage to work the next day for lunch.

My co-workers usually went out for lunch, so when I heated my food up in the microwave (which I don't use often), over the noise of the microwave, I heard one of them say, "Who's cooking? That smells good!" Because we didn't communicate a whole lot, I was excited to respond to her question, saying, "It's my food smelling so good!" and then we laughed. She asked if she could taste some, and I said sure. I thought yes indeed cause Mama Mattie always shared food, so for that training, I got an A.

Once my co-worker tasted the salad, she commented, "Jacqueline, I will buy this from you as a meal every payday. I thought, why not? So I agreed. She said, "This is a deal, I will eat crackers with it, and maybe chicken too." Well, she kept her promise and became a customer. I was tickled one day while bringing it to work, saying, "This cabbage wasn't for sale," but unique situations do occur. Because of that transaction, another co-worker bought and enjoyed the cooked cabbage. Then, one day, Kesha brought me some cabbage she saw on sale. I thought, wow, what a beautiful blessing.

By the weekend, I was ready to play with the cabbage and be creative. While adding strawberries to this salad one Saturday morning, I thought, "This is it for Willie." I started laughing and screaming out loud, so later that day, I shared with him the new recipe I wanted him to experience. He sounded interested in pleasing me but not thrilled because he was a meat and potato kind of guy; when Willie finally arrived in Atlanta, he tried the cabbage I raved about and loved it. He said, "It's better than I thought it would be." He was able to taste it one more time before he passed and expressed how proud he was of my creation. I truly feel like God gifted me with this creation. I am very thankful. My new motto, thanks to my friend Tobi, was "Have a salad Girl!"

While preparing for an event in my subdivision, I cut and steamed cabbage and some other tantalizing veggies. It smelled good, but time was running out. So, there was one bowl of steamed vegetables with steamed cabbage and jerk seasoning, and then there was the raw bowl of rainbow bell peppers and carrots. It looked so pretty to see. By the end of my event, the raw bowls were empty. I thought to myself this is it. Yes, "Cabbage on the Go" was born. Although the name may change, the taste will forever be the same. I have delivered this salad to the Healthy Heart Coalition with Ms. King, Ruby Neeson Diabetes Association with Mutima Jackson, That's My Dog in Montgomery, AL., Eye Connection with Wife LeDon and Gary, A Bite to Eat, and various Health Fairs in Alabama and Atlanta. My brother Mack even announced it at the repass for Willie. He said, "Tell the people what you have here." I thought, wow, I have the floor to share about healthy eating.

The fair in Montgomery, every Saturday with Ms. Brown, was a big door to walk through. Herbs BBQ, The Refreshing Center, Economy Jackson, Saturday Camp at Big Bethel church with Rev Bessie, and Ms. Rae. I had the wonderful opportunity to attend an Entrepreneur Class at Operation Hope. This class was held at pastor Warnock's church. While in this class, my teacher thought so highly of my salads that he wanted me to meet Ms. Shirley Banquet, owner of Grandma Gourmet Cornbread. Ms. Shirley and I have organized events together where we intertwined our gifts. Together, she makes different flavors of flapjack cornbread and pours my salad in with the cornbread. This is a great grab-and-go snack, which is delicious, hot off the skillet, and great cold, too. I am confident they would all love it.

One of my dreams is to supply CNA Nursing School Locations, Construction Sites and Truck Stops with Cabbage on the Go. It would be free for those facing financial difficulties. I can't wait to see the results. Results in mindset and in body structure. The shelf life of the salad and salad dressing is a month. I want to help people enjoy this grab-and-go item; I want to be the one to give them probiotics, Vitamin A, D, and Vitamin E omega. Ms. Shirley invited me to the Kroger Atlanta Corporate office to serve lunch for Black History Month. All the food was GREAT! Many people wanted to take the salad and the hot portions of the cabbage home. This salad struck up a conversation with LaQuita Parks, the Co-chair of the Kroger Wellness Committee in

Atlanta at the time, and me. I promised her a special container. I was excited when the Director of Public Affairs gave me an opportunity to do a sample event at the Kroger stores. I thought it was great, but I must admit, LIFE kept me busy! Then COVID changed the whole plan, but I still desired to share the many flavors of my salads. Jerk flavor, go pineapple, go curry, it's the original, go nutty, and more. Did you know that cabbage only gives you gas when heat is applied? However, if you eat it cold, you will not experience gas in your stomach. I would love to plant cabbage as flowers for decor or decorate homes with cabbage. I want to apply the dishes with a cabbage painting and make glass coffee cups with cabbage on them.

While walking one day, I found some beautiful royal blue glass stones. First, I saw them in one spot of my subdivision, and then I saw them in another place. These gorgeous stones were not just sitting on the grass or pavement; I had to take a stick and dig them up. My Sunday school teacher, Adrianna said they were a kiss from God with a notary to keep going. When I plant my floral look of cabbage in the garden, I use my royal blue rocks. I have made bags of cut-up cabbage, put them in zip-lock bags with seasonings, and eaten them right out of the bag like potato chips.

I truly thank my siblings for pushing me. My Manager /Nephew Lamont will never be forgotten for his time devoted to Cabbage on the Go and those who have blessed us financially. Including My brother James, The Bromell's

As I said, life happens, and I had to slow down. But with new awareness, I am ready to color some plates and live as an adult with wisdom. Wisdom taught me to keep my healthy numbers in balance. Eating healthy while on the go doesn't have to be complicated or expensive. With these anointed hands, I have made it simple to get your healthy blooming again.

So here I am, loudly saying, "Hey you, have a salad!" "Hey girl, have a salad." This salad will change your life and your beliefs about cabbage.

About Jacqueline

Jacqueline Jackson Homer, widely known as the "Healthy Guru," has dedicated her life to inspiring others to embrace a fun, healthy way of living—especially in the fast-paced environment of Atlanta. At 58 years old, Jacqueline has crafted a vision that emphasizes the importance of making nutritious food and balanced living accessible for people on the go. Her mission is rooted in her belief that living with wisdom and intention can lead to a healthier, more fulfilling life.

Jacqueline's destiny is not only to enhance her own well-being but also to guide men, women, and children on the path to better health. A single, driven career woman, she finds joy in reading and researching the benefits of high-quality fruits and vegetables, always seeking ways to incorporate them into daily routines.

With a career in home health and as a phlebotomist, Jacqueline extends her care to seniors, providing compassionate support in their homes and assisted living facilities. Her passion for ensuring their quality of life reflects her nurturing spirit and commitment to making a positive impact in the lives of others.

Jacqueline is a confident entrepreneur, full of creative ideas to inspire those around her. She enjoys the spiritual grounding of Psalm 91 and values sharing her journey with family and friends. Her vibrant personality, combined with her dedication to health and community, makes Jacqueline a beacon of encouragement for those seeking to live healthier, more intentional lives.

Silence Kills! Speaking Heals!

Dr. Monica Y. Jackson

One of my notable sayings is silence kills, speaking heals. Another is that we gotta be real so we can heal. I share a few of my lived truths on these pages to reach out and speak to some little girl who has transformed into a woman. Yet, she has lived in silence, has not been real, and is unable to heal. When I was a little girl, my childhood nickname was radio. It started as an affectionate term of endearment but eventually became a term to reference obnoxious chatter and a way to silence my voice. Not only would I talk and talk about anything and everything, ask questions and more questions, but I would repeat what I heard verbatim and utter what most children would not think or be bold enough to ask. Heck, most adults living today will not even ask the questions I posed. When I divulged comments that one adult said to a second adult about a third adult, I would often hear, "Turn the radio off." I knew to be quiet and not say another word. I learned early to keep silent, hold my tongue, and conform, just like many of you who are reading this.

What is inside must come out eventually, and it did. As a little chatterbox, I got in trouble in school for talking excessively. I always had something to say but maintained excellent grades. Although I received A's and B's, I received U's and S's (unsatisfactory and satisfactory, respectively) in cooperation and behavior instead of "E" for excellent. "I" often saw "A U U" and "A S S" on my report card. I and my classmates chuckled whenever we saw the latter, but it was not a laughing matter to parents. One teacher even wrote, "I don't want to have to give Monica a "U" for talking in class" on my report card. He might as well have given me an F in the subject because the word talk, a "U," or "S," meant another parent-teacher conference and punishment. I guess I always had something to say.

Fast forward 50 years; I am just as talkative and bold enough to speak up, ask questions, question answers, and ask more questions. Why? Because somewhere in the world is another little girl who has become a woman who has lost her voice, suffers in silence, and is trying to find her voice. There is also a woman who appears to have a voice when, in fact, it is actually the voice of what someone told or taught her. It is not her authentic voice. To that little girl, this message is for you. May my words unsilence the silenced, give voice to the voiceless, and encourage that "little girl woman" to stop suffering in silence. I am my sister's keeper.

While growing into womanhood, I have discovered just how immature and judgmental people are when you do not conform and align with their ways – friends, family, and foes. Your comfort (confidence) can make some people uncomfortable, but those very people expect you to accept and trade your discomfort for their comfort. Many will label your confidence as being arrogant, prideful, conceited, intimidating, and problematic. Such statements often took me back to the feeling that I felt when I heard "turn the radio off" as a little girl. That uncomfortableness only made me more discerning and confident. I say to you, walk in your confidence because you will never be able to please everyone, so learn to be pleased with yourself. Live in your truth and be authentically you.

Before you can live in your truth, you must know your truth, and it may not be what has been told, taught, or thought. Instead, it may be widely accepted views, opinions, and beliefs passed down generationally, with the truth lost somewhere in the translation. Just because something or someone sounds good does not mean it is good, and just because most people believe or accept something does not mean it is true. However, this is impressed and often imposed and sends a "turn the radio off" signal. Persuasion and manipulation sound good and remaining in certain environments long enough leads to conforming, suffering in silence, or fleeing. I often remind people that there is a difference between knowing and believing, but not many want to hear this. Listen carefully to what flows from tongues and actions.

Let us look at the definition of truth. Truth is "the body of real things, events, and facts: actuality." [1] Another source says truth is "the state of being in agreement with reality or fact. It can also be defined as the collection of real events, facts, and things, or actuality. In everyday language, truth is often attributed to things that attempt to represent reality, such as declarative sentences, beliefs, and propositions." [2]

---

[1]
[2]

These two definitions are flawed; therefore, what is labeled as truth can be subjective and misleading. Misrepresentation of truth can damage and hurt. It is why I encourage you to discover your truth, live in your truth, and know your truth. Getting there is not an easy journey and continues to evolve as you transform from a girl to a woman.

In my book, Wounds of Wisdom, I transparently shared heartbreaking truths that I sustained from friends, workplaces, family members, churches, marriages, businesses, and children. Although my very existence and foundation were rocked, truth, peace, and clarity emerged like never before, and "radio's" message could not be turned down or silenced because it resonated with men and women around the world. It encouraged many to speak their truths in coaching sessions and two summits that became my signature projects – T4: Trials, Triumphs, Truths, and Tears and M4: Men, Message, Movement. I found great purpose and fulfillment while creating platforms where people around the world – black, white, young, old, gay, straight – felt comfortable enough to speak their truths, which are someone else's truths. The things that divide us – religion, politics, sexual orientation, socioeconomic status, race – are truly baffling because not one of these groups has the absolute answers and depending on the environment you are in and what you choose to accept forms your view and beliefs. For this reason, if your truth is the truth, let it shine, and it will draw people near or push them away. They do not need convincing or manipulation. Do not allow anyone to guilt you into thinking, believing, and following as they do if it does not make sense or feel right for you. You bear the consequences of your choices and cannot blame others. Think for yourself, speak for yourself and know for yourself.

May every woman take the time to encourage the little girl within and stop trying to conform, fit in, or accept a version of the truth that belongs to someone else. Think critically, discover and live your truth, then help someone to do the same. A woman living her authentic truth is powerful, valuable, and at peace with herself.

My Journey from Girl to Woman Lesson: If I have not experienced or observed it, then I do not know, with emphasis on knowing if it is true and cannot credit or discredit another person's experience. It can be anything. Stay neutral. That is not my battle.

Speaking of battle, the battle is the battle. Think about it, fights ensue over religious beliefs, politics, sexual orientation, race, and more. Again, I say the battle is the battle. People operate as if they want you to think, do, and believe as they do. That sounds a lot like taking away someone's ability to think for themselves and choose by any means necessary – persuasion, manipulation, bullying. We are taught conformance and agreement instead of respecting differences and choices.

At the time of this writing, we are gearing up for the 2024 election, and one of the topics causing great division is reproductive rights, a woman's right to choose. That sounds a lot like aiming to force everyone to be, do, and believe the same. Regardless of the side of the fence we are on, people overlook one important word: choice.

When you start to take away one choice, in my opinion, it does not stop there. What is the next choice on the chopping board? Where does it stop? Who made us judge and jury of choice? Do we go back to where we once were? Not everyone believes the same, and we continuously aim to force them to do so, even if we will not say it aloud.

As I watched the DNC and portions of the RNC, regardless of policy, I saw one side about fundamentals and hope and the other about doom, gloom, economics, and control. There are views I agree and disagree with on both sides, but I had to look at fundamental rights and what is more important to me — choice, morals, character, economy, or money. We cannot and will not have it all. Each of us will see and view the options based on what is important to us now, but we must look at the future impact.

Following the DNC, it made me think about an experience that occurred about 35 years ago. We were expecting our first child, and I was so excited. There was nothing but tears of joy. When I went for my first checkup around four weeks of pregnancy, the doctor, a Middle Eastern man, examined me. He placed his left palm on my belly. With two fingers from his right hand, he began to tap the back of his hand, which was on my swollen belly. All I heard was one thump after another as if he were tapping a drum. At one point, he removed his hand swiftly. His facial expression was stoic. He seemed so uncomfortable and said he would see me on my next visit. During the next visit, he kept his distance, did not look at me, or touch my belly.

When I checked out, I asked the receptionist if the doctor was always so cold, distant, and unwelcoming. I then asked if

I could make an appointment with a different doctor. She asked if the doctor said anything to me about my pregnancy. I replied, "No. He just said, "see you next time." She said, "We should get you in tomorrow." I arrived at the appointment the following day with a white female OB-GYN, which was a Friday.

She walked in, introduced herself, and was both professional and attentive. She was also very warm, asked a series of questions, and said I was about six weeks pregnant. She informed me that there was a problem with my pregnancy and said I had a blighted ovum. That explained the Middle Eastern doctor's reactions, and his visibly alarmed appearance. However, it does not excuse his unethical silence and unprofessionalism by not disclosing my condition.

She went on to say that the pregnancy was not viable. She gave me two options, and I had the power and control to choose. She said that I could go home and wait to miscarry and deliver, but there would not be a baby at the end of laboring. She said after delivering at home that I should go to the emergency room immediately and take everything – sac, placenta, etc.

This was the first time I heard the term blighted ovum, and I had absolutely no clue what it meant. I recall asking if I was pregnant or not. She said yes and went on to explain. This is an anembryonic pregnancy, which is one of the many abnormalities that may occur during pregnancy. In this type of pregnancy, the egg is fertilized, the embryo implants inside the uterine cavity, but the embryo never develops. The only components that develop are the amniotic sac and placenta. 3

I could not imagine experiencing excruciating pain, contractions, seeing lots of blood, gathering bloody parts, and then transporting them to the emergency room. The mental toll that it would take and the pain I would experience without any medication or medical assistance was more than I could mentally handle. Also, I was concerned about bleeding uncontrollably, which could result in my demise. I even started to play the race card in my mind and wondered if the doctor just did not want another Black child born. She never treated me in any way that led me to this conclusion. In other words, I was looking for answers and even attempted to make sense of what I did not understand. This is dangerous, and what far too many do — create conspiracy theories, blame, and trying to create an angle for what seems senseless.

The other option was to undergo a D&C, dilation, and curettage. It is a surgical procedure that removes tissue from the uterus. It clears the uterine after a miscarriage, and mild cramps may occur. It is the same procedure performed during an abortion.4

I was torn between my faith and fear. I was concerned about being judged and living with the reality of having a D&C instead of enduring the process because it was the early termination of a pregnancy. The thought of committing this sin and murdering an unborn fetus was overwhelming, but there was no fetus to begin with. That was something that I

3
4

just could not wrap my head around. You see, what religious beliefs do not teach is that it never accounted for the science, much like the political agenda that is being pushed. As things begin to be exposed, the separation of church and state becomes muddied and looks alike in many ways.

I had a decision to make, but I was torn. I was afraid of experiencing the miscarriage at home, possibly alone, wondering if the doctor was wrong, and felt guilty based on the teachings of Christianity. I worried so much after leaving the doctor's office on Friday morning. Saturday afternoon, I went to the bathroom and saw a drop of blood. I eventually saw a second drop. I then knew that the doctor was probably right and the miscarriage was occurring. I called the doctor's office to tell her that I wanted to undergo the procedure because I started to hemorrhage. My doctor met me at the hospital and performed the procedure.

I never felt any pain, nor did I experience any mental anguish, and returned to work weeks later. Everyone tip-toed around me because they knew I had a miscarriage. This made me so uncomfortable because although I was disappointed that I did not have a baby, I also did not feel any negative emotions because I had not experienced any attachment, just an idea, and I knew that I would try again.

Reality is reality. That is what we must embrace. We create problems. The fact that everyone felt sad made me feel sad. Women said I was so strong. It had nothing to do with strength. It is about the ability to adapt, accept reality, and remain hopeful. Afterwards, other women thanked me for sharing and how it helped them look at things from an unfamiliar perspective. This is something that the world needs to learn to do instead of only wanting to see and believe what they believe, and anything that threatens it makes them uncomfortable. It is not about discrediting anyone's beliefs and choices. It is about not taking away anyone's right to choose and forcing others to conform and accept viewpoints that they do not accept or believe.

I could not imagine being unable to choose how to manage my nonviable pregnancy. My choice. My consequences. This reminds me of a church I attended that automatically withheld a tithe from every employee's paycheck, removing choice and forcing them to tithe. Even God gives us all choices, so it is written. When did man become qualified to overrule God?

Again, live in your truth and be authentically you. Do not give up; turn the radio up because we relate and bond in adversity. Everyone will face adversity. The grass will not always be green. The sun will not always shine. Terrible things happen. People do terrible things. The glass is half empty sometimes. This is not negative. This is reality. Let us discourage suppressing feelings and turning the radio off because silence kills, speaking heals, and we gotta be real so we can heal.

My Journey from Girl to Woman Lesson: There's purpose in pain, strength in struggles, and wisdom in wounds. Do not claim a battle if the battle is not yours.

Your journey from Girl to Woman, just like mine, is uniquely and incredibly yours. If you have not experienced or observed what someone else has experienced, then recognize that there just might be missing, unknown pieces to the puzzle. If you aim to credit or discredit such experiences, determine the value and purpose of engaging in such a battle that may not be yours and the price of divisiveness. Live in your truth, be authentically you, but know the truth, and afford every other human being the same opportunity.

Endnotes

[1,2] Merriam-Webster Inc. (2024)

[3] Mary Marnach MD. *Blighted ovum: What causes it.* (2023). Retrieved from https://www.mayoclinic.org/diseases-conditions/pregnancy-loss-miscarriage/expert-answers/blighted-ovum/faq-20057783

[4] Mayo Clinic. (2024). *Dilation and curettage (D& C).* https://www.mayoclinic.org/tests-procedures/dilation-and-curettage/about/pac-20384910

About Dr. Monica

Dr. Monica Y. Jackson is the proprietor of Dr. Monica Y. Jackson Education & Design Services in Southern California, providing instructional design, training, coaching, project management, and creative services (graphics, website, publishing, technical writing) to corporations and individuals. She is also an author and speaker, who transparently, boldly, and authentically discusses topics that most would rather remain silent about and oblivious towards.

Her mission is to empower, encourage, and enlighten men and women who find or have found themselves suffering in silence. Her two signature projects are the T4: Trials, Triumphs, Truths, and Tears and M4: Men, Message, Mission, Movement summits. They demonstrate her passion to unsilence the silenced, give voice to the voiceless, and create platforms to cope and regain hope. Her recent book, *Wounds of Wisdom*, is the catalyst that propels her message, mission, and movement.

For more information, visit www.drmonicajackson.com

Rising from Trauma, Reclaiming Power, and Running Toward Freedom

RENEA JONES-HUDSON

Childhood...

Growing up, I often felt unseen, unheard, devalued, and, at times, unloved. I lived with my mother, grandparents, brothers, and stepdad. My father and mother were present but not involved; my grandparents primarily raised me. I felt like I existed in two worlds—shaped by several institutions: marriage, church, and life. These institutions set the stage for my early life and would later shape the woman I am today.

Going to church wasn't just something we did on Saturdays; it was ingrained into the very fabric of our lives. It was all I knew for much of my childhood, and being at church wasn't always a source of joy. The expectations and the constant feeling of being judged (which I now realize was mostly shame) weighed heavily on me. The church was not exactly a place of refuge; I felt insignificant and out of place, as if trying to fit into a mold that never truly felt right.

My parents were not together. My father was an abuser, primarily toward my mother. What I remember most about them is how they fought, physically and verbally. My mother was around but emotionally unavailable. My brother, who is a year younger than me, had chronic asthma and was always sick; he got my mother's attention while I got her wrath most of the time. I craved connection and attention, especially from my mother, but it rarely came. My relationship with my parents was not the best. At one point, I was close to my father, but no matter what I did, it never seemed to be enough for him. When he died, surprisingly, I was deeply affected because I did not expect to feel as much as I did for him. My relationship with my mother is still strained; for most of my life, it was fueled by anger, resentment, and feelings of abandonment; sometimes, I questioned her feelings toward me.

I clung to my aunts most of my life, especially as a child. I remember when they would visit from overseas, how I would hope and sometimes beg them to take me back with them and from the emptiness that consumed me. I was desperate for an escape. Loneliness was a constant companion, but there was always a light amid it all: my maternal grandmother. My grandparents' relationship gave me hope, and as much as my childlike mind could understand, their relationship was filled with love and light. I saw my grandfather as a provider and a protector, especially towards my grandmother; their bond was undeniable. I loved when they spoke to each other in Spanish, especially when they didn't want me to understand. I loved how my grandmother's quiet strength could calm my fiery grandfather. Their marriage seemed magical, and I wanted to experience love like theirs someday.

Outside of the family and the church, participating in sports gave me refuge and became an outlet through some very trying times; sports were my escape from the chaos surrounding me, especially as a child. Every lap in the pool, every race on the track, and every goal on the soccer field allowed me to channel and release the emotions I couldn't express in words. Sports were where I welcomed the weight of expectations because those expectations, especially when I overcame them, often resulted in a reward, recognition, and acceptance.

Academically, I struggled. I wouldn't say I liked the school I attended, which resulted in me achieving poor grades, not because I wasn't brilliant but because I also felt like an outsider there. I felt like I didn't belong. I was never fully present in school; my heart and mind were always somewhere else, focused on the next moment of escape from the heaviness I felt most of the time.

Something darker affected my early childhood. The first experience seemed to last for an eternity, often right under my grandparents' watch; they were always so close yet far. This pain haunted me for most of my life, causing me to feel ugly, unworthy, and insignificant. The anguish of being sexually abused repeatedly devastated me, and because of this, I struggled silently for years with shame, guilt, insecurity, and feelings of unworthiness. Migrating to the United States was bittersweet. I loved my grandparents dearly and didn't want to leave them behind, but I desperately wanted to escape the loneliness, guilt, and shame that weighed me down.

As I write these words, I feel the weight of my past all over my body.
Reliving these experiences puts a lump in my throat and hea viness in my chest.

It is challenging to bring these deeply hidden secrets to light, especially after many years, because of
the fear of persecution, being labeled, and being rejected. Deciding to tell my truth was
frightening, but what is even scarier are the
effects of NOT speaking up, of not advocating for those who cannot speak for themselves, of never standing for something and allowing the vicious cycle of sexual abuse to continue and understanding that this is much bigger than me. I am no longer willing to drag lifelong burdens from one generation to the next, nor am I willing to continue to be available for pretenses. Living in silence almost consumed me, and at different points in my life, I contemplated suicide, but God had other plans. I know now that He kept me here for a reason: to share my story, break cycles, and empower others.

Moving to the United States was an experience unlike anything I had ever known, and I learned to adjust quickly to this new reality. Initially, it brought a great sense of relief because I would no longer be violated, and for the first time in what felt like forever, I felt free, at least for a while, and was happy that part of my life seemed to be finally behind me.

This new chapter felt easy; no longer afraid of being abused, I began to settle into a new normal. Though I still carried emotional wounds, I wasn't living in a heightened state of anxiety and constant fear. Life was better, and I was happier, and I got to rebuild my life piece by piece. Not long after, we (my mother and brothers) moved to Canada.

My time in Canada was primarily good. Canada was very different from the United States; it was much calmer and cleaner, and people seemed friendlier. Many moments made life in Canada feel like another fresh start. I made new friends in school and did not think about my past for a while. But just as I began to embrace another new reality, the abuse resurfaced. This time, by another family member, only this time, we were close; he was like a brother, which is why this time, it was different and even more painful. The peace I had started to welcome was shattered again. I was broken again, and it devastated me.

I questioned everything and spiraled, and the ugliness and unworthiness I felt about myself were amplified. I was so confused, and I contemplated suicide again, desperate to escape the weight of it all. This time, and with more people around me, no one cared, and I felt even more alone and like a castaway.

Womanhood...

But God had other plans. After the second incident, I left for the United States to live with my aunt and leave behind the resurfaced darkness. Running away to the U.S. was ultimately the best decision of my life, even though I did not know it then. When I left, I did not have a clue or a sense of direction for my life or future, but I knew I no longer wanted to be in Canada. At this point in my life, I felt the most abandoned by my family, especially my mother. Nevertheless, I finished my senior year of high school feeling very unsure of who I was.

At 18 years old, with a deep desire to experience something good and because I was promised a college education, I made a decision that would change my life drastically and enlisted in the Army.

I remember the day I left my house with a stranger and my aunt's look of fear and uncertainty as she watched the car pull away, not knowing if she would ever hear or see me again. I did not question what was happening because it felt right, and I remember being more curious than afraid.

When I look back at my journey to this point, it was as if I was always searching for the missing pieces in my life: peace amidst the chaos, belonging, and love. I decided enlisting in the Army was another opportunity to leave the ugliness of my past behind. The Army provided me with a new identity; a new version of me was born, and I was excited to learn more about her. The trauma I experienced fueled my drive and my determination to succeed and to feel worthy and valued. Looking back, I realized that things I craved came in the form of structure, discipline, and the sense of belonging the military offered; this created the foundation I needed for my future.

This journey, however, was not linear. I struggled at times with the memories of my childhood that would resurface, especially when I was stressed. I remember during a training exercise, I became very frustrated and threatened to take my own life. My battle buddy overheard me and reported what I said to our first-line supervisor, and this time was the only time I had no intention of taking my life. However, I became so accustomed to that narrative that before I realized it, I commented out loud. This incident marked a crucial point in my life and the beginning of ongoing therapy, forcing me to confront the pain of my childhood that I was carrying for years; it also marked the beginning of my journey toward healing. A journey that was anything but easy. It felt like I entered a battlefield without armor, untrained and unprepared for the fight—one filled with ambushes of guilt, landmines of shame, and the relentless crossfire of blame.

Healing required acknowledging and tearing down the barriers of unresolved issues and unaddressed trauma to rebuild a new foundation—one rooted in truth, self-awareness, and growth. As I worked through the layers of my past, I believed I was ready to start anew, to create a life filled with love and purpose.

At age 19, I married my husband six months after we met, and everything seemed great. I went into marriage not wanting to have children. Still, as fate would have it, I became pregnant—only to face heartbreak when, after I had finally accepted the idea of becoming a mother, the doctors could not find the baby's heartbeat. I was devastated. Four years later, we had our first child, and six months after having him, at the age of 24, I was diagnosed with Ulcerative Colitis (UC). This was one of the worst times in my life, but this time, I thought I would die because of the severity of the condition. Dealing with UC, I felt like I was on the brink of madness at times, and I felt as if I couldn't catch a break.

But God... He delivered me and gave me the strength I needed. Every challenge I faced reinforced that survival and resilience were embedded in my very being, part of the foundation that kept me moving forward. As I began to piece together my strength, I realized that healing wasn't just about enduring; it was about transformation.

In 2008, during a year-long tour in Korea, I embarked on a deeply personal journey to figure out who I was. I welcomed the time away from my family, seeing it as an opportunity for clarity and growth. That solitude allowed me to dig deep and explore the parts of myself I had long buried—parts tied to my feelings about my mother, my marriage, my family, and the life I had built up until that point. For the first time, I faced these truths without distraction, marking the beginning of my transformation. Confronting my past, my fears, and my self-perceptions, I began redefining who I wanted to be to step into the woman I must become.

Through that journey, I learned many valuable lessons about myself and life. I knew that to love anyone truly is to love myself first. I learned that marriage was a cycle of ups and downs, and it, too, required work. I realized my happiness was (and still is) my responsibility, that I must be happy with the way God designed me, and that it was only through him that I could have the peace and the freedom I longed for. Self-care is a personal commitment, not just in the cliché sense, but in every way (mentally, physically, emotionally, spiritually, and financially) that supports a healthy mind, body, and spirit.

I learned that how we show up for ourselves is mirrored in our relationships, especially in marriage, and that it often reflects how we see and treat ourselves. If we carry unresolved wounds, insecurities, or unmet needs forward, those will inevitably seep into the dynamics of our partnership. It's easy to look to our partner to fill those voids or to complete the parts of us that feel broken, but that expectation is not love—it's dependency. True love isn't about expecting someone to fix us; it's about being the best version of ourselves so we can show up fully for our partner.

Marriage taught me that the foundation of a strong relationship begins with the self. When we neglect our own physical, emotional, or spiritual needs, we unintentionally place the burden of our healing on our partner, expecting them to fill voids they were never meant to fill. This creates unfair expectations and strains the relationship. Realizing this, I understood that I had to take responsibility for my healing, that it was crucial for my marriage and, more so, for myself.

At the time of this writing, I have been married for 27 years; we have two wonderful children and have been through some trying times, and yet we are still here, weathering the changing aspects of the first institution God placed on man. Marriage has been a mirror for me, reflecting my strengths and areas of growth. It has taught me that the most meaningful connections come when both people are committed to having God be the head in their union and being their best selves, not just for the relationship, but for themselves. This isn't always easy, but it's worth it.

Being in the military taught me resilience and responsibility in profound ways. Leadership isn't just about guiding others; it begins with leading oneself—demonstrating emotional intelligence, humility, and adaptability in every situation. I learned that being a true leader means leading by example, showing up consistently, and inspiring others through actions. It's about understanding the people you serve, meeting them where they are, and empowering them to reach their full potential.

The challenges and the situations I encountered in the military shaped me into someone who understood that I must take ownership of my life, no matter how difficult the circumstances. I learned to handle stress with composure, face challenges head-on, and navigate adversity with determination. It taught me the value of setting boundaries, not as a way of shutting others out, but as a way of protecting my energy so that I could show up fully for those I led and myself. Leadership in the military wasn't just a role I held; it became a reflection of the resilience and strength I cultivated within. This, too, is an ongoing process.

The best part of my transformation was reestablishing my relationship with God, the most vital part of my journey. Through faith, I learned that the laws of life, the principles of love, kindness, and purpose, will affect me and my children, whether good or evil. Thus, I strive to be more mindful of my thoughts, words, and actions because it's never just about me.

I learned the importance of living congruently and aligning with my values, purpose, and truth. When we strive to live authentically, we create harmony and set a powerful example for our children. I've seen how my actions, healing, and growth have influenced my family and those around me. This journey into womanhood has been about exploring and understanding the phases of development; it's been about riding the highs and the lows, knowing that every experience, setback, and triumph brings me closer to my true self.

The woman I am today embraces the lessons ahead and walks forward with a deep understanding of who I am, how I want to live, and who I want to become. It's no longer a question of "Why me?" but rather, "How can I use this?" How can I take everything I've endured, everything I've learned, and transform it into purpose? It's about asking, "Who can I help?" and "How can I show up as the best version of myself—not just for me, but for those who look to me for guidance and inspiration?"

Life is no longer something that happens to me; it's something I co-create with intention, strength, and faith. Every experience, challenge, and triumph is part of an excellent plan. With it, I am committed to walking boldly into the future, using my journey to uplift others and shape the legacy I want to leave behind.

Shifting my perspective empowers me to move through life with gratitude and grace, knowing that every challenge is an opportunity for growth. It's not about avoiding the hard times but facing them with strength so that I can grow. Today, I walk, knowing that my steps are ordered. I understand now that everything I experienced as a child prepared me for this moment. Everything I endured, every challenge, pain, and scar, shapes the woman I was destined to become.

So many of us experience trauma, and many are still fighting to emancipate ourselves from some form of bondage, whether it's emotional, mental, physical, or spiritual. Knowing what I know now, those dark moments weren't meant to break me but to build me; they were the fires that refined me, molding my resilience, empathy, and strength. As I walk in this understanding, I accept that my journey is not solely for me; it is for everyone who feels imprisoned by their past and those still searching for a lifeline of hope and purpose. I've learned that healing is possible and starts with acknowledging the pain, facing it head-on, and trusting that every step forward is a step toward purpose.

One of the most powerful lessons I've learned in my healing journey is that forgiving yourself is a must. For the longest time, I held onto guilt and shame, blaming myself for the things that I couldn't control and for the choices I made because of my pain. But true forgiveness—starts with knowing that my help comes from God. It's about casting all our care, releasing our burdens, and acknowledging that we did our best with what we knew. It's about surrendering to His will, trusting His grace is sufficient, and allowing Him to carry what we were never meant to bear alone. True forgiveness is not just about letting go of the past—it's about trusting God to heal what is broken, restore what was lost, and lead us into a life of freedom, peace, and purpose. On this journey of forgiving myself, I can free parts of myself stuck in the past and relive old wounds. Surrendering to the process opened my understanding of true healing, self-love, and growth. Without forgiveness, I couldn't fully embrace the lessons life had been teaching me. I had to forgive myself to truly move forward, to be whole, and to show up as the woman I am today—strong, empowered, and full of purpose.

I am still on my journey to becoming the woman I am meant to be. God is still writing my story; only now do I understand that He holds the pen. There was a time when I fought for control, trying to write my path, questioning every challenge, and wondering why life unfolded the way it did. But now, I see that each chapter, even the painful ones, is by design and for a purpose. It is up to me to have absolute trust that God's plan for me is far greater than anything I can imagine. With this understanding, I am learning to walk more gracefully and confidently, knowing that I don't have to have all the answers. I don't need to know what's coming next because I am learning to surrender and trust in the Creator of my life.

I'm still becoming, growing, and learning, but I do so knowing that my story is unfolding precisely as it's meant to, and I am being shaped into the woman I was always meant to be. In truth, this opportunity to write my story has been therapeutic. Putting my experiences into words brought a whirlwind of emotions, triggering yet highly freeing. But I didn't do this just for myself. I did it for my son and daughter, the young girls I mentor, and those seeking hope and inspiration in their journey. This is for those who need to see that healing is possible, that strength can emerge from pain, and that our stories have the power to transform lives beyond our own. Who I must become is more significant than me. She serves a greater purpose and is responsible for showing others what is possible, breaking cycles, and forging new paths.

This journey isn't just about my healing or transformation. It's about the legacy we as survivors leave behind and its impact on those looking to be inspired to take a step in the right direction and be empowered the moment they do.

The woman I am becoming lives within me and the lives I touch. She embodies strength, resilience, hope, and a calling far more significant than herself. Each step in becoming her is not just for me—it is for every soul who needs to know that they have the power to rise above their past, to lift their voices and be heard, to stand boldly and be seen. It is for those who must embrace their inherent value, stay true to their worth, and step confidently into the fullness of who they were always meant to be.

This is my legacy: to inspire, empower, and remind others that their stories, no matter how painful, are not the end—but the beginning of something extraordinary. We are not defined by what we've been through but by how we rise, heal, and choose to walk forward. This is my purpose, and this is my truth. We all get to become the people we were destined to be. And it starts today.

This is my story, and this is my truth: what was meant to destroy me became the foundation of my strength, every scar carried a lesson, and God's grace restored every broken piece. My journey from girlhood to womanhood has been one of rising from trauma, reclaiming power, and running toward freedom. It has been a process of healing, growing, and becoming.

Today, I walk forward with the understanding that my life is not my own. My experiences, both painful and triumphant, have prepared me to inspire, empower, and uplift others.

This journey is not just about me; it is about the lives I can touch, the cycles I can help break, and the legacy I can leave for my children and future generations.

The woman I am becoming lives in me and through the lives I touch. She carries resilience, embodies hope, and walks with purpose, knowing that God holds the pen to her story. My life is a testament that we are not defined by our pasts but by how we choose to rise from them.

I leave you with this truth, anchored in Scripture: **"For God hath not given us the spirit of fear; but of power, and of love, and of a sound mind."** *(2 Timothy 1:7, KJV)*

May this be a reminder that no matter where you are in your journey, you have the power to rise, the capacity to love, and the soundness of mind to step boldly into your destiny. Let your story be a testament to what is possible when you trust the process and the Author of your life.

Our Journey From Girls to Women

About Renea

Renea Jones-Hudson is an Empowerment Coach with over 20 years of military service, specializing in supporting transitioning military and veteran women. Her career began with 13 years as an Enlisted Soldier and continued as a Logistics Officer for eight years, equipping her with a deep understanding of the unique challenges of military life and the transition to civilian life. Renea holds a BS in Psychology and an MS in Criminal Justice and is pursuing a Doctor of Psychology in Health & Wellness.

After retiring from the military, Renea turned her passion for health and wellness into action, opening a fitness studio in Virginia. Later, she founded Empowered Life Coaching Solutions in Georgia, offering personalized coaching programs, workshops, and community-building events to help female veterans rediscover their purpose and confidence. Her coaching philosophy emphasizes resilience, self-discovery, and holistic well-being, addressing mental, physical, and financial health.

In addition to coaching, Renea is the Vice President of DSPII Waypoint, a non-profit Veteran Transition Service Center. She serves as an Ambassador for the Griffin Chamber of Commerce and holds several leadership roles in other local veteran organizations. She also mentors 7th & 8th-grade female athletes in a community program called "Beyond Self."

Renea's influence extends beyond coaching. She is an international best-selling author, an Executive Contributing writer for *Brainz Magazine*, and a keynote speaker at veteran-focused events. Her work has been featured in various media outlets, including *I AM International Magazine, Brainz Magazine, Shoutout Atlanta, Bold Journey, Strong Fitness Magazine, Canvas Rebel*, and more.

A proud wife, mother, and member of several honor societies, Renea's dedication to personal growth and wellness permeates her professional and personal life, inspiring others to thrive in their post-military journeys.

Email: contact@reneajoneshudson.com

Website: www.reneajoneshudson.com

Phone: 678-653-6695

Connect with me on all social media platforms: @reneajoneshudson

Walking on the Edge of Purpose
Dr. Patricia Lawton

On this beautiful day, I decided to drive from New Jersey to Philadelphia, PA, to spend the weekend at my mom's. It was around noon, and I had been having indigestion all morning, so I took some Pepto Bismol and got in the car. By the time I reached the Walt Whitman Bridge, the pain had gotten worse. I was thinking maybe I'm hungry because I didn't eat much for breakfast. Before long, I park at my mom's and go inside. After we hugged, she knew right away that something was wrong. She poured me a glass of ginger ale, which did not help. She then called her best friend, Ms. Dot, a nurse, and explained what was going on with me. She stated, "Evelyn, I don't like the way that sounds, so take her to the ER now." So we went. We got there, and a security guard came to the car with a wheelchair and took me inside. Once inside, my head felt like it was about to explode. I could feel myself losing consciousness. The guard yelled, "We need help over here." The room started to go dim.

I slowly opened my eyes and was terrified. What was this pungent smell penetrating my nose? Hospital disinfect. My heavy breathing and the beep beep sound from the heart monitor indicated: "Girl, You're Still Alive!" Standing beside my bed was this handsome man with mesmerizing hazel eyes who interrupted my questions and stated: "Hi Pat, I am Alex, your nurse. As sick as I was, I remember thinking, "Damn, he's white, but I've done hit the jackpot." He then whispered to me, "Young lady, you gave us quite a scare." I then asked him how long I had been here. Alex said, a few hours. I then asked him if he had seen the man. He told me it was not time and I had something to do, but I couldn't remember what he said. Alex, did you see him? Did you hear what he said?" I was starting to get agitated and was trying to sit up. I was looking for the man because what he said was very important. Alex said, "You are the only one who could see him, and I need you to lay down and keep very still." At that point, I saw the IVs and several lines hanging from them, an oxygen tube in my nose, and a small machine sitting on my bed, which I now know was a defibrillator.

Alex said, "We will do some blood work and send them to the lab." My mom walked over to my bed, put her hand on my forehead, and said, "Baby, I'm here." I could see that she had been crying. Alex looked at her and smiled, nodding his head up and down as if they knew something that I didn't. He told my mother he had seen a lot of this in Vietnam. At that time, I did not understand what he meant. For some reason, I said to her, "Mom, I don't do drugs. I will have a pina colada if I go out to dinner, but I only have one, and that's it, Mom, I promise you." She smiled and said, "Baby, I know."

Within a few minutes, the room was packed, one doctor after another and more nurses. Then came lab techs, admission clerk, x-ray techs, and too many to count. I then asked Alex, "Am I going home soon?" He smiled and said, "No, you're going to be a guest of ours for a few days." I said to my mother, "Mom, I'm so tired, so tired." Just then, my chest started hurting again, and the monitors were beeping louder and louder. I watched in disbelief all these people coming around me. And I'm thinking to myself, am I really this sick? I just have heartburn. The room started spinning, and a nurse brought in a syringe full of medication. I could not tell if they stuck me or put it in the IV. I could hear the doctor tell my mom that they were giving me some Morphine. I could hear him ordering more tests and an EKG, but the rest was blank. The doctor told my mother that they were moving me to the ICU as soon as I was stable enough to be moved.

I was supposed to be the strong one for her and the rest of the family, and yet here I am, fighting for my life. My body was engulfed in pain as if objecting to my decision to get up. More people started to surround me, and out of impulse, my hand traveled to my chest. I was naked from the waist up, but at that point, I didn't care. I just wanted the pain to stop. Soon, I was moved to the ICU floor, and my room was right across from the nurse's station. After getting settled in my bed, I received more medication, and off to sleep I went.

It took two days for me to fully wake up, and even then, it was still a blur. A nurse came in and said, "Hello Pat. My name is...," but it sounded like she had marbles in her mouth. I couldn't make out what she was saying. She left the room and came back with some Jello and soup. But, my arms felt like bricks, and I couldn't lift them, and back to sleep, I went. I woke up the next day, and this time, I started to remember the man, and it was not a dream. I knew him!

*****

You see, when I was in the ER, I died. I saw myself lift up out of my body and began floating in midair. I was thinking about how light I felt and how my hands looked different. Then, all of a sudden, I heard this loud wind as if something was coming really fast. I then saw this hand as big as a house take my body and turn it and push me down into my flesh body so fast and with such force. It startled me, and I remember thinking what was that? A few minutes later, I started to come out of my body again, and I was floating towards the ceiling. Just then this man appeared in midair with me and started talking to me and I knew him. The thing is, he never moved his mouth, nor did I move mine. We were having a conversation with our minds.

I was furious when I saw him. I didn't yell, but I pointed my finger at him and said, "You don't understand how they have been treating me here, and I've had enough, and I'm going home!." He then said, "But it's not time." I then said, "I don't care, I'm going home." I proceeded to go towards the ceiling, and just then, my mother screamed and was bitterly crying. He and I looked at her, and I said, "Oh, I don't want her to cry; I just want to go home." He folded his arms across his broad chest and just looked at me. I knew then that it was my decision. I looked at him again and said, "Ok, I'll stay, but I don't want to." He began to tell me the reasons that I was here and what I had to do. Then that wind sound started again, but this time, the hand was more gentle, and it pushed me down again into my body.

*****

After a few days in the ICU, the nurse helped me up to take a shower, and that's when I saw the dark marks on my chest, and I knew that they came from the defibrillator. I noticed the conversation would steer to something else whenever I asked. It took several weeks for those marks to go away.

As God would have it, the time had come to have a one-on-one talk with myself. I asked myself, how in the world did I get here? I pulled the tray over to my bed to comb my hair, and a mirror popped up in the tray. I looked into the mirror, and I saw a mess. For a brief moment, I saw that little girl in me looking back, and I started to cry. I cried for that lost little girl who had been hiding inside of me for years. I cried for the lost dreams and the fake relationships. She dreamed of becoming a lawyer one day, but at sixteen, she was pregnant and had to drop out of school. The expectations of walking across a stage in cap and gown were now out of reach. In the 1960's, you had to leave school once they found out that a student was pregnant. I made the mistake of telling my best friend, and she told a teacher, who, in turn, reported me. So now, as a teen, I am a mother and a wife. What does a sixteen-year-old know about being a mother and wife? Nothing, so I went to work to take care of my family until I realized this so-called marriage was not what was best for me or my child.

Years later, now married for the second time and having had four children, I had the opportunity to go back to school, but my then-husband told me you don't need all of that; just work your job and come home. I was already working two jobs then, and I was thinking of getting my education and working one job. One day, I was washing the dishes when I heard a strange noise coming from the next room. I walked into the room and saw him tearing up my books. There was no taping them back together. Ironically, many years ago, it was against the law for a black man or woman to read or write. My GOD, did he not get the memo? It took me years to admit that I was not in a healthy relationship and that I was doing a disservice to my children and myself.

So, I made the difficult decision to raise the white flag and said, "I surrender," and I signed the papers to dissolve the marriage. This was bound to happen when two children in adult bodies came together; we were both selling one-way tickets to a trip going nowhere. I can only speak for myself, but I didn't have a clue and couldn't buy one. One day, I was on the city bus going to work, and an amazing thing happened. I was eavesdropping on a conversation where two women sitting in front of me were talking about a program offering people to go back to school, and they would help pay for it. I quickly got a piece of paper and pen out, and as she was giving the lady the phone number and who to contact, I wrote it down. She told her that she didn't know what classes were being offered but to call them and check it out. Well, I did! When I got to work, I called the number and was able to make an appointment for the next day. Of course, I had to call off from work the next day, but I was a girl on a mission. The next day at 9:00 AM, I was sitting in the office of Mr. Bradley, who was heading up a new state program for people with low income. I fit the bill for that one!

He asked me how I learned about the program; I paused momentarily and decided to tell the truth. He laughed and said, "Good for you." He handed me a packet with a list of classes that were being offered. As I flipped through the pages, low and behold, they were offering a Paralegal program. I almost fell on the floor. I said, "I would like to take this one." He looked at me and said he would have to test me for this class. I said, "ok." He then asked if I had time to take the test now, and I said yes. Mr. Bradley got up and went next door to set up a space for me to be tested. I started sweating and asking myself if I would pass the test or if I was crazy for trying this, but after all, it was one step closer to becoming a lawyer. Now I want to pray and ask God to help me in this one. Well, I took the test and passed. He filled out the paperwork, had me sign, and explained that I would have to pay three hundred dollars to the school and that his program would pay the rest. He also explained that the school had a payment plan and that they would work out the details with me.

He gave me the paperwork, my start date, and where to report. I shook his hand, thanked him for everything, and left. I got outside, shouted, "Thank You, Jesus," and didn't care who heard me. The following year was very tough, but I completed the program. The day after graduation, I went back to the office with my diploma in hand and found Mr. Bradley. I said to him, "I came to thank you for your help and to show you that I completed the program, and again, thank you so much." He walked over, shook my hand, and said that I was the first to come back and say anything. His eyes began filling up, and he said I had made his day. I left and started the process of filling out applications for a job as a paralegal. Every day for weeks, I applied, and it was the same answer each time, you need to have three to five years of experience. Lord, how can I get experience if no one will hire me? Everywhere I went, they wanted me to volunteer. So, In my mind, I said, I'll do that to get the experience and get a job at night to pay my bills. I did this for some time and now was the time to apply again. What I was told this time is that you need to have paid job experience. I felt like a mouse on a treadmill and couldn't get off. Once again, my dream was deferred, and I felt like I was in quicksand with no way out.

I became weary! This little girl was never taught limitations, but that didn't stop others from imposing them on me. The things that happened to this little girl, I cried for her because she couldn't. So what do I say to this little girl inside of me who is screaming, "Let Me Out."

Do I try to explain that what happened to her was not her fault? Do I dare ask her to forgive being raped, beaten, and to suffer in silence? How do you tell a child that those acts will carry over into your adult life, causing you to make wrong decisions over and over again? Back then, asking for help could land you in a psych ward. So you keep your head down and your mouth shut. Now I was ripe for the picking, going to school and getting more degrees and diplomas than what was on a thermometer. What was I trying to prove? What was missing in me? And why was I feeling so empty? We as women try to fill this space with food, the wrong men, people pleasing, or jobs that will cause us to be so tired that we don't have to think. And there lies the danger of marrying or getting into the wrong relationships because now you want someone else to handle it, and unfortunately, you have met your twin. You want to close your eyes and just sleep and not have to think. You don't trust your basic instinct because you don't know who you are, or somewhere along the way, you lost yourself, and some of us gave ourselves away freely. Smiling all the way like sheep being led to the slaughter. How do you come back from that?

It took me years to climb out of that well. I felt dirty, not smart enough, and not good enough, so I accepted any scraps thrown my way. The wrong friends, the wrong men, the wrong jobs, and the enormity of the impact can't be overstated. I could only see who I was and not what I could become. I felt that GOD had left me, but I was the one that walked away. I was the one who forgot my teaching of who God was. I learned the "Now I Lay Me Down To Sleep" prayer and never got up for years. Do I tell her that broken crayons still color?

Yes! I would tell that little girl, who is now a woman, to hit the pause button. You should not date anyone or make permanent decisions about temporary problems. You must begin the work before bringing anyone into your life. Why? Because your life depends on it. And if you don't, you very well could end up in an ER with a blood pressure of 200/116 in full cardiac arrest!

*****

The heart specialist came into my room, sat beside my bed, and said, "Pat, I'm the heart doctor assigned to your case, and we need to talk." He stated," I have all of your tests back and have viewed them. You have all the signs of a heart attack, and yet your heart is fine." So what's going on in your life? He and I began to have that conversation. I told him all of the things that had happened to me from a child up until that day. And how lost I felt. He listened to me intensely, and the things that poured out of me that day I had long forgotten. The doctor explained that I was experiencing stress, depression, and anxiety and that this was causing the chest pains. Had they not caught it in time, I would have had a heart attack and how bad it could have been.

Laying there and hearing his words, I thought, "I'm walking on the edge." I had no idea. He also explained that it was time for me to take my life back and do what I wanted. Then he said something even stranger: "Pat, if you have to curse someone out and go back and say that you're sorry later, at that time, get it off of you. You were not meant to carry someone else's foolishness." It was strange hearing a doctor say that. Sitting before me was this well-educated, soft-spoken man telling me to curse folks out if they were talking to me crazy. After being discharged, I learned how to take my life back one day at a time. I haven't had to curse anyone, but I have learned to stand my ground and know how to say "NO."

If I may, I would like to take you on a short history trip. We have all heard of the Roman Empire and the treatment of criminals. The story goes as if someone killed another, and then the dead body was strapped to the criminal. This term was known as "Dead Weight." They were forced to live out weeks of their life carrying a maggot-infested corpse strapped to their bare back. During the process of decomposition, it slowly leaked poisons into the criminals, making them sick until they finally died a slow, painful death.

I know this sounds disgusting, but I'm telling you this because it happens when we carry unforgiveness, anger, bitterness, and resentment. We slowly become infected over months and years and die a slow death. My question is, "What are you carrying?" Can you imagine getting married and walking down the aisle in your beautiful gown, him in his tuxedo, and pulling two wagons each full of trash? What a way to start a new life together. My, My!

If you are reading this, I ask that you begin to; "Do The Work."

Doing the work means cleaning the house! You, my friend, are the "HOUSE." Look within yourself and clean out fear, anger, guilt, and shame for some of us. We, as women, have carried this baggage for years, and it's time to release this dead corpse so that it can be buried. Ashes to Ashes and Dust to Dust!

So how do we do this? In my humble opinion, I would like to offer the following steps:

1. Pray- ask for forgiveness for the past and be willing to change. Understand that God is your first love, and then learn to fall in love with yourself. You can't love others if you don't love God or yourself.

2. Take a hot shower or bath, and after you dry off, stand in a full-length mirror and truly see yourself. Look at what God made. You were not put together with a sewing machine. Psalm 139:14 You are Wonderful and Beautifully made. The human body is an extraordinary work of art by God. We should not take our existence for granted. We must get comfortable in our own skin and see ourselves as God sees us.

3. Learn to Breathe - Be quiet and listen to your heartbeat.

4. Self-Reflection—Be honest with yourself and release the negative self-talk. If no one speaks kindness over you, then speak it over yourself daily until you begin to believe it.

5. Get a Journal, and this one will be for gratitude. I know everyone says to write down everything you want; house, cars, job, husband, wife, kids, and so on. But how about thanking God for what you already have and truly meaning it. You don't have to get deep about a book; you can get one at the dollar store and start with that. This process will start to help you get centered. And by the way, if you can't think of anything to say thank you for, here's one: "BREATH."

6. Self-care Routine—What rejuvenates you? Walking, music, reading, or meditation. Here's one: getting your nails done.

7. Sleep—Get enough rest! This is so important because if you don't, everything falls apart.

8. Personal Growth—Set goals and work towards them. With this one, start out with short-term goals and do them. What is one thing you have always wanted to do but never could? You will like how you feel when it's done.

9. Know your strengths and work on your weaknesses, and if you need help, don't be afraid to ask for it. Think of this: When you walk into a strange room, you walk to the nearest chair, and you sit down. You, like most of us, never question whether the chair will hold you. With blind faith, we sit down. Learn to do that with God, and yes, it takes time.

10. Look within, you may find what you were born to do. What are your core values? What are you passionate about?

Doing these steps will keep you busy for a while. As you clean your house, if you get "stuck," go back to step (1). In doing the work, you will find yourself going back to step (1) several times, but that's okay —you're on the right track.

In closing, I would like to leave you with the words of Maya Angelou;

"When you know better, you do better."

About Dr. Patricia

Dr. Patricia O. Lawton has more than twenty-five years of experience as an educator. She is a court appointed advocate for Guardian Ad Litem (GAL) as well as a trained mediator in conflict resolution. As a spiritual life coach and motivational speaker, she advocates for those who find themselves voiceless to gain the courage to speak up and out. She has helped hundreds of individuals for both their personal and professional lives, which she sees as her ministry.

Patricia holds a doctorate degree in Philosophy in Religion allowing her to be used as God's vessel telling her story to the masses in the hope of saving others from following the same dark path that she once walked.

Throughout My Journey, God Was There

CECELIA MYERS

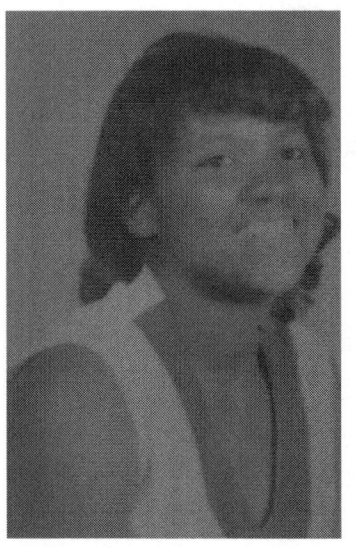

One thing that I am now sure of is that God has been with me throughout my life. I've felt His presence, asked for His guidance, and, at times, heard Him answer me directly.

Born and raised in Chicago, Illinois, by a single mother with a 6th-grade education, we mostly survived on government assistance. I had five sisters and a brother, who was the oldest. We had two older brothers who passed during their childhood due to illnesses before my birth.

We grew up in the inner city, where neighborhood gangs were the norm. Gang members were territorial and would protect their neighborhoods from rival gang members. We would sometimes witness drug deals in front of our apartment building. However, they never bothered us as we went to school and came home from work at night. My sisters were associated with some of them. They would look out for us even when we weren't aware.

We weren't allowed to wander the neighborhood because it wasn't safe. We spent a lot of time playing in the backyard or at our aunt's house, who lived in a somewhat safer neighborhood. Although my mother remarried during my childhood, her husband, who was the father of my two youngest sisters, was never a positive influence or presence in my life.

The trauma of witnessing domestic violence towards my mother by my stepfather took a toll on me as a child and teenager. Once we were older, my sisters and I would try to intervene and would jump him when he hit our mom. Those incidents always occurred when my older brother was not around. But we girls would do our best! During those times, she would put him out, and it was like a weight was lifted off her and us.

The laughter and lightheartedness would return to the home. We may have had less food, clothing, and things we needed, but we were happy to have our mom because, during those times, she was fully present for us. They separated in my late teens. She was our biggest cheerleader, encouraging and celebrating our victories in school and life.

She spent time with us and was there whenever we needed her, which was invaluable to me. She was proud to be a mother and homemaker. She said that being an only child, she always wanted to have lots of children. She aspired to be the best she could be with her limited resources.

I appreciated her being there for me when I got home from school. She was here on earth for me for 39 years. I could always call her, and she would give me good advice. She was my friend and confidant. I know she is in Heaven, watching over me and my siblings. May her soul rest in peace.

However, I was confused whenever she allowed my stepfather to return. The tension in the house would return in anticipation of our stepfather's next attack on our mom. I once asked her if she loved him more than she loved us. She said it was a different love, which only confused me more.

I would sometimes visit my birth father at my aunt's home, but I never felt loved or cared for by him. From my observations, his one and only love was his liquor bottle. He and my mom broke up when I was 4yrs old. I have no memory of him living in the home with us. The only memories I have of him as a child are when we visited him at our aunt's house. He was usually inebriated. He was a natural comedian at those times.

The trauma of not having a father in my life who loved and cared for me had a negative effect. It led to promiscuity, at times, to not ever wanting to get married or have children. However, my big brother was the positive man in our lives who was present. He loved and cared for us and disciplined us when needed. Although he was just 11 years older than me, I looked up to him as a father. I am forever thankful to him for always stepping up and being a positive male influence on me throughout my childhood and teen years. He would also buy us things we needed for the house, such as appliances, bikes, and TVs, and just be a present, positive influence. He showed me the qualities that I should look for in a man. So, when I saw similar qualities in my husband of 40 years, I knew he was the one for me.

Although my mother was raised by her mother as a Catholic, my mother was Baptist. She raised us as Christians, but we did not attend church. She said it was because she didn't have the right clothes for us or herself. But she told us about God and His son Jesus. My older sisters attended a local church briefly, were baptized, and joined the choir. They would come home, sing songs they learned, and teach me the songs. I remember one of my older sisters introduced holy bible scripture to me when I was eleven. I memorized and recited it often, and it gave me hope.

KJV. Psalms103:1-5:

"1. Bless the Lord, O my soul: and all that is within me, bless his holy name.

2. Bless the Lord, O my soul, and forget not all his benefits:

3. Who forgiveth all thine iniquities; who healeth all thy diseases;

4. Who redeemeth thy life from destruction; who crowneth thee with lovingkindness and tender mercies;

5. Who satisfieth thy mouth with good things; so that thy youth is renewed like the eagle's."

It was the light that I needed to know that the Lord was my provider, healer, and merciful caretaker. That was the beginning of my Christian foundation. It answered the question that I had about whether there was a God in Christ who cared for me and my family.

I loved school, although it was not easy for me. I had to study and get tutoring. Due to poverty, we moved a lot during my childhood. That also played a role in school and was not easy for me. Having to start over at new schools, sometimes in the middle or end of the semester, hurt my grades. I had to repeat the 4th grade. I now realize that was truly a blessing.

My second 4th-grade teacher was Mrs. Brown, a petite, bright-eyed, brown-skinned woman, barely 5ft. tall, full of positivity, energy, enthusiasm, and love for her students. She encouraged me to do my best. I discovered that I loved reading and writing poems. She introduced me to black poets and instilled black pride in me and a sense of being able to accomplish any life goals. I can still see the intensity of her face when she recited poems from my favorite poets, Maya Angelou and Langston Hughes. She would often tell us to be proud of our skin color because "God gave you that."

I was about nine years old, and we lived near what was then Chicago's Teacher's College. I would see the college students walking to class, wearing jeans and backpacks. They didn't have to line up and could come and go as they pleased. That was so very cool to me and inspired me to want to go to college. I attended Simeon Vocational High School. I was laser-focused on my education and was determined not to let anything get in my way. Not even the harsh cold and snow of Chicago. I remember that sometimes there would be as much as 10 inches of snow on the ground, but as long as the school was open, the main roads to school were cleared, and the big green Chicago Transit Authority was running, I was going to school!

Sometimes, my mom would try to get me to stay home because I had to walk almost half a mile to the bus stop. However, I would bundle up, head to the bus stop, and go to school. Years later, she told me that she would watch me out the window for as long as she could until I disappeared from her sight.

Once I turned 16, I got a part-time job at McDonald's on Grand Ave. near the Gold Coast. The CTA train would take me directly to the restaurant. I was making money and now could help out at home. I still got decent grades and was able to go to college. I chose Chicago State University, which was the new name for Chicago Teacher's College. Now, I was walking around campus, going to class, wearing jeans, and carrying a backpack, just like the students I saw when I was 9 years old. It was a dream come true! Thanks be to God!

I planned to go to college for two years, but I was still working part-time. I worked on the Gold Coast in Chicago as a security loss prevention officer at several different department stores, including Marshall Fields, Bonwit Teller, and Saks Fifth Ave.

However, at the end of 2 years, I decided to finish college and obtain a degree. By then, I was working full time and attending school full time. In my Junior year, I pledged the best Sorority in the world, Alpha Kappa Alpha Sorority Incorporated. I was accepted by Beta Chapter, however Chicago State University was starting a new chapter, Xi Kappa, and since I attended, I was now on their new line. So, as it turns out, I'm in the history books as a founding member of the Xi Kappa Chapter of Alpha Kappa Alpha Sorority Incorporated. Being introduced to the Sorority's commitment to service in the community and sisterhood outside of immediate family awakened the desire and satisfaction of service to others for the common good and betterment of mankind.

It was an honor to pledge and serve with 21 other beautiful black women, and now I can see how the Chapter has grown in service, excellence, and membership beyond my expectations by leaps and bounds!

I obtained a bachelor's degree in Corrections and Criminal Justice from Chicago State University. I was the first of my siblings to obtain a college degree. One week after graduation, I got married. My husband was in the US Navy, and we relocated to Jacksonville, Florida, where he was raised. I lost contact with most of my ships (Sorors) until reconnecting a few years ago through social media.

In Jacksonville, Florida, I had the opportunity to meet and connect with my bonus son. It was truly a blessing to get to know and love him. He was beautiful and brilliant!

We also had the support of my husband's parents, who positively influenced our marriage and my Christian development. They were truly Christians who loved and served the Lord. My father-in-law was a Deacon, and my mother-in-law was a Deaconess. They demonstrated and showed me what it was to have a beautiful marriage blessed by God. They loved me as a daughter, and my mother-in-law was my spiritual mother. She was truly a Virtuous Woman whose mission was to please God and serve her husband, family, and community. She took me under her wing and showed me how to make my husband's favorite dishes, especially his favorite homemade biscuits.

My father-in-law was the father that I never had. We also had a great connection. He taught me things that my birth father didn't. He was my spiritual father. He and my mother-in-law took great care in visiting, encouraging, and caring for the sick, shut-in church, and family members. I was witness to their genuine, sincere love for God and how God's blessings overflowed in their lives. I was encouraged. I desired these blessings and came to faith in Christ. I committed my life to the Lord in 1985 and was baptized at Second Missionary Baptist Church in Jacksonville, Florida. Once again, God provided me with exactly what I needed when I needed it.

My favorite scripture is Romans 8:28: "All things work together for good for those who love God and are called according to His purpose."

We had our son in 1986. We were very happy about this blessing from God and the addition of our family. When our son was 4 years old, I took him to Chicago to visit my family. We had been going every year since he was born, but I took him alone this time. It just so happened that my birth father was in town and had an apartment. My aunt, his sister, said that he wanted to see me and was sober. I was so excited to visit him to show him my beautiful, brilliant son and let him know of my accomplishments: graduating from college, having a good government job, happy marriage, and all.

As I began sharing my life with him, he seemed disinterested and said, "Are you still hanging out on doorsteps?" I just kinda laughed it off, and he didn't have much else to say. Needless to say, the visit was short. I have to admit that it was not until some months later, after I got back home, that it hit me that he implied that I was found on the doorstep!! Thank God my mind allowed me to slowly process what he said without being angry and lashing out at him in front of my son.

I thank God for peace of mind and for knowing that I have a Father who is in Heaven and cares for me!

He passed away a few years later due to alcoholism. Surprisingly, it had an effect on me that I didn't expect. It hurt to know that he could not love me as I needed him to and also that he and my mother wouldn't reunite. I didn't realize that I had those feelings until his death. My mother always said that he was the husband she was meant to have, but she just wasn't strong enough to deal with his alcoholism. I was struggling with his death, and the realization that I wouldn't be able to tell him how he hurt me and how his not being in my life affected me.

I read that someone wrote a letter to their father who passed, expressing their feelings. So, I gave it a try. I wrote a 5-page letter to him, wrote his name on it and put it in a mailbox! It was such a relief! I was able to get my thoughts and feelings out! It was the release that I needed to be able to move on. Although, I knew he'd never get it. I now realize it was probably a blessing that he wasn't a part of my life. God knows!

In 1989, my husband was stationed in Atlanta, and we relocated. That's when I fell in love with the weather in Georgia. I loved all of the seasons and became obsessed with learning the names of every flower, shrub, and tree that bloomed amazing flowers. I developed a green thumb. I would look for any excuse to go outside and enjoy the weather.

In Chicago, I still had to wear a jacket sometimes in the evenings in June. I couldn't understand how anyone could take a beautiful day for granted and not enjoy being outside.

In Atlanta, my husband and I found a church with a bible-based preacher and teacher. I became active in several ministries. Because of my love for children, I became involved with The Children's Chapel as a teacher and later co-coordinator. It was a blessing to get to teach, interact with, and learn from the children. They brought me closer to God. Children still have what I call God's sense. Their hearts are pure and not yet polluted by the noise of the world. They tell the truth without filters and keep you on your toes. They are truly a blessing from God.

In Georgia, I began my career as an adult probation officer with the Department of Corrections in Dekalb County. I supervised probationers with convictions from shoplifting to murder and everything in between. I was the only black probation officer in the North office. It was challenging, but I was up for it. I knew that all eyes were on me. I enjoyed the work and, a few years later, transferred to the Cobb County Probation office, which was closer to home. I developed a good rapport with my assigned probationers. It got to the point where some of them would tell me that I should be a social worker. Some years later, the Department transitioned towards mandating that probation officers carry 40 calibers, Glock Smith and Wesson. Although weapon training and requalifying every year was not a problem for me, it was never mandatory to carry a weapon. The atmosphere was changing. It became obvious to me that I needed to make a move. So, I went for it when I was made aware of an opportunity to transfer to a position with The Department of Family and Children Services as a Foster Care Case manager.

It was hard to believe that there were so many children in the Foster Care system without families who either were not able to provide proper care or could not be approved due to criminal records or other circumstances. The work was challenging but so worth it. It was a great feeling when I was able to place a child back in the home of their family or other caretakers who could care for them properly. Sometimes, that also meant finding a good fit with a family who wanted to adopt them.

In the 90s, my mother and paternal aunt were both diagnosed with breast cancer a few years apart. They both underwent chemotherapy and mastectomies. They both survived it. I knew my sisters, and I were at high risk due to breast cancer being on both sides of our family. I always encouraged them and my friends to do self-examinations and get yearly screenings as I did.

However, I had to reschedule my yearly mammogram appointment one year due to a work conflict. I was working long hours then as a supervisor with The Department of Family and Children Services, ensuring that children were being cared for properly by their caretakers. Before I knew it, three years had passed. I felt a lump, went to the doctor, and obtained a mammogram. It really wasn't a big surprise when, after a biopsy in 2010, I was diagnosed with breast cancer. Thankfully, it was in the early stages, which, in my opinion, was a miracle considering that I went 3 years without a mammogram. I remember thinking that since I had it, that would lessen the chance of my sisters getting it. That was a relief. One in 8 women develops breast cancer in their lives.

I opted to get a mastectomy as there would only be a 5% chance of the cancer returning. If I opted for a lumpectomy, there was a 40% chance of it returning, and I was not willing to take that chance. I underwent reconstruction. Praise God, I have been cancer-free for 14 years!! Lesson learned: make time and take time to care for yourself so that you can be there to take care of others.

During my recovery, I made a commitment to spend more time with God, reading my Bible, and praying more in an effort to increase my faith and prove myself worthy to God in Christ Jesus to use me as He saw fit. He is still with me. I truly believe that when we align ourselves with His will, seek His guidance, and rely on His strength, He will bless us abundantly. It is a gift from God.

Throughout my life, God has been with me. He has made a way when I couldn't see a way. Just seek His face and guidance and rely on His strength. In times of weakness, know that God cares for you, and if you trust Him, He will carry you through whatever comes. Just put it in His hands and leave it. He can fix it! In my life, I have experienced that everything that happens is not all good. But all things truly do work together for the good of those who love God and are called according to His purpose.

About Cecelia

Cecelia, a devoted Christian, has been a loving wife for more than 40 years, a proud mother of two sons, including her bonus son, and a doting grandmother to six grandchildren. With a heart for service, she spent her career as a Social Worker with the Department of Family and Children Services, providing support and care to families in need.

Now retired, she enjoys her time working part-time, delighting in the company of babies a few days a week, and cherishing moments with her grandchildren. A dedicated member of Ebenezer Baptist Church in Atlanta, GA, she serves as a Deaconess and shares her love for worship through singing in the church choirs.

Her faith is central to her life, and she firmly believes that with God at the center and a positive attitude, anything is possible. She encourages others to stay focused on their goals and trust God to guide their path to fulfillment and success.

Life Was Good
NINOTCHKA PHILLIPS

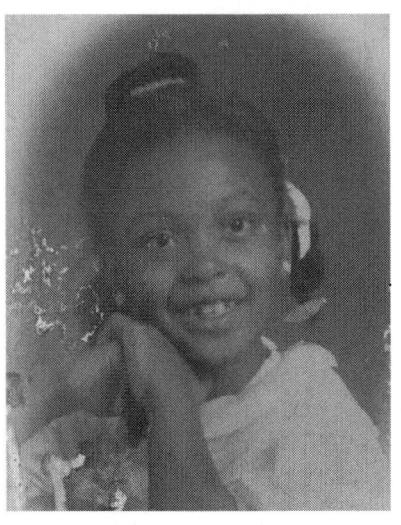

I grew up in a two-parent home with a working, amazing father and a wonderful homemaker mother. As an only child of one of my parents, I always had their attention, and their love poured in like no other. Haywood Phillips, my father, was a hard worker who loved and cared about his family, near and far. He would take me with him to ride along in his "big rig" 18-wheeler truck. My beautiful mother, Sammie Phillips, would always be in the kitchen cooking a nice dinner for us or helping me do my homework. My childhood was perfect until the demise of my father came suddenly as his health took a turn for the worst. He developed cancer in his body. My mom nurtured and cared for him until his final day. I was devastated. I cried until I could not cry anymore. I wanted to die with him.

My mom is amazing! As her role as a housewife and mom changed drastically, we dealt with the loss and continued on with living. I am sure she did not understand why this happened, but she knew things were changing quickly. She developed contentment and immediately went into the work field, where she worked a job that allowed her to be home in the evenings. My mom eventually had to acquire another job as she began to struggle to meet the monthly bills on time.

I hated this new move. Leaving my home became so stressful and created hate in my heart. I was okay until my mom began working two jobs, ultimately leading to my new home. My Aunt's home was filled with so much hatred for me and no love. I have no memories of happiness. I grew up hating my Aunt, my uncle, and my Aunt's two daughters. I had to learn from my mom how to love them as adults. Many nights, I cried for my dad and my mom to rescue me from what I thought was abuse. I became afraid to say anything. My behaviors at school changed as I was a fighter, suspended multiple times, paddled by men's principles, and ultimately had to leave the school. I lost my voice and spiraled into whatever was next.

Whew, I graduated high school! Now what? Again, my loving mother expressed her concern regarding my future. "Get a college degree," she would say, not knowing I had no clue what I wanted to do with my life. We packed the car and drove 11 hours to Grambling State University. No, I was not a part of their great playing band. This is where I was to grow financially, become my adult self, and begin creating a life. I failed. After three years, I came back home and started working odd jobs. My mom could not understand my transitions; therefore, I had to make a decision for us both. I was asked to leave her home. Then, I thought she hated me because why would you want me to leave instead of talking or sharing your feelings. Only now, I understand why. There is always a way, but you may not get that answer.

Adulthood is nothing shy of being a child with no guidance. At this point, I had no understanding of my life. Everything kinda "floated" around me without any words. I would see my friends excelling, family members getting married, and then there was me. No thoughts on my life, just a new follower of worldly people.

My dad introduced my mom to the Church of Christ. After his passing, she became more active in the church as she was my Sunday school teacher. I grew up in the church and only left once I became an adult. The reality is I wanted to submit to activities I knew God would frown upon and also kept those activities away from my mom. Well, I'm not good at keeping secrets. Literally almost everything I encountered, she knew. From juvenile cases to some of my adult incarcerations. I have never considered myself a "wild card," but if I were to list everything, this would take longer. I get it; we have all made mistakes. I have one that stayed with me for years to come.

Substance abuse and mental health are a perfect combination for the disaster of your life. I found what I considered to be fun in substances from marijuana to cocaine and ecstasy. Not knowing any effects, let alone the long-term. I was still dealing with the loss of my father, not ever expressing how I felt. I could not understand the transition from girl to woman. As I type this with real tears, I must say it has taken me 27 years to become Ninotchka Phillips, the woman you see today.

When I was asked to resign from a position with the state, I knew I had not become a woman. I had to submit to annual drug testing and gave a positive for marijuana. Out of all thing separated, marijuana stayed with me through my life. Mainly, because everyone was smoking it and it appeared they were all fine. For me, it changed the way I interacted with people. The positive testing at what I considered a "real job" under my degrees was now obsolete. My good friend once asked, "How can you tell if the person is a representative of the real person?" these words have been true ever since. I created a "representative" for my real self. Today, I believe this disorder is called "imposter syndrome." Among other possible diagnoses, this was the most relevant to say I identify.

Looking onward and upward as I continue to navigate this wonderful life, I see my errors. The repairs began with my spirituality. Strengthening my faith, not as an imposter but as a genuine and serious Christian, I stand with God. This is a requirement in my life. Next, I listened to my children and effectively communicated my errors. My goal and hope for them is to learn from my mistakes, as I lived there for years, and prosper off the seeds sown. My mom is the main character to whom I owe it all because she stood firm on God's law. Now, what have I gained from this? I'm not an imposter anymore. My truth could save you from failure and death in sin. I have committed my life to God again. This time, not as an imposter, but a child who became weak and needs strength.

Through all the tumultuous turmoil, trials and tribulations I still stand. I am still here to make it right. I am still here to help someone or be of some encouragement in tough times. I am still here to put in the work for Jesus. I am still here to show I have changed. I am still here to show my growth from a little girl to now what I call a woman. I now know I was never left alone. I now realize my role. Clear and Present. I will share that I felt I have always had clues of "what to do," but that, combined with other struggles, was vastly ignored, causing the life I lived.

Listening is a skill. A lot of times, people aren't heard. My voice left a long time ago, and it was buried with addiction. After facing life's trials, I began listening. I still have a long way to go with relationship building, but I am ready for all the tasks God puts forth. My mom has always been there with her unconditional love. I love her so much. She appreciates my growth and continues to be a light of encouragement as I begin a new chapter in my life. This next chapter is very personal as my better years are behind, and the best is to come.

My best years are to come with a full understanding of my new goals. Set them goals and follow through. Be clear and precise, along with specific details. This is my (your) life; you can create ANY life. There is no time limit on your success; however, like anything and anyone, time is not on our side; therefore, your body ages.

A lot of mistakes have been made. If you are still alive today, you can make those necessary changes, whether big or small. I put a lot of my responsibilities on others. After losing my career, I have focused more on the woman I am becoming. I appreciate all the "no's" and all the help I have received, and even when I didn't have anything, I was helped. It is now time to return those blessings. A newfound contentment, a new way to handle downfalls without substance use. If you or anyone you know suffers from addiction, no matter how big or small, seek help. 211 is a national telephone line available in each state where immediate assistance is offered

About Ninotchka

Ninotchka Phillips is a dedicated Christian and proud mother of two who embraces life with gratitude and purpose. She has a passion for outdoor activities and finds joy in helping and working with others to achieve their goals.

In her free time, Ninotchka activates her "self-worth mode," using those moments to explore new ventures and foster personal growth. She loves life and all it has to offer, seeing each day as a blessing in the journey she has been assigned.

Connect with Ninotchka on social media:
- **Facebook**: Ninotchka Phillips
- **Instagram**: @HaywoodCleaning
- **LinkedIn**: Ninotchka Phillips

Grace Through The Storm A Journey of Redemption and Self-Love

LETICIA REEVES

I was born to a teenage mother, just 15 years old. From the beginning, my life was a series of uphill battles, and my grandparents became my saving grace. They took me in and raised me as their own, sacrificing so much to ensure I had opportunities they never did. They enrolled me in private school until 10th grade, after which I attended public school and graduated. They gave everything they had to support me, and even after their passing, their love and efforts continue to inspire and uplift me. I will forever be grateful for their love and dedication, which became the foundation of who I am today.

Growing up, I found joy in dance. I started learning when I was just seven years old, and ballet quickly became my first love. The grace, the discipline, the feeling of freedom—it was like I could leave all my worries at the studio door and lose myself in the music. I danced passionately, pouring my heart into every plié and pirouette. But when high school started, life changed, and I had to let go of ballet. I still miss it sometimes, that feeling of belonging to something beautiful and precise.

Then there was basketball, which became my new obsession. I got my first basketball when I was eight; from that moment, it rarely left my side. I'd wake up dribbling it around the house and fall asleep with it by my bed. It wasn't just a sport; it was my way of staying connected to myself, giving me purpose and focus during times when I felt completely lost.

Growing up without my father was a pain I didn't fully understand until much later. For most of my life, he was just a missing piece of my story. I spent years wondering who he was and why he wasn't there. During the height of the COVID pandemic, I found out he'd been in a terrible accident—one that nearly cost him his life. It was then, in those raw and vulnerable moments, that I met him for the first time. It was surreal, meeting the man who had been a ghost in my life for so long.

Along with him, I met my Aunt Cornelius, whom I lovingly call Aunty Boo Boo and her kids. They welcomed me with open arms, and for the first time, I felt a sense of belonging on that side of my family. But despite that connection, my father and I don't speak often. The distance between us lingers, leaving behind a complicated mix of sadness and acceptance.

My mother, too, was absent in her own way. She struggled with addiction, and our relationship was never close. I didn't even call her "Mom"; I called her by her first name, even though she was my birth mother. I saw her more as a sister—someone I would call to catch up with and have casual conversations. Our interactions weren't like those of a typical mother and daughter. While our relationship was unconventional, it was still a connection, just different from the norm. It hurt growing up feeling like I didn't have parents in the way other kids did. I carried that pain quietly, often feeling alone even when surrounded by people. I was popular but never felt like I truly fit in. A lot of people knew me, but I didn't always feel seen.

On top of everything, I was born with deformed feet. It's something I rarely talk about because, for a long time, I was deeply embarrassed. I hated showing my feet in public, terrified of being laughed at or judged. I hid that part of myself, never letting on how much it bothered me. Even when I danced or played basketball, I always felt that quiet shame, like a secret I couldn't fully escape. Despite my outgoing nature, there were many times I just wanted to be left alone, hiding the parts of me that felt unworthy.

My journey through love was no less complicated. I've been married twice and have three beautiful children, each with a different father. My children are my heart and soul, the reason I keep pushing forward. But my path to motherhood was filled with its own trials. My relationship with my oldest child's father was abusive, and it nearly cost me my life. He shot me in the leg—a moment that still haunts me. It was then, in the hospital, that I learned I was pregnant with my first child. I was terrified, facing the reality of bringing a child into such chaos. I couldn't take pain medication because of the pregnancy, and I had to endure not just physical pain but the emotional weight of everything I'd been through. I realized how strong I was in those moments, stronger than I ever knew I could be.

Surviving that ordeal was nothing short of a miracle. I felt God's hand guiding me, sparing me when I wasn't sure I deserved to be saved. I made a promise to myself and to my unborn child that day that I would never let anyone make me feel small or powerless again. That was the turning point, where I began to see my worth and started fighting for the life I wanted, not just for me, but for my children.

As I grew older, I realized something was missing, a deep emptiness that nothing seemed to fill. I'd been looking for love and validation in all the wrong places, trying to find someone who would make me feel whole. But every time, I ended up with men who didn't love me for who I was but instead for what I could offer them. I was tired of being used and mistreated, tired of feeling like I was never enough. That's when I turned to God.

I started seeking a deeper relationship with the Lord, finding comfort in His word. I was baptized as an adult, an experience that transformed my heart and soul. I surrendered my pain, my past, and my insecurities at His feet, and in return, I found peace that I had never known before. Jesus became the head of my life, guiding me with His grace and mercy. Through Him, I found the strength to stop being with people who didn't value me. I began dating with purpose, no longer settling for less than what I deserved. I learned to love myself, seeing myself through God's eyes—worthy, beautiful, and deeply loved.

God's love filled the void I'd been carrying for so long. His grace lifted the burdens I'd placed on my shoulders, and I finally began to understand that I am enough. I stopped allowing people to use me and started setting boundaries that protected my heart. I let go of the need to be perfect and embraced the woman God created me to be, flaws and all. I found refuge in the Lord, and through His strength, I began to heal.

Today, my faith is the cornerstone of my life. I wake up each morning knowing that I am loved by a God who sees me, knows my heart, and has never left my side. I am no longer that scared little girl who feels like she doesn't fit in. I am a woman of God, a mother, a fighter, and a survivor. My journey hasn't been easy, but every step has brought me closer to the Lord, who has been my anchor through every storm.

I still struggle with acceptance and nerves sometimes, especially in business meetings or around my peers. But now, I remind myself that I am walking in God's purpose. I am not defined by my past, my mistakes, or the pain I've endured. I am defined by the love of Christ, who has redeemed me and given me a new beginning. I am still learning and growing, but I am not afraid anymore. I know I am never alone, for the Lord is always with me, guiding my steps and holding me in His loving arms.

My story is one of redemption, finding hope in the darkest moments, and trusting in a God who makes all things new. I am proud of who I am and where I come from, and I know that with God, my best days are still ahead of me. I am living proof that His grace is sufficient and His love can heal even the deepest wounds. I am still here, still fighting, and still standing in the light of His glory.

About Leticia

Leticia Reeves, born and raised in Detroit, Michigan, now resides in Georgia, where she brings a wealth of experience and passion to the real estate industry. As a Real Estate Professional specializing in new construction sales with Piedmont Residential, Leticia is dedicated to helping clients find their dream homes and guiding them seamlessly through every step of the process.

The oldest of five siblings, Leticia has three sisters and a brother on her mother's side and one sister on her father's side. Family is a cornerstone of her life, and she is the proud mother of three amazing children—two daughters and a son. Outside of work, Leticia enjoys watching sports, traveling, and spending quality time with her family. Her enthusiasm for real estate extends into her personal life, as she loves exploring new construction homes, consulting with new agents, and connecting with people from all walks of life.

Leticia holds dual Master's degrees in Business Administration and Human Resource Management, giving her a unique blend of business acumen and interpersonal skills. These qualifications, combined with her passion for client relations and team development, make her a standout professional in her field.

Currently single and dating, Leticia embraces each chapter of life with positivity and purpose. Whether she's assisting first-time homebuyers or mentoring aspiring agents, her goal is always to leave a lasting, meaningful impact in every interaction.

Born Fabulous

DENICE RICHARDSON

I knew at a very young age that something was different about me: my outlook, perspectives, needs, and enjoyment. Also, I was born a Twin. So, what I've learned and discovered about myself, I am passing on to you!

As a little girl from Detroit, Michigan, I started my first mobile business when I was 5 years old (selling candy, soda, and chips to my neighbors). I financed my business by running errands (like going to the store and collecting soda bottles), which eventually led me to set up my first lemonade stand from home (which I count as my first tangible win).

In 1960, the world was different. When I was eight, I was a natural-born entrepreneur, always paying attention to how many customers were shopping in the neighborhood retail store and how much money they put in the cigarette vending machine. I wanted one in my home to make money for my business, so I asked the store owner how I could order one of those vending machines; she said the number was on the machine, so I wrote it down, went home, and ordered it.

My Mother, Lucille Frances Richardson, was shocked to see a vending machine being delivered, so when it came to my door, she promptly turned it away. Imagine the look on her face! I got the bright idea to order a cigarette machine because my Mother and her friends would constantly send me to the store to buy cigarettes for them. As I said, the world was a different place in 1960. I figured she and her friends might as well buy cigarettes from me. I was done walking to the store eight times a day. While I stood in the doorway and watched the delivery man load my cigarette machine back onto the truck, my Mother informed me I was too young to enter the tobacco vending business. Seeing that I was only eight, I had to agree with her.

As I entered my early teenage years, I began crafting jewelry. I created a display box to showcase my earrings and necklaces. I was a walking billboard wearing all the merchandise in school and around my neighborhood. Soon, my teachers, friends, and, once again, neighbors were my customers, another win! My Father, James Richardson, told me I was destined for greatness.

He recognized my entrepreneurial spirit and talents and encouraged me to continue walking my path. Though she thwarted my budding career as a tobacco executive, my Mother passed me her fashion sense. She was my inspiration; I loved to watch her dress! She wore the most exciting outfits with the best accessories. Everyone who met her would say she had pure elegance and grace.

The keen fashion sense I inherited from my Mother helped me get the attention of a Diamond Broker when I was 16. By this time, I was deeply invested in my next business, dog grooming. I ran a dog grooming salon in my parent's basement and used my poodle, Easy Money, as my show dog.

Easy Money was my best friend and favorite accessory; I regularly dyed his fur to match my outfits. This particular day, I was wearing lime green, and Easy Money was sporting a lime green poodle puff. I caught the attention of Chava Bernhardt, a high-profile, sought-after show dog groomer. Chava admired my stylist's ability to turn heads and gave me a business card to come to her home, and she would teach me how to advance as a groomer. I was charging $50, and my price increased to $150.

My business leaped to a new high, another win. It wasn't long before I was buying and selling show dogs. About a year later, she shared another family business with me. The Bernhardt's were also in the jewelry business, diamonds and gold, to be exact. Her husband, Mortimer, was one of the largest diamond brokers in the business. We began to develop a business relationship that would span decades. Mortimor taught me how to master my skill as a wholesaler and visualize success as a Jeweler. Why have average when you can have extraordinary?

At 17, I developed an interest in modeling; I attended several workshops and took classes with thoughts of starting my own company (still on the path of discovery). This was an exciting time in my life. In high school, I was voted the most likely to go to Hollywood! WHICH I WENT! I wore full ostrich feather boas and long-sleeved gloves in high school. I was influenced by Diana Ross and the Supremes, who set the tone for my life.

Around this time, I went to Florida to visit my brother Larmarr, a professional athlete turned high school principal. I had always had a love for monkeys! So, when I had an opportunity to visit a pet store, I purchased a monkey with money from my mobile clothing business. My monkey's name was Famous, and he became my newest showpiece. I encourage EVERYONE, if you're passionate about something, get it! Yes, I wanted my own monkey. It was my childhood fantasy. Now in full armor, I was ready to perfect my modeling career, teach myself how to become an entertainer, commentator, and coordinator, and make a living while perfecting my skills. This took focus, dedication, and tenacity! Another win was that I picked up some ideas from the Ebony Fashions Shows.

Modeling, styling, and hosting fashion shows became the business that took me to California. Moving to California, specifically Hollywood, was a lifelong dream.

Let me introduce you to The International Originals: Twelve High-Fashion Models, Ten Women, two Men, four Poodles, and one Monkey! We performed at the St Regis Hotel (we received several 5-star reviews), and it was time to introduce myself to Hollywood.

I ran an ad in the local newspaper and hired nine models. My first show was at the Beverly Hilton, with many shows to follow.

At the age of 21, I opened La Decouverte of Beverly Hills (a high-end, one-of-a-kind) Boutique. When God places you on your assigned path, many doors will open! This was divine intuition, an inner resource for my hopes and dreams. I met the shop's owner as we walked towards each other, and she said, "I'm turning one hundred today!" "I'm retiring. Would you like to take my shop?" I purchased the shop on the spot for $100 monthly and signed a year lease for $1200. For those of you who have heard of The Rat Pack (Sammy Davis JR, Frank Sinatra)....she was their interior designer.

I was blessed with an investor and my twin sister, Denette Richardson. We were the first black-owned boutique in Beverly Hills in 1977. Within two years, we opened a larger shop around the corner with the same name. We brought out a manufacturing company from Denise Rossi, which included a warehouse of fabric sewing machines and supplies. We began designing our own line as well and sold her brand. We would also sell International designer clothing from Paris and local designers in the community.

Years later, good fortune came my way when Roger Mosley walked into the shop and said wow, this is a black-owned shop. I will give you an opportunity to be my wardrobe stylist for the hit TV show Magnum PI, another win. Now, this little girl from Detroit was receiving checks from Paramount Studios. I decided to go to the studio and join the union to start doing Tom Selleck's wardrobe. By now, my life was flowing with one opportunity after another! To my surprise, this was the second time I faced RACISM! At the studio, sitting with the family members from MGM, Paramount, and Universal Studios, I was told by the Producer I wouldn't qualify to style Tom Selleck's wardrobe, basically because of my skin color, and that I wasn't in the "in" crowd. However, I didn't let that deter me.

I had many Black supporters and friends of all different nationalities.

Another supernatural blessing was right around the corner! LA 'DECOUVERTE BOUTIQUE made history! In 1977 I was featured in Black Enterprise Magazine Women Who Retail. We closed the shop after 7 years. We styled various celebrity wardrobes for two years and did fashion shows part-time.

In 1982, I was featured in Contribution of Black Women to American by Author Marianna W Davis

God had another plan for my life! In 1983, I gave birth to my first child, Bernisha Waller. My second child was Bernetta Waller in 1986 and Denard Waller in 1987. Bernard Waller, their Dad, and I were very excited. Now, as a mother of three, I had my family! Another win! Now, my focus was raising my children and giving them a head start in life.

I had accomplished my dreams and went to Hollywood. I even sang with Diana Ross in Las Vegas. I achieved my goals! I still thank God every day. I never thought in my wildest dreams that God would allow me an opportunity to introduce my children to their grandparents because all my children were born in California.

I had plans to open a mini-mall in San Bernardino. However, my Dad needed me, so my life took another path that I never expected.

Detroit, here we come!

My Father had Diabetes and had to have half of his leg amputated, and he was severely depressed. This trip extended his life by two years, and he met his grandchildren!

I got to share love with both parents and spend time with them. My Mother was born fabulous! I inherited this gift from her. Within three years, she passed away from cancer. I was devastated and had to learn how to grieve. There is no right way to grieve. It's a painstaking experience, and we all must endure. I tried to relieve my pain with alcohol!

After gaining thirty pounds and becoming depressed for years, I recovered. I fought to overcome this with prayer, discipline, and determination. My first experience of losing loved ones was too painful for tears! I was blessed to take care of both parents.

I learned the gift of massage at a very young age. I took a massage class, and I still enjoy it. I've been anointed with HEALING HANDS. I am in the Guinness World Record 2001 for the longest massage chain. Another win!

My children went to college:

- Bernisha went to Law School.
- Bernetta went to Spelman College.

And Dernard is an entrepreneur.

In 2007, I was a proud Mother with a new career: Candles, a retail and wholesale manufacturing company. As a family business, our first account was Motor City Casino. Our second account was Motown Gift Shop and then came the hospital, high-end boutiques, the Charles Wright Museum, and celebrity stores in seven states. Look at God—He is the Almighty!

In 2014, we moved to Atlanta, relocated the candle business, and expanded the family. Over the next eight years, I had five grandchildren: Bella, Whitney, Trey, Johnny, and Phoenix.

Everyone had families of their own, and I helped raise my grandchildren—another Win!

In 2020, the world was turned upside down with uncertainty. I took this time to renew and enlarge my spiritual wisdom for personal growth and development. As I reinvented myself, I had to stay on a high vibrational frequency, rooted and grounded.

In 2023, at the age of 71, the FAB-Fabulously Aging Backwards movement was birthed to help bring global awareness to everyone on the planet about how to stop slow or reverse chronic diseases with simple lifestyle changes! I've noticed how my movement has impacted the earth from my social media family, friends, and even myself. This movement will outlive me. This is the legacy God has birthed in me! I had a biometric assessment and was diagnosed with a 38-year-old body. I'm 71, I've reversed 33 years!

May I be the inspiration and encouragement you need when you're struggling to find your God-given purpose? This is my story from a humble living legend. You're welcome to join the movement and reverse how you think and feel about aging and start living a longer, healthier, happier life. Remember, you start aging at birth!

Thank You

About Denice

Denice Richardson is a living legend. She was born in 1952 in Detroit, MI, the oldest sister of a set of fraternal twin girls. She and her sister are the 4th and 5th children of James Richardson Sr. and Lucille Taylor (formerly Richardson).

Denice is an entrepreneur, beginning her business endeavors as a 5-year-old child in Detroit, then traveling to and residing in Hollywood and Beverly Hills for 20 years while in her early 20's. While in Beverly Hills, Denice owned an upscale clothing boutique and was also a celebrity wardrobe stylist. In addition, Denice formed a 12-person modeling troupe, whom she traveled across the United States with, hosting, commentating and coordinating fashion shows.

In 1977, Denice was featured in Black Enterprise, "Women Who Retail." Shortly after that in 1982, Denice was featured *Contributions of Black Women to America*. This book is recorded in the Library of Congress, ensuring Denice's place in history!

Years later, Denice returned to Detroit, to care for her ailing parents and raise her 3 children (all born in California). While in Detroit, Denice made a pivot into candle manufacturing and created A Proud Mother Candle Company. A Proud Mother Candle Company became a staple in Detroit and gained nationwide clientele in clothing boutiques, gift shops and bookstores.

After successfully establishing that business, Denice relocated to Atlanta, GA, where she currently resides. All of her children and grandchildren also live in Atlanta, and they enjoy a very close relationship. Denice is a very active grandmother and supports all of her grandchildren in their academic, musical and athletic endeavors. While in Atlanta, Denice founded, "Fabulously Aging Backwards Movement" in 2023.

Denice has a goal to heal the planet and help everyone age backwards! The Fabulously Aging Backwards Movement was created to bring awareness about stopping, reversing and slowing down most chronic diseases caused by lifestyle choices. You can follow her and joining the #FABM on Instagram at @aproudmothercandles.

Contact Denice:

313-415-1703 cell

apmcandles@gmail.com

IG @aproudmothercandles

The Darkest Grey
VANEEKA ROBINSON

It took years of denial and suppression to understand why I could not get along with my mother. After all, little girls always wanted to be like their moms. Utopias of elegant style and class are visions of little princesses worldwide, but not mine. Even as I lined pretend utensils on cold, hard ivory tiles that held up her two-inch Candies pumps, I was a mature version of myself, the eldest dependent of a single parent with two kids no one else claimed. We already depended on other family members to help with school clothes and Christmas; now, another baby wiggled into the picture. My brother was just plum delighted. He was only four and thought Mom had a baby doll. Finally, he'll be a big brother. On the other hand, three years his senior, I looked at this little wrinkled, bald-headed baby, who everyone said was a girl, as a threat. With yet another mouth to feed, Christmas Day looked incredibly somber.

We spent three days at our aunt's; because she was blind and didn't work, she volunteered to take care of us. My mom had spoken with us on the phone and said we had a sister. And upon her arrival, I ran to the door like a lovesick puppy to greet its provider, its master. See, up until that point, I still worshiped my mother.

"Hey," she whispered. "Shh," she motioned with her index finger to her lips. "You'll scare the baby," she told my brother.

"Hey," I greeted the tall, dark man behind her. I had met my sister's daddy. This man was not him.

"Hi," he answered warmly. "I'm your Momma's friend, Nate."

We all gathered at the kitchen table while my aunt questioned my mom about her ordeal during delivery. She even felt the baby, trying to get an idea of what she looked like.

"Ooh! She is bald-headed," she gasped, giggling as my little sister squirmed from foreign and unexpected touches. My brother had pulled a chair alongside my mother. He sat close enough to smell the formula on the baby's breath.

"Sit back some, Chris. You can't breathe on, huh. She'll git sick," Mom cautioned.

I rolled my eyes, not enthused about the special attention she already received. Mom didn't seem even the slightest bit interested in knowing how things went with my aunt. She didn't even seem interested in knowing how much I missed her.

I walked into the living room, pouting while the fiesta carried on in the kitchen. Occasionally, I glimpsed out the corner of my eye to see what she did whenever she made a strange noise. Once, I looked over and caught the attention of my mom's boyfriend. He seemed to notice that I was more than a little crabby. He smiled and quickly said, "I'm thirsty, anyone want a drink?"

In the South, a drink meant a soda. My mom and aunt declined in harmony, but my brother and I accepted. Since Play Momma seldom let us drink sodas because she was convinced they would mess up our kidneys, we were more than willing to take him up on the offer.

"Squirt, why don't you go and get Nate a drink?" Mom suggested.

I was named Squirt when I was just a few days old by my mom's then-boyfriend because he said I was short and round, like a squirt or a drop of water.

Great! I thought, now I can get out of here and away from all this madness.

"I wanna grape!" shouted my brother, who startled the new baby enough to make her cry.

"Shh!" Mom said angrily. "I told you to be quiet."

"Well, what kind of drink do you want, Squirt?" Nate asked, singing my nickname as if to tease me.

"I don't know. What kind do you want?"

"I asked you first," he replied.

"I asked you second," I said with a smirk.

We both laughed, and I was just thrilled to see the attention on me, even if it came from a complete stranger. "I'll have whatever you have, then," he said with a settled grin on his face as if he had won the game.

We decided on Sprite. I turned up my nose, taking the change from him. He turned up his nose to mock me. I could only laugh as I walked to the door, stirring the four shiny quarters in my hand like marbles.

Once I opened the door, forgetting what Mom said about silence, I screamed, "Ima git a earnge!"

Nate patronized my childishness by screaming back, "I wanna orange, too."

I let out a big laugh and skipped down the hill to the store on the corner.

We took the baby home, and Mom reminded my brother over and over that night that her name was Denise and not "Baby." "But you can call her Dillie," she added.

I don't remember much about what went on in the house around me. Everything seemed fine. Weeks went by, and I had a new friend.

I got the attention I wanted and felt I deserved. After all, I was mainly the one who took care of my little brother. My favorite TV character was Shirley Temple. A chubby and cute little girl with strawberry curls. Most of the time, Shirley Temple played the role of an orphan or fatherless child. In that, we were alike. I didn't know my father either. I wanted a complete family with a mother, father, and children. I wondered if Nate would stay or love me like the men in Shirley Temple stories.

Mom began working again soon after she returned home from the hospital. But as always, she had trouble finding a babysitter. It wasn't hard getting someone to keep little Dillie; her father's side of the family delighted in keeping her overnight. But my brother and I were not family to them; either they never offered or my mom never asked. I guess Nate must have been a real loser because he never worked or left our house. So he agreed to babysit us.

The first day, my mom left him with us. He played games with me and laughed as I sang and danced like Shirley Temple. He was more fun than my little brother.

"It's such a good trip, lollypops. It's just a cool trip to the candy shop. Where gum gums play..." I sang and pranced around.

"You wanna play old maid?" I asked. Nate never turned me down.

We played old maid for about an hour while my brother played with his garage and car set. Eventually, we both grew tired of the card game, and I went into my room to find other things to play with. I searched my toy box for a coloring book. I only had about five crayons, but I felt it would be enough to make some pretty pictures.

"How bout we play something else?" Nate inquired from my doorway. I was startled to see that he was standing in my room. He had never come to my room, or any grown-ups for that matter.

"All right, what?" I asked timidly.

"House," he replied.

I looked over at Chris, asleep on the floor. We had always played House together. I would pretend to have plates and cups and, lining them up on the floor, I'd pretend to prepare Chris' dinner. He would come home from work, and I would be dressed in my mother's robe with a towel on my head to make it seem like I had long hair. We would have a baby, my Holly Hobbie or Baby Alive doll, that I held most of the time. We would eat and talk, and he would leave for work again.

"It ain't a lot of fun," I said with a grimace.

"It is—my way," Nate replied. "I'll show you."

House started just as it did when Chris and I played it. It became boring as usual, then Nate suggested he take over with directing the rest of the script. He said he wanted to show me how to play "Momma and Daddy" but that I had to come to my mother's room with him. I really wanted to learn a new game. The games my brother and I played had grown monotonous a long time ago. School, Grocery Store, we even owned our own business from time to time. However, Chris was no fun because he had to be told everything: where to sit, what to do, and even what to say. Nate was different. He was grown up. He could teach me some things I didn't know, some new games.

"Why do we have to go to my momma's room?" I asked.

"Because that's what mommas and daddies do, don't they?" Nate replied.

When I thought about it, he was right. Almost every man who entered our house eventually ended up in Mother's room. And so I followed him there.

Once inside the bedroom, Nate closed the door. I was scared because I felt uncomfortable, closed up, and alone with him. But my heart pounded from both fear and excitement, as I was eager to find out what my momma did with the men she brought into her room.

"My brother might wake up," I said, attempting to get out of doing something that didn't feel right. I have never done this before, I thought. I only closed the door when I changed clothes. My mom would burst through any closed door when I played with my brother or friends. She would say we were up to something if we were being secretive. Mostly, she was right.

Sometimes, Chris and I would close the door to jump on the bed like acrobats. Once, she even caught my brother playing with matches. But for some reason, I did not feel as though this grown man wanted to jump up and down on the bed with me. And I knew that an adult wouldn't encourage me to play with matches; at least, that's what we were taught in school. Still, I did what I was told. Not just because he was old enough to be my father but mostly because I didn't want to upset or disappoint my new friend. I'd never met an adult who wanted to be my friend and play with me.

"He won't wake up," Nate assured me.

He started his game with smooth talking and gentle touches. He whispered how pretty I was, brushing his fingertips along my arm. The touches felt nice, and I became more relaxed. He said he had liked me from the first time he saw me. "You remember when your mom came home from the hospital?"

"Yes," I answered with a smile, remembering how he was the only one who paid attention to me.

He kept saying nice things to me, things I had never heard another human being say. With a sudden motion, Nate pulled up my shirt. I caught his hand.

"I-I don't know," I started again. But he put a finger over my mouth.

"Am I hurting you?" he asked.

I shook my head.

"Well, trust me," he said, "You'll like this game. I promise I won't hurt cha. It'll feel good." So, I trusted him ... my friend.

As he laid me down on the bed and kissed me like the grown-ups I'd seen on television, he took off my pants and underclothes, then his own. I remember feeling and hearing my heartbeat with such force I thought it would explode at any minute.

"How old are you?" he asked.

"Six." I had to think about my age at first because I just had my sixth birthday.

He started talking about how big my vagina looked. Now, that felt wrong. I have never seen Shirley Temple in such a predicament. So I lay there trembling. "Trust me. I love you." Those were three words no one had ever said to me before.

He loves me? I thought while being distracted. I kept saying to myself, calm down, don't be scared; he loves you, and he'll never hurt you. I closed my eyes and tried to be a brave little girl for him because I believed he loved me. But what came next would change the course of my naïve, hungry life.

He opened my legs, and as the pressure of his body weighed heavily on mine, I felt a pain between my thighs that I had never felt in my young life. I gasped and screamed in sheer agony! I pushed him with such force that he jumped up and looked at me, shocked. By now, I sobbed uncontrollably.

"I'm sorry," he said nervously.

Even after he jumped up, I never looked at his penis. I had once overheard some of the older kids in my building talking about penises. I had wanted to see one. Then it would be something if I told them I'd seen a real one. But what happened in my momma's room that day wasn't worth bragging about. I was ashamed—and afraid—to even look him in his face. I feared seeing a monster rather than my friend.

"I din mean to hurt you, Squirt," he said, as he reached out for me. In an instant, I snatched away from his grasp.

That was no Mommy and Daddy, I thought. That hurt. And if men were hurting my mother like that, then why did she take so many of them to her bedroom? That was not House; he hurt me! And as I stood pulling my clothes on and weeping, I thought of how much I hated him. Nate could no longer be my friend because he had lied and hurt me!

Nate jumped to the door before I did and said in a desperate and frightened voice, "Listen!" "You can't tell nobody what happened tonight." "Don't tell nobody we played house."

"Why not?" I asked as I began regaining some sense of control. Despite Nate insisting that he hadn't done anything wrong to me, his eyes, big and stunned beneath his sweaty forehead, told their own tale.

"Because," he stammered, "you'll get in trouble. And if your momma finds out, she won't love you no more, you understand?" He sounded very sure of this.

I didn't need anyone to tell me what happened was bad. But to hear him say that my mom, who I felt barely loved me in the first place, would love me even less if she found out was enough to make me dry my tears and agree to never breathe a word about that night to another living soul. So I nodded my head and reached for the doorknob.

After that horrible experience, my childhood ended. The place that Nate touched felt funny now. He never offered to watch us while my mom worked again. Occasionally, he'd stop by, and I would avoid him like cold spinach.

Mom noticed the big changes in me. For instance, I didn't want to play with my friends anymore. In fact, I only left the house for school. I isolated myself in my room and kept the door closed. I had a secret now, and I felt the more people saw me, the greater the chances of someone discovering my secret.

A babysitter named Sheila watched us. She was 19, and my mom had some problems with her in the past. Sheila told my mom she owed her money, but Mom didn't seem to think so. After her plans to have Nate house-sit fell through, she paid Sheila the extra money and once again, I was somewhat safe, though I was never safe from myself.

Sleepwalking and nightmares shadowed nearly every night now. Soon, my behavior revealed more about that night. I visited my Aunt Nannie. She informed my mom that I appeared to be walking funny. Suddenly, I was off to the free clinic.

I don't know what Mom told the doctor, but he said he was just examining me. For some reason, I was positive they wouldn't find out what happened to me. They would never guess, I thought. They're too stupid, but how I wished they would.

I lay on the table naked, covered only by a cloth gown with the Berenstain Bears printed on it, as the doctor examined me. I realized they must have known something, for I couldn't recall an exam like that.

After the examination, I was certain they would all learn my secret. The doctor left then, minutes later, reappeared and asked Mom to step out of the room with him. I lay there looking up at the white ceiling, my heart pounding like it was about to burst right out of my chest.

When my mom returned, her eyes were watery, and anxiety masked her face. For sure, she knew now. I stared at her for some sign of anger but saw none. I was relieved but, at the same time, disappointed. It seemed she was not angry at all, just upset. But her eyes did not meet mine. Just then, someone tapped lightly on the door. Before anyone could answer, a stout, dark-skinned lady with gray and black hair entered. She held a few items in her hand that she carried with latex gloves. She wore a frown that seemed stuck on her face with cheap fuchsia makeup. Even as she talked, her facial expression stayed the same. To me, she was a mean clown.

"Okay, sweetie, I'm going to have to give you some medicine in this needle."

"A shot?" I asked, looking at the syringe in her hand and then at my momma.

"Be good now, Squirt, it'll be over in a second," Mom whispered.

She choked up between her words, and tears flowed from her eyes, but she never looked in my face. I lay over the table like the lady with the frown asked me, and she stuck the needle in my butt cheek. It hurt, but I did not cry out loud, yet I couldn't control the teardrops.

I didn't understand why I had to get a shot for playing house with a grown man. At the time, I thought that was my punishment for being bad. I told my brother when I got home that I had gotten a shot. When Mom overheard me tell him, she got very upset.

"Don't chu ever tell anyone else that again. You could have died!" she screamed. "Do you understand?"

I nodded my head like I understood, but I knew little about what happened to me or even whose fault it was. All I knew was that what happened to me greatly upset the one person whom I wanted to love and accept me. Keeping her pain in mind, I made it a point to never mention it ever again.

A couple of times after my examination, I would return to the clinic. I talked to a lady named Mrs. Barnswell. I remember her name because she told me, when she introduced herself, to think of a barn. It didn't take long before she asked me who touched me on my pocketbook. (She explained that pocketbook meant my vagina). Then I wondered why she just didn't say 'vagina.' It was obvious she thought of me as a stupid kid who didn't know how to express herself. But I did, and I was forced to go through an entire session of questioning about Nate. Yes, I told her Nate had hurt me. I just wouldn't tell anyone how. Among other things, I was just plain embarrassed and wished I hadn't found out what mommies and daddies do.

Now, I was supposed to talk about that disgusting stuff?

"Did Nate put his hands in your pocketbook?" "Did Nate put his mouth on your pocketbook?" "Did Nate put his fingers or hand in your pocketbook?" "Did Nate put his lollipop in your pocketbook?"

"No. No. No. No," I repeatedly lied because among all her stupid questions and comments. Despite her attempts to turn my ideal into a Walt Disney movie, no one ever told me it wasn't my fault. I assumed I was in trouble. After all, why was I there and not Nate? So, I must have been the one who did something wrong. And if Nate was right about that, he must have been right about my mom not loving me if she found out. And so, at six, I was prepared to take my secret to the grave.

Shirley Temple never went through that!

The possibility of losing my mother's love blinked in front of me like a yellow caution light. I waited for her to come to me and hug me, but she didn't. She cried, but she didn't cry with me. She never reached out to console me. So I returned to my miserable, twisted little life with many questions I dared not ask. Left like paper blowing in the wind, I would have to figure it all out on my own.

My pattern remained the same, except for the funny walking. The nightmares never stopped, and the sleepwalking continued for months. Mom would tell me the next day how she caught me walking with my eyes closed through the house and rambling in the refrigerator. My pain compelled me to eat everything in sight. When I ran out of things to eat, I ate odd meals: frozen Kool-Aid, jelly toast, dry cereal, and anything edible I could get my hands on.

Mom never woke me as I wandered through the house because someone told her it wasn't safe to wake a sleepwalker. But what about in the morning, throughout the day? Numb and purposeless, I still slept. My grades plummeted as I became more distant. I constantly slept, never fully awake again. I observed the world through an hourglass, wishing time would stand still for me so I could figure out why everything was always turning.

Yet, I remained the same.

When I look back on that year, that incident, I realize why they call molestation a sex crime. I was victimized. To this day, I believe the moment Nate saw me, he decided to prey upon me. All he needed was the time...and the opportunity.

The moment he observed me in the living room, pouting, he knew I was starved for attention. He realized then that I was desperate for love, and so he set out to manipulate me, thus making me his victim. He sat in the trenches and waited. He waited until I fully trusted him. He waited until my mom became comfortable enough to leave us alone with him then, like a leopard, he revealed his true self. He attacked, and I was his victim.

My name is Vaneeka Robinson, and this is my testimony, the story of my life. I lost myself in 1977, at six years of age.

My heart was heavy, and I couldn't get out of my head. I couldn't believe I was given gonorrhea by my abuser, and my mom did nothing about it. I looked at my bottle of anti-depressants. Maybe it would've been better if I felt like it worked.

I walked into the kitchen and got a Coke from the refrigerator. Then I took three Effexors. With a gulp of soda, I chucked down three more. I did this about four times, and as my head felt woozy, I thought, this is it. I'm finally going to do it! I cried now, really hard, because deep down inside, I didn't want to die. I just felt powerless against whatever it was that controlled my life. Was it God? Could He be so cruel a God to let me suffer this way? And if so, well, to hell with Him, too! I did manage to pray to Him one last time. I prayed that he would forgive me for what I'd just done.

People are so quick to hit you with quotes and phrases. Tell you that God wouldn't put more on you than you can handle. If I heard one more person tell me that, I would've gone postal! First of all, they're saying that God indeed makes us suffer. If that's the case, then he's not the loving God I was introduced to. As for the saying, "God won't put more on you than you can handle," well, that's just a bunch of bull! Who decides what another person can handle? If everyone could adequately manage their stress, hundreds of thousands of people wouldn't be killing themselves—and others.

Now, I was faced with a dilemma. I did not want to die. That voice was still with me, saying, Hang in there. It'll get better. But the voice that guaranteed me that things wouldn't get better always spoke the loudest. And so I thought the encouraging voice was gone forever and for good. But I began to hear it again—soft—like a sweet, somber breeze in the willows.

I called my friend, Selene. I had stayed in contact a lot more than anyone else, mainly because she was the only person who would at least listen and try to add insight, even if she had no answers. She answered the phone. I told her I was tired and couldn't go on. She kept asking me what I was saying, but I never explained. I just said that I was giving up and to tell my family farewell. I wanted to say: Tell them that they caused my death. Tell them that I felt I had no reason to live because they didn't love me. But I couldn't. I didn't want to leave this life angry and resentful. That was the only way I could have the last laugh. As my family approached my casket, they would see, they would know, what their uncaring, insensitive, and unsupportive asses did to me!

Selene asked me not to do anything until she got to my place. I told her it was already in the making, but if she could get here in time, whatever happens, happens. She said that was fair enough and hung up the phone. Now, I prayed that Selene would arrive in time. I really wanted her to stop me from taking the remainder of the pills. But as I took three more Effexors, I wondered if she wasn't already too late.

By the time there was a knock on the door, I had taken over twenty anti-depressants. I opened the door, and she asked what I had done. She glanced at the tablets on my coffee table while waiting for my response. And I told her the truth. I told her how many pills I had taken. I figured it would all kick in regardless in a matter of minutes, and there was nothing she or anyone else could do to save me. To me, it was the inevitable. God didn't want me alive, or He wouldn't have let me suffer, so I was certain I was supposed to die. What will I tell him on Judgment Day? I figured, let me be judged, for He knew my troubles, and I'm sure He knew my burden. Yet he had the power and did nothing. When did I have the power? NEVER!

Now, as she picked up the phone, I ran to retrieve it, stumbling onto the coffee table, yet I was so woozy and doped up that I felt very little where my knee had hit.

"No police!"

"I'm not calling the police; I just want to call Poison Control so that I can find out what it is these pills may do to you."

I let the phone go, but I told her, as she dialed with one hand and examined the bottle of Effexors with the other, that it was no use in calling. As she talked to the people on the other end, I hollered not to give out my address. She told the lady how many pills I had taken. I just sat slouched on the couch. I could barely sit up straight. The room wobbled from side to side like a ship and words seemed to hum around me like a foghorn. This ship was sinking! Selene never hung up the phone, but it all happened in minutes. Soon, there was another knock on the door. Unable to even stand now, I was stretched out on the couch. "Don't answer it," I called, but she was already headed toward the front door.

"What did you do?" she yelled.

I opened the door. "What did you do?" she immediately asked.

Her words circled around me from all directions. I wobbled toward the couch, which sat like a mirage in the center of the room.

As she glanced at the coffee table with the remaining pills scattered about it, I was asked how many I had taken. Slumping down on the couch, I tried to stabilize my balance. It was as though I was aboard an imaginary ship in a turbulent sea of despair.

"I don't know...twenty maybe," I heaved with exhaustion as she went toward the telephone. "Don't call the police!" I yelled at her.

"I'm not calling the police. I'm calling Poison Control to see what those pills could do to you." She promised. I was so tired, and all I wanted to do was go to sleep, so I laid my head down and closed my eyes.

There was another knock on the door in what seemed like a short moment. I reached for her to prevent her from opening it, but I moved in delayed time, slow motion. I tried to stand, but my legs were too weak. When she opened the door, Atlanta Police stood there. I was upset with Selene, but I was more thankful she did what she did. I wanted someone to intervene all along, and it just let me know she cared for me.

A policeman walked in and looked at me. He asked what the problem was, and Selene told him. He then began talking to the person from Poison Control before radioing on his two-way.

I don't know who he called, and I didn't ask, but an ambulance pulled up within minutes. The paramedics took my blood pressure, asked if I had insurance, and escorted me to the vehicle. I asked Selene to lock up my house, and once inside the van, I was given an intravenous line. While they drove, I felt relieved that people would take me seriously now. I remembered the concerned look in Selene's eyes. It felt good knowing that someone cared. My problems would be addressed.

I arrived at West Paces Ferry Hospital emergency room. I was asked questions like: What's the date? Who's the president? Then they prepped me. I looked around, curious to know why they were prepping me. One nurse kept a watchful eye on the heart monitor as my blood pressure elevated; another nurse collected information from me, including my psychiatrist's name.

Finally, the emergency room doctor came in and explained to me that Effexor was a fairly new drug and that doctors were not fully aware of the side effects of an Effexor overdose. She gave a lot of small talk, but I heard loud and clear: "We will have to get it out of your stomach." Soon after, a nurse came in with a rubber hose just like the one used to spray your lawn.

"Wha chu gonna do wit that?" I asked, staring in shock at this long rubber device.

"This is what we'll use to pump your stomach," she simply responded.

"Now, don't give them a hard time. Cooperate, Ms. Parker," commanded the lady doctor upon noticing the expression across my face.

"Cooperate?" I screamed.

Before I could contest any further, a medical assistant stood on either side of my arms, and the six-foot hose was on its way down my throat!

I heard the physician's assistant yelling that I had to relax and swallow or that it would be worse. I felt as if I would pass out. The hose choked me, and I heard everything in my stomach making its way through the hose into what resembled a vacuum. This went on for what seemed like an hour, but I'm sure it must have been only minutes as I cried in pain. I actually thought they were choking me to death as I gasped desperately for breath.

"Just breathe. Breathe out your nose!" the doctor yelled as others kept me pinned down.

I remember looking up at the doctor, who stood watching over me and the heart monitor, and uttering with the rubber still clenched between my teeth, "I'm sorry."

"We're not doing this to punish you," she replied.

Afterward, my mom and grandmother walked in with bloodshot red eyes. I asked my mom why was she crying.

"Because I love you."

And that was when I saw her look into my eyes again. It was the first time since my childhood that I had noticed. Months later, when I left the mental hospital, I learned of how my family worried and prayed for me. Well, everyone except Chris, that is. One day, the kids even told me that they prayed for me when the ambulance came.

Soon, things returned to normal, though. Remember what I said about my people coming together in death? Well, they were convinced I wouldn't make it. It felt assuring to know they would all be right there to honor me in the event of my demise. But still, it was in life that I needed them most.

I received therapy through the years. I took pills. Nothing alone seemed to save me from the cancer I call PTSD/Depression.

But knowing the gift God gave me, 'my writing,' was my saving grace.

I can speak at functions now, even as nervousness tussles in my gut. I am always queasy at first, but if I keep my composure, looking above the audience's heads and not in their faces, I can deliver my message with prestige without losing my way on stage. I use God's gift to me as my survival mechanism. There's no hand I could not reach. No heart I could not soothe. No mind, I could not tame.

The Darkest Gray Revised is a book I've written about my life. Through my story, I can reach out to others from my hometown, Atlanta, California, Sri Lanka, and Japan. The miles my words traveled are limitless. My first written document displayed my ability.

I was suicidal as early as the age of nine. But eventually, realizing God's gift to me. There wasn't anybody I could not touch, and I am grateful for that.

People would come up to me after speaking engagements. They shared how my story helped them, giving me handshakes and hugs.

All I want is to help victims as well as abusers. I need everyone to understand I matured along with my knowledge. That pain may last a night of pure blackness with little hope to see your way through, but joy cometh in the morning! On my journey from a girl to a woman, I know that the spirit of the Lord never leaves you. I'm delivering the message that life is the only thing worth the fight!

The only thing final is... Death. Dark blackness is conquered by the slightest bit of light.

Do what you must to keep going.

Pour your soul into something positive.

What was once pure black with the slightest speck of light can easily turn your darkest gray into your guiding light!

About Vaneeka

Vaneeka began her writing career as a performance poet and rapper in the 90's under the name, V Lyric Parker. She appeared at various venues and on local radio stations in her native Atlanta, GA, immediately becoming an audience favorite.

In 2001, she self-published an earlier version of The Darkest Gray under the title Who Has Lived My Life. She hopes to serve as an inspiration to others battling depression and to those who've survived childhood sexual abuse.

The eldest of three siblings born to a single mother, the thirty-something author still resides in her hometown with son, Torrey, and daughter, Ciara.

I Carried Her With Me

CHYANNE THOMAS

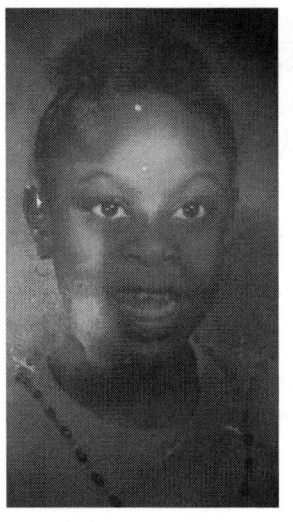

She was there screaming until I heard her and began to heal H.E.R....

The bed was cold, and the space around me was dark and quiet. Outside my room, I could hear voices, screams, and movements echoing throughout the hall. It was not so much fear that I began to feel it was apathy, yea, apathy. I felt numb emotionally; this numbing sensation transitioned to my physical as well, or at least I thought it did. A sense of discomfort flowed through my entire body, from a tightness in my chest and clammy palms, and my legs felt heavy, unable to move. All the while, I could feel my internal self-shaking violently. These feelings and physical responses correlate to many pivotal moments and days in my journey from a girl to a woman. Still, it was also the 1st time I realized I carried my little girl or younger self deep within my subconscious.

As far back as she remembered....

Beautiful Trinidad and Tobago, the place of my birth and the beginning of my journey. I love everything about being Trinidadian, from our accents to our clothing and culture, a rich mixture of many other cultures, and our curry. I think that for a very long time, I assumed that some of my experiences were just part of our culture, and as such, you suck it up and drive on. As I have gotten older and wiser, I have realized that sometimes, what we accept as culturally acceptable can still be wrong. The first time I heard the word bystander and connected to it, I felt like one my entire life, I had sat back and watched myself being tormented never once speaking up. At times it also felt as though I had been surrounded by bystanders, which was like being on the field alone. The silence of those family unit bystanders kept me quiet and confused, so I delved deeper into being a bystander in my own life beginning with those Sundays...

"HIM"

It was always a Sunday; that's what it always felt like. The house was silent; no lights were on, and no other electricity was used. I remember doing whatever chores or cleaning needed to be done the day prior (Saturday), and so on Sundays, we were always just returning from Sunday service, which meant that we took that day to rest and relax. Us, kids being, me, my siblings, and my cousins were outside running around in the yard, playing under the house, making mud pies, and playing what we called Dollie House. Our grandmother "Mami" was on the front porch in her rocking chair with what I perceived at the time to be a look of adoration maybe contentment as she looked over her grandchildren. I can recall the cool breeze, the sun, the laughter, and the joy of those moments. It was a feeling of serenity, just the calm before the storm. Whenever this skit or memory played out in my mind, I could never help but smile as I was often overtaken by the sense of peace and happiness it provided. The transition from that moment to the next caused an extreme amount of confusion, fear, and anxiety. I remember being in the middle of running around with a smile on my face, only to look up and see him standing there in the doorway. It wasn't a full door. It was one of those that could open at the top, bottom, or all together. Every time I looked up and saw him, it was like everything froze; time stood still, laughter turned to crying, smiles turned to frowns, the sun would disappear, and instantly darkness would consume me.

I would feel numb as a knot grew in my throat. I could feel the tears forming but not falling and my screams growing loudly but not being released. I would stand there frozen, hoping that someone, anyone, would see me disappearing into the house and then the washroom with him. This may not make sense, but I would stand there internally paralyzed, watching the external part of me, the little girl, follow him obediently. For as long as I could remember, this was a figment of my imagination, not something that happened, not a memory, but just a thing that would pop into my daydreams through the years. Those Sundays ended when I left Trinidad in 1990 and moved to the U.S where I was reunited with my parents. My internal bystander stayed behind on that island, and I carried that six-year-old girl with me into the next phase. She was truly all I had and all I knew without even knowing it.

My Father

The first time I feared him was while reciting the alphabet. I was about seven years old and still getting familiarized with this man I was made to call dad. One evening we were practicing our alphabet, and all of us were saying it so fast that L.M.N.O.P. sounded like we were singing the word ellemennop instead of saying the actual letters. I am not sure if there was any consideration given to our ages, the fact that we had just arrived in the U.S. and still had solid accents, or that we were also scared. He (our father) was infuriated and had us repeat it several times before pulling out his belt (aka Tiger). Yes, the belt had a name that correlated with the damage it caused physically, mentally and emotionally. This may not have been the first time I saw his rage, but it is the one that I always remember first. At that moment, and many that followed, I wondered why my siblings and I had come to the U.S., It felt like our lives had ended when we got off that plane on March 10, 1990.

We went from running in the yard, playing with our cousins, each other, and our friends, having nothing but everything, to having something yet feeling like we had nothing. You can say we had each other, but after a while, I think we ended up just having ourselves independently. Our father was a very interesting man, a tyrant for sure, a drunk, a gambler, an abuser, but also an intellect and a thinker. When I first met him, I had no feelings as he was unfamiliar to me, and as I got to know him, I disliked him tremendously before I liked him yet alone loved him. He was a force to reckon with, and if you asked me what his impact was on my life a few years ago, I would have told you that he single-handedly ruined it. He was vicious, so much so that he contributed to a house where everyone wanted to escape his wrath to include his wife.

Our mother worked what seemed to be 24/7, 365 days a year. This left us with him for the few hours that he was home sober or other. His beatings were daily for small things, for big things, and sometimes it felt like we got beatings just for being kids and alive. At some point, we started charting the intensities of our beatings; we noted the colors our hands would turn after every lash, with purple being the max. If you came back to the room with purple hands, everyone was trying to find a way to comfort you. His punishments escalated and he started integrating sleep deprivation even on school nights. We would have to stand and watch him sleep for hours on end, sometimes standing while holding books over our heads and other times kneeling or holding our hands out to the side. I often stole moments of rest when I thought he was in a deep sleep. I hated this man! I hated that we had to live in the tiny 1.5-bedroom apartment and that my mother chose to stay with him. I did not know what it meant to be a kid and to do kid things without repercussion. We weren't allowed to go anywhere, have friends, receive phone calls to the house, and certainly not watch television. At 8 years old, I knew how to make a full-course meal and did so often for my siblings and myself. Looking back, we were home alone so much that we parented ourselves, but somehow, we were always in trouble when our parents, mainly our father, was home.

There are a lot of not-so-great memories and things that transpired during the time I was with my parents. I often find it extremely difficult to identify times when I was happy or content with life other than the good days at school. I found some pleasure on the days when my father would come and tell us he needed his white linen suit ironed. Firstly, it was mostly me who would be tasked with the ironing. Secondly, this meant he was in a good mood and going out for hours. If we played our cards right during his preparation, we could probably get a yes to watching one movie out of this. I remember one day, my mother (and my aunt) snuck us to Coney Island; acknowledging how we all lived in fear is sad and eye-opening as to all the issues I may have bottled up but also that my siblings and mother may have internalized as well.

Externally, I was existing, but internally, I was numb. I channeled my anger into academics, winning spelling bees and excelling in math. My dad didn't acknowledge any of this; at 8 years old, there was no way to make sense of it. I would be lying if I said there weren't any days, I wanted him gone, not just gone as in left and didn't come back. I mean gone, as in ceased to exist. There were days when that desire became passive enough for the thought of rat-poisoned water to cross my mind or him walking under an iron as it fell from above. I often wanted to scream that you brought me/us here to this strange world that you didn't understand and didn't try to learn it with us or guide us through it. You added to our confusion and disorientation by physically, emotionally, and mentally oppressing us. No matter how good I tried to be, I was still just a thing... The same thing that the little 6-year-old was to **"him # 1"**. It felt like I was just there with no real significance. She was there with me during my father's reign; she safeguarded my feelings, blocked out the things we couldn't process, and began to harden us to the world around us.

The Streets

My older brother and I were sent back to Trinidad for a few years. I had started stealing from my mom, taking things to school to be something that I wasn't. I was tired of being the kid with the Lion King sneakers from Payless. I am not sure if being sent back was supposed to be a punishment, but to me, it was the best thing ever. I went back to an environment and life that was familiar. The people were familiar, the food was familiar, and the way things worked was familiar. I was able to enjoy this. Unfortunately, it was short lived. When I returned to the U.S., I finished 6th grade with straight A's and went to the local middle school. From there, things went from bad to catastrophic. I excelled academically, but socially, I struggled to find my place. There is a huge culture shock and difference between the ways of a 3rd world country and the ways of Brooklyn, N.Y. The inability to have guidance, support, and a nurturing space while navigating that social gap can and did increase my vulnerability to the streets. The Brooklyn streets offered many things that our small 1.5-bedroom apartment did not. So, I started giving into the streets and allowed it to partake in raising me, exposing me to people, places, and things that I will never forget and pray to never be exposed to again.

I made enemies, and even worse, I made questionable friends. I hurt people, and I got hurt. I went from being a straight-A student in elementary and middle school to trying to fit into the streets at all costs. In April of 1998, I entered the juvenile system and would be a part of that for many subsequent years. In the summer of 1998, a few months after my first encounter with the law, I ran away from that tiny Brooklyn apartment and refused to look back. I slept on park benches at a male friend's house and was violated by him and his brothers. During this time, **"him #2"** made his mark; he was a family friend whose child I often watched before running away. He taught me the meaning of quid pro quo while simultaneously awakening the little six-year-old.

At 14 years old how do you comprehend a man in his 30s and a family friend handling you that way? You don't, because you have no idea since your experience with **him # 1** had already made it clear that you have no voice and that your only job is to oblige and go with the flow. This family friend saw me a few times while I was on the streets and gave me money; it was his way of "helping me out" while helping himself. I bounced around the streets for a while, sleeping here and there and spending a few days with my friend, her siblings, and her mom, but they struggled as well, as her mom was hooked on crack.

I had some life-threatening moments, and I also had some experiences that I am not sure I would have had if I had not run away. I attended my first block party, joined a dance group, and won a competition. These moments meant the world to me. They felt like moments where I was able to just be a kid. A few weeks later, I was back in the system, picked up on a Person in Need of Supervision warrant (PINS). I went from one juvenile center to another while going back and forth to court until I was finally sent to a group home (Wayside Homeschool for Girls) in Valley Stream, NY. I was in the group home for a while but still very angry and lost. After a few months my behavior got me sent to a Maximum Facility Lock-up (Tryon) in upstate NY. My love for writing and learning continued during this time. I wrote short stories and tons of poems. I learned a great deal about myself and some interesting things about the U.S. I was intrigued by the surrounding city and learned about the Erie Canal while upstate (which was fascinating then).

On August 31, 1999, I was released from Tryon on probation. I was 16 years old. A few months later, I found myself pregnant by a 26-year-old man who wanted no parts of me. I am not sure anyone believed that he was the father nor that I even knew who the father was. The assumption of my promiscuity made it easy for them to question me. However, I could tell you down to the date of conception, Sunday, November 7, 1999, because it was the first time in my life I willing had sex. I ran home that night and wrote it down in my diary. Uneducated about the entire thing, I didn't use protection, I did know that I was attracted to him, and while there may have been some manipulation, it was something that I wanted to do. Two weeks later, I was sick and pregnant. Four days before my seventeenth birthday, I became a mom; due to the strained relationship between me and my parents, as well as my anger and rebellion, I was not living at home.

My parents (to this day I am unsure who spearheaded this) contacted the Child Protective Service (C.P.S), and because I was a minor with a minor, my son unfortunately had to move back with my parents when he was only a few months old. This situation only created more resentment and anger towards them, but it also had a lasting impact on my son and my siblings who were still at home. Looking back, I wish I had handled that better because my son was fed stories that impacted our relationship in his early years, and I am certain he still processes some of it today. For most of my life in N.Y I never felt like I fit in any situation except one that involved learning. I had never finished H.S., truthfully, I had never really started. I did not make it past the first month or so of 9th grade before getting into the system. This love for learning made it easy for me to pick up wherever needed. After having my son, I studied for a month before passing the test for my General Education Diploma (G.E.D.). Unfortunately, my love for learning did not fill the void that often kept me intertwined with the wrong people, places or things.

The first time she tried to speak.

It was a Friday night, and the girls and I were out and about like any other. We checked into our hotel room and waited for Ben to show up. When he did, Vee and two other girls left the room to grab snacks and drinks as we prepared to hit the town. Chelly and I stayed in the room, and Ben was on the bed across from where I was sitting. These weren't random people; this was not the first time we stepped out or grabbed a hotel room together. These were friends that I had physically lived with in Bushwick. Ben was also not a stranger; we adored him, and I probably loved him more than the other girls. I appreciated how much he looked out for us whenever we hung out or spent time with him. We never had to worry about anything. As a matter of fact, some of the best times we had were on trips to visit him in Long Island. I felt the need to remind myself of these things as my mind bombarded me with questions that would imply, he was up to no good. I sat there looking at him, slowly building up with fear. I was uncomfortable, afraid, and getting more and more anxious; something just felt off as I sat there, becoming hypervigilant. Was I being set up? Did the girls leave me so that Ben could have his way with me? Were other men coming to the room? I remember asking Chelly why it was taking the girls so long and was shocked when she said it had only been a few minutes. Even though Chelly was in the room, it felt as though I was left alone with Ben. Though he was familiar, something made me feel extremely vulnerable and afraid.

Suddenly, the daydreams of "him" that I thought were figments of my imagination began to replay over and over in my mind. It was as though I was reliving those moments; I could not tell what was real from what was not. I felt sick as I slowly began to realize that the thing I thought was my imagination appeared to be a reality that I had lived through, and for whatever reason, being in this room, at this moment with Ben, made me feel like the six-year-old girl who had to comply, it was as though I knew I was sitting there waiting to be summoned. I remember jumping up frantically, grabbing my things, and running through the hotel. I saw the exit and must have blacked out or zoned out because when I came to, I was back in Bushwick in our apartment. I do not recall how I got there, but I was there with a knife under my pillow. At some point later, the girls came home equally as frantic, worried, scared, and unsure as to what happened or why. I must have been in and out because I had no idea what or how the conversation went. When I opened my eyes again, I was in the psych ward of Kings County Hospital.

I was 18 years old when I realized, remembered, uncovered, and accepted that I had been sexually abused by a male relative. That realization is what brings us full circle to my waking up in the King County Hospital's psych ward. I had a nervous breakdown induced by post-traumatic stress; the specific trigger was unknown. My family dynamics were not excellent; I didn't live with my parents and hadn't done so for a while. Unfortunately, even though I was 18 years old, it was my mother who had to come to sign me out of the hospital for me to be released. Let me be frank, I found it useless at the time, and over the years, I have come to realize how trauma begets trauma and how secrets and the status quo acceptance can be handed down through generations just like wealth. I was a bitter 18-year-old full of resentment, discontent, anger, and everything else without a clear understanding of why. I was furious that my mother had to come to sign me out, but there she was, trying her best to be a mom. I am sure that her best has never aligned with what I felt I needed. We spoke about the situation that landed me in the hospital, me defensive, aggressive, and probably abrasive to her. I am unsure what she felt then, but she came off dismissive. I recall sharing my new clarity about what I thought were daydreams that turned out to be flashbacks. It wasn't my imagination playing tricks on me but a family member having their way.

I went as far as to tell her who would stand in the doorway beckoning me. The response that I received was not expected, but at the same time, it was expected. I am not sure where in the cycle of womanhood that sexual abuse in some manner becomes a right to passage, but the impression I got was that it was a thing that happened, and you'd be ok. She matter-of-factly shared her experience, briefly and without much detail, just that it occurred. In addition to that, she questioned my certainty about the individual that I named. She insisted that it was not him but maybe someone else who she remembered to be very sexual at a young age. I still cannot say what receiving that response felt like or what it feels like now while recalling the conversation.

Nothing came out of that conversation, no follow-up conversation, no one was called out, and nothing was addressed. I did come to find out that I was not the only one, and this lack of regard for females at any age by family and friends is something that many knew happened. I found out that other females in the family my age and younger fell victim to him as well. Saying lack of regard may be harsh and a gut punch to a family member who reads this. The reality is that it should not have happened and knowing that it did and not getting me or any of us help didn't do us any good. It's like it was something you would get over with time, but I didn't. I was six the first time I left the island, so it's safe to say I was six when that specific situation ended. I cannot tell you when it started. Still, I can tell you that it has had a lasting effect on my ability to navigate sexual situations whether wanted or other. It was also not the last time that the little 6-year-old was violated because of that 1st situation. Without knowing, I carried her with me internally as I grew externally and her inability to feel supported or cared for transitioned with me into my adult years.

Frenemies

When I was about 19 years old, I received word that someone who I had previously wronged was planning to kidnap me (this sounds crazy to write and even crazier to acknowledge as my truth). Upon hearing this, I moved and found myself in one of the worst situations ever. I escaped one situation only to barely escape another. I learned the true meaning of deceit and how loving someone can create a level of comfort that causes you to overlook cues and warning signs. I left this situation badly beaten, bruised everywhere, and in excruciating pain, physically, mentally but mostly emotionally. Someone that I trusted with my life allowed some gang members to come into her home where I was living at the time, and they gave my cousin Vee and me the business. I didn't fight back; I just lay there and took the stomping and the hits with whatever was in the socks they held. The entire time, I only wanted to know why. Why and how could that individual do this to me, to us. In that moment, I was forced to acknowledge who I wasn't, the situations I was better than, and the people who meant no good. I ended up leaving New York shortly after that situation. I was tired of fighting and trying to be for the streets. I embraced my street smarts, but my book smarts kept tugging on my senses.

There was so much more for me than I was giving myself space to be. I remember being in a juvenile center in Brooklyn called Crossroads and spending my time writing poetry. The staff there always encouraged me to get them published. This affirmation followed me in the group home and the lock-up. There was never a space where some random adult who didn't know me validated the light that burned brightly within me. I just was not able to see it for a very long time. Leaving NY that summer was the first time I had seen that flicker and its possibility of becoming a flame. For the first time ever, I ventured outside of the Big Apple. I turned twenty that summer (2003). Though my departure was under emotionally painful circumstances, there was also some hope for what the future held.

Mr. KJ

In the summer of 2003, I joined a company that traveled from state-to-state selling books, magazines, and encyclopedias. They always said that people from NY had the gift of gab; I would have to agree since I never had any issues making my sales. This segment of my life opened my eyes to more than door-to-door sales and the concrete jungle. I learned about Southern hospitality, racism, a hot Christmas in Arizona, and met a forever friend in Olympia, Washington. I went to North Dakota, known to me through the movie Fargo. I visited the Mall of America in Minneapolis. I drove on the I10 in St. Louis while Chingy sang about meeting at the Holiday Inn. I experienced various people, personalities, belief systems, and upbringings. I learned from an exceptional boss who was an islander and always reminded us that he came to this country with nothing. I made lifelong friends who will smile reading this segment in remembrance of our time together. These are also friends who saw me low and held me until I could stand. This segment also introduced me to domestic violence and the reality of how difficult it could be to leave. It enhanced my ability to be empathetic towards my mother amid my anger that she stayed with my father.

One day, I watched my dad chase my mom down the steps of our apartment building; she was running from him and trying to escape to work. I remember him grabbing her in the doorway and thinking to myself she almost made it. In that moment I told myself that NO man would ever put his hands on me, and if he did, I would fight back. His name was KJ, and I never fought back. He was a handsome fella from Chicago. From the moment I saw him, I was taken aback by his accent, the way he walked, and how he carried himself. He must have been on the crew for a while before I got there because he was a van driver. I heard stories about KJ and had been warned to stay away from him; at the time, staying away was easy because he was in a relationship. Within a few weeks of me being on the crew, KJ and his lady (K) broke up, and she left. Again, I was told that he was very abusive and that if we pursued each other, I would put myself in a violent situation. I am not sure what it was, but at twenty (and a few years later), I thought there was something so unique and amazing about me that this man would see the errors of his ways and change for the better. I found out that I was wrong very quickly. I endured physical, verbal, and emotional abuse at his hands. Here I was, all but 100lbs, 4 ft 11", getting handled by this man. That feeling of being frozen and disappearing inside of myself activated without warning or without being summoned. There she was, 6-year-old me, protecting me yet again from the outside world.

I remember having an asthma attack and ending up in the hospital while I was out working. After being released, I decided to stay back the next day and stay in bed with nothing to eat. One of our friends, EF, stopped by and bought me some food; I think it was Jack in the Box. Now, EF was a very good friend to me, but he was a mutual friend to KJ and me. At the time I saw no harm in him stopping by to check on me while also bringing me something to eat. Well, KJ came back that evening and was upset about my visit. Without consideration for my condition or the fact that I had nothing to eat this man grabbed me off the bed, dragged me over to a window, and threatened to throw me out of it. I was so confused and scared I faked an asthma attack just for him to have mercy on me. Writing this, while therapeutic, awakens feelings that I have yet to deal with in totality. My self-esteem was nonexistent, and I believe he saw that. Even with me talking and acting big, he saw through my defensiveness or defenselessness, feeding into my inferiority fear. He had me locked in and he knew it. I was afraid of him and would never dare to cross him. He would have his ex (K) call MY cell phone to speak to him. I would answer politely and then hand the phone over to him. He would find some privacy, and they would talk for hours. What was I supposed to do, tell him no? In hindsight, my naiveness and desire to be loved at any cost is upsetting; however, I can give grace to the young lady I was. We make decisions in moments based on what we know at the time. She did what she thought was best based on her experiences, her exposure and the little she truly knew about life and love. I cannot recall exactly what state we were in when my cousin Vee returned to the crew. She had left New York with me in the summer but only stayed a few weeks, leaving before KJ and I became an item.

When she arrived, she quickly caught on and asked me some questions; of course, I avoided them, lied, and came up with stories blaming our cat for my scratches. KJ didn't really care about who had an opinion and was very open about his violent tendencies; Vee, however, was here for it and was just as open about her disdain and discontent for him. One morning, I was ironing and must have mindlessly said something that he found disrespectful, he went on a rampage. KJ was in the doorway yelling at me, while I was still ironing his shirt between the bed and the window. I remember putting the iron down, and I must have been

pumped knowing that my cousin was close by because I was not backing down. He yelled, and I yelled, and before I knew it, he was running over to me, trying to grab the iron to do God knows what. Vee hearing the commotion came around the corner, and as he snatched the iron, she snatched me. I am not sure if it was just her words or if she had a weapon or what; I just remember what felt like mass chaos and my rescue. I stopped staying with him that day and tried to refocus myself and my energy. I am grateful that I was able to get out before the situation got worse. Forever thankful to Vee for using her voice when mine was frozen. Looking back at these moments or situations, I can see the little girl who had learned to disappear inside while being obedient and submissive outside. I carried her deep within my subconscious into these spaces and places because she had become familiar with showing up and shutting up.
She stayed small and accepted that she was inferior and had no choice and no voice.

She cried out, and this time, I heard her.

Somewhere between 18 and 20, something changed in my relationship with my father. For whatever reason, I no longer hated him. As a matter of fact, he became the only person in my immediate family with whom I would have a decent relationship with. We would often talk about books, music, and sports here and there. He referred to me as daughter and had adopted this melancholy way of speaking. It was very peaceful and inviting (to me). We spoke about some of our past experiences with each other, and it was done without malice, blame, or any type of negativity. He would say," You know, daughter, we live and learn". My hatred for him turned into love, adoration, and empathy. In the spring of

2004, while I was still traveling with the magazine company, my dad ended up in the hospital. I do not recall all the details except that his blood pressure was 218 over something. That was the number that I needed to know. The significance of how high it was and what it meant for his health prompted me to move back to NY. Not only did I move back, but I enrolled in a technical college while trying to join the military. The idea of losing him before getting my life right frightened me into action. I may have glanced at my past since then, but I have not stopped fully looking back until now and even still there are things that have been left out. I finished my associates with honors in June 2006 and shipped out to the Army that July. The Army replaced the streets and became my life's new teacher with enforced boundaries and standards I didn't have to create for myself. If I stayed within the parameters, I excelled and didn't need a voice to hold others accountable; I had the outlined standards to reference. I did not know it then, but my ability to succeed in the military was because of the boundaries.

Had I been left to navigate society without guidelines or preset boundaries, I am not sure that I would have been able to succeed. I cannot imagine navigating this world with the mindset of a six-year-old afraid to speak up. I began to face life with the security of the military. I was able to stand on my own, learning about credit, finances, building wealth, and establishing myself for the future of me and, at the time, my son. In 2008, I met my ex-husband. I gave birth to our daughter in 2010 after experiencing a traumatizing miscarriage in May of 2009 and my 1st military sexual assault experience. I somehow navigated the military, motherhood, and wife life, all while excelling professionally and educationally with internal trauma brewing daily. I had my 1st home built in 2010 and moved into it 9 days after my daughter was born.

Consider life from 1990 – 2004 I felt like things were looking up. That was until little cracks and holes started to become noticeable. In Jan of 2012, my ex-husband was significantly injured overseas. In addition to his injuries, our marriage and life together were taking their toll and running to the end of its course. This period of my life left me absolutely depleted. I am not sure how I made it through those years, and I honestly cannot articulate what it felt like because the only thing that comes to mind is utter emptiness with a desire to cease living. I woke up every day and mindlessly lived. From 2012 to 2016, I was a living ghost or just a human shell. Emotionally, I had nothing; I was losing friends to death, losing my marriage, in and out of court for custody and still in shambles and ashamed of my military sexual trauma (MST). It was way too much, yet somehow, I kept going, just moving along aimlessly without a desire to even exist.

Looking at the place where things made some kind of sense I returned to school and earned my bachelor's degree with honors. I followed up with my first Master's, graduating with honors in 2015. I achieved several promotions and made it to the rank of Sergeant First Class (S.F.C. or E7). Then 2017 came and there went my life falling apart yet again. At this point having made it to 34 years old I can tell you that living was exhausting! I found myself going through a medical evaluation board for the second time. My dreams and aspirations of being the first female Sergent Major of the Army came crumbling down and it felt as though I just had to take what was being handed to me. I was back in court for my daughter all while trying to have a civilized co-parenting situation. If things couldn't get worst in Jan of 2018, while going through the medical board process, I had my 2nd military sexual assault trauma experience, and it was this experience that made her voice loud and clear. This experience made me see a side of the military I tried to protect my Soldiers from. I went from being an advocate to needing an advocate. I went from hearing about things getting covered up or handled incorrectly to watching my accuser retire with full benefits as punishment. I ended up in the hospital for two and a half months following this experience, trying to get myself back to a place where getting a massage would be enjoyable again.

During this time, I had some exceptional therapist and was able to find solace with some of the other ladies that shared similar experiences, I had time to sit down with six-year-old Chyanne. I asked for forgiveness, comforted her, and realized how proud I was of her. That six-year-old could not stand up for herself, but she did what she could to keep us safe and did so all by herself. With her, I acknowledged that we didn't know how to be a kid and that a lot had been taken from us without our permission. None of this had anything to do with us or our value. We transferred that responsibility. Childhood trauma work is what this experience led me to. It made me accept that I was not showing up in many situations because I did not learn how to handle them.

Additionally, my fight/flight/freeze response was the only response that the 6-year-old me learned, so in situations when I should say no, I became and at times now still become afraid of the consequences so complying seems to be the best option. In defense of this response, I crafted a hard-core exterior; once penetrated, I am back to freezing and feeling small like the six-year-old girl. That hard-core exterior has kept me safe but has also damaged relationships and made it difficult in personal and professional spaces. I am often misjudged, overlooked, or perceived as difficult to deal with. Every so often there are the people who take the time and put in the work to get through the exterior. Those individuals get to see and experience all the goofy, silly, fun, down-to-earth, loving, emotional parts of many. I have been told on so many occasions "I would have never guessed you were this type of person" or "I really thought you were a b....,"

Where am I /we are now

That MST experience eventually taught me what space I want to hold in the world and why. I am still doing "the work," but I am also contributing to the work of others. I just needed to figure out and refine how I would accomplish this. In 2019, after getting medically retired, I started working on my purposeful life parallel to the life I needed to live to continue surviving. I earned my 2nd master's degree with honors and was inducted into the National Society for Leadership and Success (in 2020); I earned my Project Management Certification and a few others to support my professional career, which I use to fund my purpose as I develop and grow into it. It took me a while to conceptualize what that purpose is. I toyed with so many variations of it. Was it therapy, psychology, or social work? Each of these avenues would have allowed me to work with individuals who have experienced trauma in their life specifically in childhood. However, I also quickly learned that I am a true empath (which some consider a trauma response) which could lead me down a path to secondary trauma.

I started looking at other options where I could support without living through the past of others and was being pulled in the direction of coaching. I was initially turned off because I perceived it as an over-saturated market. Then a few months later, I noticed that I was still being pulled in that direction. I took a few courses through Fielding University, including their evidence-based coaching program and other courses from different programs. I fell in love with the philosophy of coaching. I fell in love with the notion that we already possess everything we need to thrive. It's all right there, embedded within each of us. Unfortunately, just because it's there does not mean we have the know-how to bring it out. As a coach, I help my clients find the keys to unlocking their greatness and fullness to optimize their living and thriving. This awakening kicked my imposter syndrome into full gear; questions about my abilities and personal struggles became cons to my pros. But my desire to step into that purposeful life was stronger than my imposter syndrome.

Suppose we can assert that life is a continuum of learning. In that case, we can also assert that knowledge is endless and ever-growing. Suffice to say that none of us have reached our limit of learning in our pursuit of knowledge. My experience is enough to pour into someone else and I am enough now until I learn more, and I will be enough then as well. I aim to assist where I can comfortably, and for me, that is through trauma coaching. Trauma isn't something that just goes away; it's like a virus that hides within our system, lying dormant until activated. It may never be cured, but we can find ways to acknowledge its existence and move beyond its limitations. I believe this, and I love this for us. Today, you can find me managing a program while wearing my professional hat; In school somewhere adding to my knowledge base; Mothering my two kiddos and building my brand in passion and purpose as C.E.O. of B.E. H.E.R. (Hopeful – Empowered and Resilient) coaching.

My personal notes:

I am grateful not just for the opportunity to share parts of me but also for the experience that it provided. There were moments of healing, crying and processing through this and I embraced it with grace, sympathy and compassion for myself. Sometimes the hardest thing for any of us to do is forgive who we were or who we are now. Never forget that you are a being that will consistently evolve, be a part of your evolution and don't just let it happen to you or for you. Acknowledge that some things are outside of your control while being present for the things that are within your control. Treat yourself the way you want others to treat you, then treat others the way you treat yourself. If you have experienced some type of hurt or trauma, take a second to honestly reflect on how it informs you how you show up daily. Lastly no one is without flaws so give yourself a chance by taking a chance.

Things I acknowledged while writing this:

I was not a resilient child; I was just a child, and I became an adult carrying the trauma that the child did not bounce back from.

I am not a strong woman; I am a capable woman with the mental agility and willingness to keep moving. I can neither do it nor be it all, I need my person or my people.

I am not an angry woman; I am afraid to be handled as an object with no voice. So, my defense mechanism is to automatically project assertiveness in fear of being seen as an opportunity or weak. It is never to project anger. This is something that I am challenging myself to work on by setting healthy boundaries, knowing my limits and using this amazing voice of mine.

Dedication:

Naturally I dedicate this to my kids, my sister who has been a huge proponent in my life over the last few years, her extended family and the people who have loved me through it all. I also want to acknowledge anyone who is living through the residuals of trauma, I send you love, light and uplift you in my thoughts and prayers.

A silent note to my friends who left my side way too early, I love and miss you all so much.

To the reader, thank you for embracing my words and my life.

Stay in touch or update:

I am currently working on two anthologies myself and will be a co-author for a military anthology due for release in May 2025.

You can connect with me on Instagram, Facebook, LinkedIn or via email using the information below.

IG: iamchyannet

FB: Chyanne t Thomas

Linkedin: www.linkedin.com/in/chyannet

About Chyanne

Chyanne Thomas is a devoted mother of two, a proud Army veteran, and a passionate advocate for women's empowerment. Her journey is one of resilience and transformation, proving that no challenge is insurmountable. After becoming a mother at 16 and navigating the challenges of young parenthood, Chyanne earned her GED at 17 and found her purpose in the United States Army. She served honorably for over 12 years before a medical retirement ended her military career.

Determined to continue making an impact, Chyanne pursued higher education, earning two master's degrees—one in Business Administration and another in Project Management. She is now the CEO of BE H.E.R. Coaching (Hopeful, Empowered, and Resilient), where she works with women to overcome trauma, embrace empowerment, and transform their lives through mindset shifts and positive psychology.

Chyanne's mission is fueled by her belief that every woman's story is worth sharing and every strength worth celebrating. She uses her own life experiences as tools to help others break through barriers and rewrite their narratives. Through BE H.E.R. Coaching, Chyanne inspires women to uncover their resilience and step into their power.

To connect with Chyanne, email her at inquiry@b-her.com.

When You Ask God Why

DESIREE WILLIAMS

When I graduated from school, like MOST teenagers, I wasn't quite sure of what I wanted to do as far as college. I knew there were certain things I was interested in, like Marine Biology, Fashion Design, and acting. There was really nothing at the top of my list. I was just so glad to be graduating from high school. I just needed to kick back for a while. I needed a serious break. But I kept hearing that same song playing in my head from every adult I've known. Don't rest too long after high school because you'll become lazy, thus never continuing your education. The pressure was definitely there.

My best friend, with whom I graduated, said she was considering the military. The Navy, to be exact. She suggested that I join at the same time she did. "Maybe we could be on the buddy program together?" It sounded like a good idea, but I needed to figure it out. After checking it out, I thought I would have to lose some weight, and more importantly, I would be leaving my younger siblings behind, and I was scared. I just wasn't sure. Anyway, she went in, and I decided to take a few classes at a local university. I had been talking to a college recruiter and decided to just take a few classes to start. That would be fine as long as I was doing something. A year and a half later, school started getting expensive, so I said, "Maybe my friend was right; why not just try the military?" They can pay for school; I could save money and travel. Also, they would pay for my living expenses as well. The thought of doing boot camp without my best friend made me sad. I kept thinking, "I should have joined when she joined," but there must have been a reason why I didn't. After talking to a recruiter, I decided to go ahead and go in. My prior college experience came in handy because I went in as E3 instead of E1. That just meant more money in my paycheck. My best friend walked me through the process, and next thing you know, I was on a plane to Orlando, FL, headed to boot camp. Eight weeks later. I graduated and got my orders. After a short vacation in Atlanta, I would report back to Florida to work at the Naval Air Station.

I arrived on a Friday and spent the weekend settling into my barracks room. When Monday came, I promptly reported for my first day at work. I spent the first hour getting to know all my coworkers and waiting for my senior chief (Senior Chief Harris), who was in charge of the day shift at NAS, to arrive. My direct supervisor, Petty Officer 2nd Class Silver (PO2 Silver), walked me around the station to explain my job duties.

I was what you would call an AVIATION BOATSWAIN'S MATE. [ABH] This meant that I was responsible for crew and passenger manifests, loading and unloading cargo, making sure planes were mechanically fit for flight, keeping the runway clear of debris, and, as I soon learned, many other things.

"Do you have any questions for me?" asked PO2? "Yes, I'm curious,"..... (my mind full of anticipation & worry). What is Senior Chief Harris like? (I couldn't help but ask because, being fresh out of BOOT CAMP, I was so used to being harassed and yelled at every single day. I just wondered if work was going to be the same way.

It was as if he had read my mind and knew what I was thinking. He said, "Don't worry." This job is very laid-back. Chief Harris is cool as long as we do what we're supposed to do. "You won't have any issues."

Sometime later, Senior Chief Harris walks in. PO2 Silver says, "Good morning, Senior Chief. Our new airman is here." "Good!" he says. "Send her to my office."

PO2 motioned for me to walk into the office. I must admit, I was a nervous wreck. He had" THAT LOOK." He was tall, had dark, frazzled hair, and proceeded to stare at me with these very dark, piercing eyes. With his forefinger and thumb, he played with a thick, black mustache. He hung up his jacket, fumbled with some paperwork on his desk, then read the name on my uniform, speaking very loudly, said. "So, you are "Williams." "Well, Airman Williams, I should say." "Welcome to N-A-S. Did Petty Officer Silver show you around?" "Do you know what your job is going to be?" "(his questions coming out faster than I could answer them....")." Are you ready to work?" "Yes, Senior Chief!" I said, (my voice cracking, meanwhile, trying my best not to sound so nervous). "I hope so."

Noticing my rank on my sleeve, he said, "I see that you are a higher rank than most of my airmen here. How did that happen? He asked." "Isn't this your first duty station?" "Yes, sir, I responded." "I came in as (E3) instead of (E1) because of my college experience." "OK, well, I hope you know that means you will have more responsibility here than most of my airmen. Just so you know." I had no idea at the time what that could have meant, but as time went on, I soon found out.

Everything started out good. Then, after about six months, things started to get very tense. PO2. Silver approached me one day while we were standing around. We had just sent out our last flight for the day and were preparing to go home. He said, "Hey, Williams, do you want to go out after work?" I politely declined, saying I was tired and wanted to go back to my room and relax." "OK, he said, I'll see you tomorrow." The next day came, and many more days after that, the same question came up. From the little things that he said and the way he stared at me, it was clear that he was becoming increasingly interested in having a relationship with me outside of work. I finally told him I had a boyfriend stationed in another state, and we were pretty serious. "Oh, so that's why you never want to go out with me. Well, anyway, how would he know what you're doing? He's in another state." "Well, like I said, I am in a relationship; it's serious, so, no, thank you. I do not want to go out with you." I had tried to be as nice as possible, but after all that time, he still would not take NO for an answer, therefore making me very uncomfortable. Finally, the day came when I had to get him to back off, but the question was, HOW? After all, I had told him several times that I was not interested, and even by now, our coworkers were telling him as well, and, at the same time, teasing me about it, all the while making my work environment so much worse. Going to Senior Chief Harris was my only option because we were always taught the "Laws of Working in a Hostile Work Environment" and "Using Your Chain of Command," which simply meant, when reporting anything, ALWAYS go through the proper steps/and/or people to report an issue, starting with the person directly over you, then whomever is over them, etc., etc., until the problem has been dealt with in some shape or fashion.

I decided to take a different route. I was so focused on keeping things peaceful and not letting this situation affect my job more than it already had that I asked a couple of the girls for advice on how to proceed. Both said, "Well, if you don't make your complaint official and get it on record, they will assume his behavior was ok with you simply because you did not report it." In my heart, I knew this was true, but I also knew how real life works. This whole thing could backfire and blow up in my face. My final decision,.... I will talk to PO2 Silver face to face and just let him know that I will be having no more of his harassment. If that didn't work, I would have no choice but to talk to the Senior Chief, and I told him just that. Of course, when I finally approached him, he acted like I was blowing things way out of proportion. He even went as far as to call me a DRAMA QUEEN. I overheard him telling one of our coworkers that I was acting like a "stuck-up B!" I thought this sh$$ would never go away. I'm just going to have to talk to the Senior Chief directly.

I got up one morning, went to work, and waited for the Senior Chief to come in. When he finally arrived, he stormed past me as if he didn't see me sitting there. Part of me did not want to do this because he already had a certain attitude towards me. I felt he didn't like me much anyway, but now I'm desperate. I needed some assistance, and I figured this whole thing could get resolved with him being the boss. I told him what was going on and how long it had been going on, and I just wanted it to stop. I didn't want this to affect my work. I was very uncomfortable at work, and I didn't like the fact that everybody at work knew what was going on, and they chose to make me the butt of every joke because of it. One thing I refused to do was to have to come to work every day and be miserable. A big part of being successful in my job depended on me being in the right state of mind for the safety of EVERYONE. So, with all this said, I asked my Senior Chief to just speak to him and get him to treat me fairly like everyone else and leave out the negative comments. For me, it seemed really simple. However, for the Senior Chief, not so much.

He told me I didn't need to let everything bother me, "This is life, and I need to just do my job and stop being a crybaby." "With all due respect, Sir, I have the right to complain to my superior officer when my workspace is being violated, I am not being treated fairly, and I am being sexually harassed." that's pretty much what was happening. It's been going on for several months. "Why are you just now telling me this he asked?" "I've been trying to deal with this myself because I did not want to make my work environment any more hostile than it already is." "I figured if I talked to him personally, he wouldn't feel like I was trying to get him in trouble by going over his head when I simply could have just had a conversation with him." I also knew the #1 rule of reporting harassment of any kind in a work environment. If this conversation had ever gone higher, that would have been the first question I was asked. "Did you let the person know that they were making you uncomfortable?" The Senior Chief dismissed my complaint, making me feel like I wasted his time. He was even so bold as to confess to me that this is one of many reasons why he hated women, especially BLACK women in the military. He said, "y'all are just TOO DAMN SENSITIVE; you cause TOO MANY PROBLEMS! "and you need to stay home and take care of your babies; you don't belong here!"

My mouth literally dropped open, and it was impossible to keep the look of shock from appearing on my face. Then, he proceeded to dismiss me from his office. Of course, when PO2 Silver found out about the conversation and the result, it gave him even more ammunition to come after me, therefore keeping up the foolishness. At this point, I was so miserable I didn't want to go to work. I thought about anybody else I could talk to, but in reality, there was no one, not even at home, to talk to for support. I've never felt so alone. So, for the time being, I just let it go. I would not go over the Senior Chief's head and report him because all these higher-ups were in bed together. Little did I know this was just the beginning of the disaster that was to come.

I just concentrated on work for the next few weeks and went home. During my time at work, I formed great work relationships with the pilots who came into our naval station. They knew I had a boyfriend at another base and started offering me empty seats on the plane when they were available to fly and visit him. I was off every other weekend, and when a flight was available, I quickly jumped at the opportunity. It was nice to just get away. Each time, the opportunity came. I told PO2 Silver. I wanted to let him know my plans in case they needed to reach me for some reason. I only told him where I was going and when I would be back; of course, I left out the specifics, like (WHO) I was visiting." He always approved. I was always careful to ensure I was back in time for work. I always came back the day before, and the pilots and I had always communicated about the importance of me being back on time.

I had been taking flights for about 2 months. One Friday, an officer I often flew with offered an available seat, which I quickly accepted. When I landed, the Lieutenant Commander who flew me there approached me and said, "You have a phone call from your Senior Chief back at your Naval Air Station." I thought to myself, "A phone call? Why on earth would the Senior Chief be calling me? My first thought was, "Maybe I had my work schedule confused, and maybe I was supposed to be at work this weekend; "OH GOD!" I thought, FEAR immediately set in. I walked inside the air terminal and grabbed the nearest phone, "Yes. Senior Chief, I asked, (voice cracking) …This is Airman Williams." Before I could say another word, he started yelling at me, calling me every name except a child of God, then asking me, "Did you sign a chit before taking these flights out of town? "A chit? Sir?" "I didn't know I was required to sign a chit." Most of my coworkers traveled out of state on the weekends or wherever; as long as they were back in time for work, I've never known them to sign a chit. I thought I was only required to sign a chit if I took leave and went on vacation. "No," he said; I see the log of every flight you've taken." "You've been doing this for a couple of months now." Each time you flew out, you violated Naval Policy. "Now! "Get your sorry ass back here. ASAP! I will deal with you then, and I promise it won't be pretty." Then he hung up.

Now, let me explain what a CHIT is. A chit is a piece of paper, basically, what you would call a" permission slip." You pretty much need one to do ANYTHING in the military. There was a popular (catchphrase) that we used. "You need a CHIT to SH$$! "To this day, I don't know why I never filled out a chit to fly out of town. I guess it was because I ALWAYS let PO2 Silver know what my plans were, and he NEVER asked me to sign a chit, nor did he ever oppose my request to go. I even got permission from the Officers who were flying out. But, I missed the last step: the MOST IMPORTANT step... Fill out a chit and get approval on paper with the proper signatures. My lack of owning such a document would ultimately become a problem. But, at the time, I was thinking, "I have communicated with my supervisor; this is my weekend off, and as long as he said OK, everything was good." I later found out that he was well aware from day one that I was supposed to fill out a chit, but he never advised me to do so. In fact, I also found out that he bragged about letting me take those flights for the last two months, therefore giving me enough rope to hang myself; then he decided to go to the Senior Chief to report me. Based on our previous dealings, it wasn't hard for me to figure out why.

After the Senior Chief hung up on me, I immediately started crying. I was in another state, in major trouble, and the flights were not returning home until Sunday. I was stuck for the weekend! My boyfriend met me at the airport, saw me crying, and said, "What's wrong? "I explained the whole situation to him and the phone call that I just got. "He said,

"Well, there's nothing you can do about it, so while you're up here for the weekend, you might as well just enjoy yourself till your flight leaves on Sunday, then just go back to work on Monday and face the music." That didn't make me feel any better, but he was right, so I stayed until my flight left Sunday to return to Florida. I spent the whole weekend in my hotel room miserable, anticipating the reprimand I was facing on Monday morning.

Monday came, and I was back at work earlier than usual, just to be safe. As I sat there waiting for the Senior Chief to arrive, PO2 walked in and said (with a smirk on his face), "Aah, I see you made it back." I gave him the look of death. As I spoke to him angrily, "You could have told me from the very beginning that I needed a chit to keep flying in and out of town. Why didn't you ever say anything to me? "Is this because of the problems we've been having?" I don't know why I even asked (I already knew the answer). "As my supervisor, you would think you could be bigger than that, do the right thing, and inform me of what I was doing wrong." He walked away, mumbling, "This is your problem; you deal with it." About two hours later, the Senior Chief walks through the door, shouting loud enough for the world to hear. "WILLIAMS, IN MY OFFICE RIGHT NOW!" I literally jumped out of my seat, VISIBLY TERRIFIED, and followed him into his office. He slammed the door shut.

"So, Airman Williams, you wanna explain why the hell you proceeded to fly out of the state without permission?" "What the hell were you thinking?" All I could do was tell him the truth: I had gotten verbal permission from PO2 Silver, and the officers always offered me a seat if one was available. I really thought you only had to fill out paperwork if you were taking vacation time. He went on from there, mostly just talking about how stupid I was, how he was tired of having me around, and how he just couldn't wait until it was time for me to leave this place of command because, AGAIN, according to him, I don't belong in the Military. I think I had been in his office for maybe 20-30 minutes, but it felt like hours, and still, he hadn't yet told me what kind of punishment I would be facing. Finally, the moment came. Not that I wanted whatever stressful, unnecessary, awful punishment he would give me; I was just ready to get out of his office.

"Well, Airman Williams!" the senior Chief shouted, "Since you like to break the rules, I think you should stay at work and think about all the problems you've caused since you've been here!"

WAIT!

WHAT?

PROBLEMS I'VE CAUSED?

(In my mind, I'm thinking…Do you mean being sexually harassed, having no choice, but to report it, because I couldn't stop it on my own? Or maybe, … given low-end jobs way below my pay grade and being retaliated against because of it. OR, perhaps it was being told by my superior that because I am a woman, and a (black woman at that), I don't belong in the Military) Is that what he meant by ALL THE PROBLEMS I'VE CAUSED?

That statement sent a surge of PURE ANGER through my spirit. That was one of the few times I actually felt HATE towards another human being. I tried to speak but needed to defend myself, so he stopped me. "Just shut up! Just shut the hell up, Williams!" he barked. I'm sure everyone in the building could hear him scolding me by this time. "You will be staying here at work, doing double duty." "When your shift leaves this afternoon, you will stay and work with the night shift crew." "You will not go home, do you understand?"

"Yes, sir", I said. He continued...." When your shift returns in the morning, you will work your shift as well." I was scared to speak, but I had to ask. "So, sir, when can I go home, bathe, and change my uniform? He said, "I don't give a sh%% about that; that sounds like your problem!' You better work that out because you will be pulling double duty till further notice. "Now you're dismissed, and this is considered STRIKE TWO! STRIKE THREE, I will be kicking your ass out of the US Navy, FOR GOOD!"

That day, my shift ended, and everyone went home except me. I stepped outside the terminal in a low-key area where some of my coworkers often took a break to smoke. The tears started rolling. The next thing I knew, I was in full breakdown mode; you know, that real ugly cry where you just completely let it all out, and you don't care how you look or who sees you. It was way overdue. I asked that ultimate question (the one we ask when at our lowest point): GOD, WHY? WHY IS THIS HAPPENING TO ME? I was raised with the understanding that everything happens for a reason, but I needed him to give me some answers. I'm here by myself, away from home. Feeling COMPLETELY ALONE with no support. I had just turned 21, starting life on my own, and this had been nothing but one disaster after another. I had only been in the Navy for less than a year, and this experience was not going well at all. I had expected some difficult times along the way, but this? Did I make a mistake joining the military? I was starting to think so.

I was so consumed in my feelings that I didn't notice the night shift senior chief approached me. Senior Chief Davis, a cool, laid-back man who always had jokes, was serious about the job; otherwise, he was probably the most easygoing person I've ever met in the military. He was always nice to me, even kinda flirtatious at times, but he was that way with every lady who crossed his path. He was always careful not to cross the line or take his words too far, unlike PO2 Silver. "Airman Williams, (he smiled as he spoke, puffing and blowing smoke from his cigarette) you've been a busy girl, huh?" I tried to hide my face; my eyes were red and watery, snot was coming from my nose, and I had no tissue to get myself together for conversation. "Yes sir, I guess so, but I swear I had no idea I needed a chit to leave town for the weekend; I was back every Sunday, which was a whole day before work, and I always told PO2 Silver when I was going. I thought that was enough." "Well, why didn't Silver remind you to get that chit-signed? As your immediate supervisor, that was also his responsibility to ensure you followed proper procedure." I said the same thing, but Senior Chief Harris wasn't even interested in that; he basically issued the full blame to me, read me the Riot Act, insulted me, and told me he was ready to get me out of the Navy altogether. I had one more time to screw up. On top of all that, I can't even go home. I have been ordered to workday & night shifts till he says otherwise. "How is that even possible, Senior Chief Davis?" I can't even go home to change clothes tonight or bathe. When will I sleep? This entire thing is so stupid! I started crying all over again.

Chief Davis gently placed his hand on my shoulder. "Don't worry," he said. "I got you covered on the night shift, and until this is over, we will work something out." "Thanks, I said! My head hurts! This is too much. So what now?" I asked. He said to me while laughing, "Just go in the bathroom and wash your face; you don't look too cute right now with a snotty nose and blood-shot eyes; you look like you've been crying!" I couldn't help but laugh. Even in the worst of circumstances, Chief Davis always had jokes.

Over the next several weeks, I worked my regular shift during the day, and Chief Davis formed an arrangement for me at night. I would sleep and shower in the "Officers' Quarters," a room where pilots who occasionally flew in freshened up and rested between flights. It was a built-in' Hotel room" of sorts. I kept a spare uniform and made sure to be up and ready by 5am every morning, an hour before my shift started. I continued on as if I worked double shifts just like Senior Chief Harris had ordered. Being the inexperienced Airman that I was, I didn't know at the time that this punishment was illegal, and Senior Chief Davis never said anything, but now, when I think about it, I think he was just trying not to ruffle any feathers by speaking against it, and, at the same time, helping me as well. To get me out of that building, sometimes, he would even send me on "errands," which sometimes took hours to complete. I was amazed when it came to helping me get through all of this, and to keep from getting too depressed, Senior Chief Davis became very creative. I must admit, it helped a little, and I didn't cry as much.

A little over a month had passed (36 working days, to be exact). Senior Chief Harris finally lifted my "jail sentence," and I returned to my regular shift. From then on, I kept to myself and conversed with coworkers only when necessary.

We welcomed in a new airman, Airman Kimmy. She was a petite, Caucasian blond-haired, blue-eyed girl straight outta Michigan, complete with an accent and very animated. Even the Senior Chief became fascinated with her. Every time she walked by, he stared at her a little too long, and I think I even saw him drool a few times, which was great for me because that would take his focus off of trying to make my life miserable. I was responsible for training her, and over the first couple of weeks, that's what my focus was. Kimmy wasn't hard to train at all and was very eager to do the job, but the only bad thing about that was she wanted to move too fast.

We had been only two weeks into her training, and she was already asking me to do my job. I explained to her that promoting to my level of work takes time to build the experience. I had been there for six months or so before I could perform such tasks. She thought things were so easy, and she was eager to do more. "Be patient," I warned her, as you will soon see, that accuracy and detail are our biggest responsibilities. "It's not as easy as you think; one wrong move and people can die!" Kimmy was somewhat spoiled and used to getting whatever she wanted because that entire conversation went through one ear and right out of the other. She wasn't trying to wait at all. She skipped right over PO2 Silver, went straight to Senior Chief Harris, and complained. Lord, just what I needed!

The next thing I knew, Senior Chief Harris was calling me into his office, which was a regular occurrence by this time. I swear there was a chair in his office with MY NAME on it. He started in on me (with his same accusatory, overbearing tone), "Williams! Airman Kimmy tells me she wants to train and have more responsibility, and you refuse to comply." (In my mind, I'm thinking about all of our past exchanges, and how this was getting really old). I spoke firmly, determined not to be disrespected this time. "Sir, what Kimmy wants is not as simple as assuming more responsibility but to perform my leadership job. Having been here for three weeks, she is hardly qualified to do such, and that is exactly what I told her. "Sir, I think you would agree, knowing how crucial it is to do our job correctly."

He proceeded with his usual disrespect, telling me that NOBODY asked me to think and that I had better assist her in doing my job for today, and he trusted that she would do it well. Even though I was totally against the idea, I knew there was no point in saying anything because I already knew how that would go. I walked out of his office, right over to Kimmy, and, in as calm of a voice as possible, I said, "You obviously have your mind set on doing my job, so today, YOU will become ME! Let's go!" We headed to the front desk; I instructed her to fill out and sign the usual flight manifest and other paperwork for all incoming flights, took it into the Senior Chief's office for his signature, and went outside to wait for our first aircraft.

The aircraft arrived, and we saluted the pilot (Commander Lea.) She was a frequent flier to our terminal, and I knew her well. She would be there for about three hours, so we immediately got to work on her departure while she retreated to the officer's quarters to refresh herself. Our job was to get the aircraft fueled, checked for safety, loaded with cargo, belted, secured, and ready for departure. Although we did this every day, all aircraft were not loaded quite the same. This is where it could get difficult.

We had to consider weight, cargo type, and several other things. This is mainly why two weeks was not enough time to learn this job. Of course, according to the Senior Chief, I was to let Kimmy do most of the work. I was to stand back and guide her, which took longer than usual because I had to go over things several times until it was right. We had only three hours, and that wasn't much time. I told her we had to move faster because it was unacceptable to send out a late aircraft, and a late aircraft resulted in facing severe consequences. To make things worse, I had other responsibilities and was needed elsewhere. I had other team members help because we were almost out of time. They had been there longer than I had, so I depended on them to help her.

It was time. Commander Lea came outside and boarded her plane. We saluted and saw her plane take off. She wasn't in the air for ten minutes when we suddenly got a message over the air conditioning radio.

"MAYDAY! MAYDAY! PILOT IN DISTRESS! THIS IS COMMANDER LEA! AIR CARGO BROKE FREE, I AM PINNED DOWN TO MY COMMAND BOARD, AND I AM IMMOBILE; I NEED HELP TO PREPARE FOR AN EMERGENCY LANDING! DO YOU COPY? "

The distress alarm was sounded, and we were all off to the runway. In more simple terms, the cargo that was loaded onto her airplane had broken free from the belts/nets holding it down during flight, rushed forward, and piled on top of her, leaving her unable to fly her plane. She was about to crash, and she needed us to save her.

Now... Do you wanna guess whose job it was to load air cargo onto each aircraft safely and securely? MINE OF COURSE!

Once we got to the runway, we got the (Arresting Gear) together. That's the Big adult-sized chain link wire that is wound up tightly to catch an airplane flying down the runway when an aircraft has lost control and landing gear has failed to assist in landing. Once we succeeded and the aircraft was stopped, we all went back to the terminal, and tensions were more than high! A plane with an officer and very expensive military cargo almost crashed that day, and some questions needed to be answered.... Most of all, SOMEONE WAS GOING TO BE HELD RESPONSIBLE.

Commander Lea walked into the terminal. We all stood on command. The rage on her face was quite obvious. The room was so quiet you could hear everyone's fear. She stood there looking at all of us. Then she showed a side I had never witnessed in as long as I've known her. Using every curse word known to man, she said.....

"I ALMOST F-ING DIED TODAY! I WAS LITERALLY CRUSHED WITH THOUSANDS OF POUNDS OF CARGO ON TOP OF ME WITH NO CONTROL TO FLY MY AIRCRAFT! MY LIFE FLASHED BEFORE MY EYES, AND ALL I COULD THINK ABOUT WAS THAT I WAS GOING TO DIE, NEVER SEEING MY HUSBAND OR MY KIDS EVER AGAIN, NO ONE! WHO IN THE HELL WAS IN CHARGE OF LOADING MY PLANE?"

"SPEAK UP NOW!"

PO2 Silver, our immediate supervisor, spoke up. Without hesitation, he confidently said, "I believe Airman Williams would be the one you need to talk to." On any given day, he was correct. I was usually the head of that job, but it would not be that simple that day, and I would make sure the Commander knew it.

Senior Chief stepped out of his office, "Airman Williams, in my office." He turned to Commander Lea; "ma'am, if you will allow me, I need a minute to speak with Airman Williams; then, if you will, please join us and the base Captain for a meeting." I walked into the Senior Chief's office, and Deja Vu hit me....... HERE I GO AGAIN. My heart was beating so fast I thought I was going to have a heart attack at any moment. However this meeting ended, my life would be changed FOREVER.

"Well, Williams, you really did it this time!" He said. "Do you realize how much trouble you're in? You almost killed a Naval officer today and destroyed millions of dollars of military cargo." "Do you know what the punishment for that is? I'll tell ya! You are going to Fort Leavenworth (this was the official military prison located in Kansas)."

"Three strikes, NOW YOU'RE OUT!! I am finally getting rid of you! You are going down for this! After today, I will never have to look at you ever again. You are a disgrace to the United States Navy, and you will be dishonorably discharged! Your career is over!"

It was the way he spoke to me......It was different this time; it was calmer and even a bit more exciting. It was as if the chess game was over, and he had won.

He called for Commander Lea to join us in the office. "Ma'am, I have counseled Airman Williams; she will assume all responsibility for the incident today." I was in total shock, stuck inside my own body, unable to speak. I could not believe this was actually happening. That same feeling came over me; my eyes became foggy, my head felt like a vice was crushing it, and tears streamed down my face. I'VE NEVER FELT MORE POWERLESS OVER MY OWN LIFE THAN AT THIS MOMENT. If there was one, my future was in someone else's hands.

Commander Lea spoke. "Senior Chief Harris, before you move forward with Airman Williams, I need to talk to her privately." He quickly left the office and closed the door behind him.

"Airman Williams, all the time that you have been here, I never thought you would have made a mistake of this magnitude! You almost cost me my life today!" "What the hell happened?" "How could you be so careless?" I sat here in silence, still stuck and unable to speak. I shook my head and moved my lips, but nothing was coming out. I was so hot like my body was on fire.

"AIRMAN WILLIAMS!" She yelled. "ANSWER ME!"

Something in the way she screamed at me woke me up. I jumped and yelled at her, forgetting she was my superior officer. "I need you to hear me, Commander; seriously, hear me! Please!" "I have nothing to lose now, and my life and career are at stake. I need to tell you everything!"

She didn't even get upset at how I spoke to her. She just told me to sit down and talk, and I did. I confessed everything from the sexual harassment, the things the Senior Chief said to me in his office, the discrimination, the illegal work ethics, and, just recently, the catastrophe that almost caused her life. Today, I wasn't in charge of your aircraft. Airman Kimmy was, and the Senior Chief gave her permission to take over my job. She hasn't even been working here for a month. I was called away to work on other things, and for time purposes, I had to hand off the job to the rest of the crew.

Commander Lea's face turned red, "Are you f-ing kidding me! He left an inexperienced airman in charge of my aircraft?" "How the hell does that happen?" I said, "I feel that the Senior Chief got caught up in his disdain for me and that he just wanted to go against me when I spoke against the decision for Airman Kimmy to do my job and be in charge."

Commander continued… "Airman Williams! WHY???? Why didn't you get everyone involved to sign a chit as proof of this job switch?"

{Whelp! There's that word again!! CHIT is the very "item" that played a heavy role in this.}

"Actually, Commander, I did!" I was suddenly feeling a small piece of hope. "When the Senior Chief first ordered me to let Airman Kimmy do my job for the day. I filled out a chit stating my objection and added it to all the paperwork that he had to sign for your flight manifest. He signed all the papers in the file, Airman Kimmy and I signed them, and I put everything in the file cabinet, but not before I made copies." I reached into my left front pocket, pulled the paper out, and showed it to her. Commander Lea opened the door and called the Senior Chief back in, along with Airman Kimmy and PO2 Silver. We had been in the office for at least four hours or so. The Commander had summoned the base Captain and a few other officers in our command. Before I knew it, I was in a room with some of the Navy's biggest Brass. This was intimidating, to say the least. The entire investigation lasted three days. Commander Lea made me and Airman Kimmy testify to the events of the flight disaster and also asked me to talk about everything I had experienced since I'd been at the air terminal. She even spoke positively on my behalf. After three days, I was called into the office, the Senior Chief offered an official apology, and I was officially absolved of any responsibility that led to the flight disaster. In the words of the Commander of the base,

"I'm Glad you were smart enough to get that chit-signed; that's what ultimately saved you. You're dismissed!" I gave a final salute to all the officers in the room, thanked them, and left. When I got back to my room, I fell to the floor on my knees. I had just realized why..... Remember when I asked God, "WHY IS THIS HAPPENING TO ME?" Now, it was clear.

Less than two weeks later, by (my request), I was transferred to Air Operations—another part of the Air station, where I could finish my last year in the Military. I had wanted to make it a career, and knowing what I know now, I would have. My environment would not always be with people like Senior Chief Harris or even PO.2 Silver. I had suffered enough trauma to last me a lifetime. I was just in my early twenties and just getting started in life. I needed a drastic change, so I moved back to Atlanta and worked for a law firm before finally becoming a professional Chef. I had some good times in the Navy and met many great people.

It may sound strange, but I don't regret joining the Military. It taught me some important lessons in life that I still use today.

"Be still and know that I am God. I will be exalted among the nations; I will be exalted in the earth!"

PSALM 46:10 ESV

About Desiree

Desiree Williams is a proud US Navy Veteran who was born in Rockland County, New York, and later relocated to Atlanta. She graduated from high school in 1990 and is the proud mother of one son, who has inspired her to become actively involved in the Clayton County and Coweta County school systems for over 20 years.

Throughout her career, she has served in various roles, including as a para-professional, part-time caterer, and childcare provider. Desiree has received several awards, including Clayton County's Parent Volunteer of the Year and recognition for her commitment to parent involvement through the PTA.

In 2005, she earned a degree in Culinary Science & Arts from Le Cordon Bleu Culinary Institute."

Afterword

As we close the pages of *Our Journey From Girls to Women*, we reflect on the collective strength, courage, and resilience that unite us all. This anthology is more than just a book; it is a testament to the power of storytelling and the profound healing that comes from sharing our truths. Each story you've read is a beacon of light, illuminating the path from pain to progress and, ultimately, to victory.

To the women who poured their hearts into these pages: thank you. Your vulnerability, honesty, and courage will undoubtedly inspire countless readers to embrace their own journeys, no matter how challenging the road ahead may seem. You've reminded us that every scar tells a story, and every triumph is worth celebrating.

To our readers: thank you for allowing these stories to touch your hearts. May the words you've read ignite a spark within you, encouraging you to rise above your challenges and claim your victory. Remember, your story matters. Let this anthology serve as a reminder that you are never alone, and the power to rewrite your narrative lies within you.

As we leave this chapter, let us carry forward the lessons of love, perseverance, and unity. Together, let us continue to uplift one another, celebrate our journeys, and inspire the next generation of girls to become strong, fearless women.

With gratitude and hope,
LaQuita Parks
Publisher

Ready to write your story? We are ready to help you take your story from a "thought to a realization!"

www.paprovipublishing.com to schedule a FREE discovery call with us today!

Email: Support@paprovipublishing.com to schedule a 90-min strategy session